C. L. Crouch
War and Ethics in the Ancient Near East

Beihefte zur Zeitschrift für die alttestamentliche Wissenschaft

Herausgegeben von
John Barton · Reinhard G. Kratz
Choon-Leong Seow · Markus Witte

Band 407

Walter de Gruyter · Berlin · New York

C. L. Crouch

War and Ethics in the Ancient Near East

Military Violence in Light of Cosmology and History

W DE G

Walter de Gruyter · Berlin · New York

⊗ Printed on acid-free paper which falls within the guidelines of the ANSI
to ensure permanence and durability.

ISBN 978-3-11-048596-7

ISSN 0934-2575

Library of Congress Cataloging-in-Publication Data

A CIP catalogue record for this book is available from the Library of Congress.

Bibliographic information published by the Deutsche Nationalbibliothek

The Deutsche Nationalbibliothek lists this publication in the Deutsche Nationalbibliografie; detailed bibliographic data are available in the Internet at http://dnb.d-nb.de.

Printed in Germany

Cover design: Christopher Schneider, Laufen

for my grandmother

Foreword

The following represents the revision of a thesis for which the degree of D.Phil. in the University of Oxford was awarded in 2009. Thanks are due to my supervisor, John Barton, for his unfailing faith in both the thesis and myself, as well as to a number of individuals who read and commented on parts or the whole of earlier drafts. Among these are Hans Barstad, Kevin Cathcart, Stephanie Dalley, John Day, Paul Joyce, Shalom Paul, Francesca Stavrakopoulou and Jonathan Stökl. Finally, a debt of immense gratitude is due also to my family, without whom the entire endeavour would have been long since lost.

Carly L. Crouch
Fitzwilliam College, Cambridge

Contents

Part III – Ethics and history

1. Introduction

To what extent are the ethics of the Hebrew Bible, insofar as they reflect the ethics of ancient Israel and Judah, commensurate with the ethics of these nations' ancient Near Eastern contemporaries?

This was the starting point for this examination of the ethics in the ancient Near East, which has taken the actions of warfare as its case study. The hypothesis to be tested was that ancient Israelite[1] and ancient Judahite[2] ethical ideas were not as distinct from those of their neighbours as generally supposed.

From the beginning of comparative study of ancient Near Eastern cultures, there has been a tendency among biblical scholars to want to emphasise the uniqueness of the biblical nations of Israel and Judah. From the Bibel-Babel controversy sparked by F. Delitzsch, through the biblical theology movement characterised by such works as G.E. Wright's *The Old Testament Against its Environment*, to the so-called "pseudorthodox" scholars of more recent times, there has been a longstanding concern to retain an ultimate certainty in the incomparability of the biblical ancestors' beliefs.[3] This bias has persisted despite the attention drawn to it by scholars such as M. Smith and M. Malul, no doubt encouraged by both its original source – the desire of the religious to secure the special place of their faith in history – and by more scholarly assertions of the importance of "Bible first" interpretation.[4]

---

1 As has been emphasized by P.R. Davies and others, biblical scholars have a tendency to sloppy terminology when it comes to their more historical endeavours. This study will distinguish as far as possible between the nations of Israel and Judah, and persist also in using both "Israelite" and "Judahite" in tandem, to emphasise that these nations, though clearly related by history and culture, developed along different historical trajectories. The nature of our sources makes unambiguous differentiation between them difficult, but it ought nonetheless to be pursued in principle; the use of clearly defined terminology is designed to keep this attempt constantly in mind.

2 The terminology of "Judahite", instead of "Judaean", is employed to emphasise the differences between the pre-exilic, national culture of Judah and the post-exilic culture of the province of Yehud (later Judea) (see also n.1).

3 G.E. Wright, *The Old Testament Against its Environment* (London: SCM Press, 1950). For the term "pseudorthodox", see M. Smith, "The present state of Old Testament studies", *JBL* 88 (1969): 19-35.

4 M. Smith; M. Malul, *The Comparative Method in Ancient Near Eastern and Biblical Legal Studies*, AOAT 227 (Neukirchen-Vluyn: Neukirchener Verlag, 1990). See e.g., S. Tal-

Even those scholars who pursue comparative study are frequently influenced by a desire to distinguish the biblical culture from the culture(s) of its ancient Near Eastern neighbours – a need which at times lends itself to the uncritical pursuit of methodologies which, though faulty, produce the desired conclusions.[5] Ethics has not been immune to this concern: if anything, it has been more susceptible, given that most study of ethics in the Hebrew Bible is pursued for the purposes of enlightening modern believers as to the relevance of these texts for their own lives.[6]

As an antidote to the persistent bias against the other cultures of the ancient Near East, this study has been conducted from the opposite starting point: it has asserted that Israel and Judah were first and foremost part of a broad ancient Near Eastern "historical stream", and that, though they did have unique qualities which differentiated them from their neighbours, they also shared more characteristics than they disputed. As a more familiar analogy, one might compare the cultural relationship between Britain and the United States: though any traveller or expatriate between these countries would affirm that there are cultural differences which distinguish these nations from each other, they would also recognise that a great deal of the intellectual and cultural background of these societies is shared, as are many values and ethical beliefs. Indeed, the more astute observer might also notice that the similarities and differences which one had thought occurred on a

---

mon, "The comparative method in biblical interpretation: principles and problems", in *Literary Studies in the Hebrew Bible: Form and Content* (Leiden: Brill, 1993); reprinted from *Congress Volume: Göttingen 1977*, VTSup 29 (Leiden: Brill, 1978).

5 For a rare instance of the reverse – a scholar apparently determined to cast the biblical cultures as less-developed morally than their neighbours, in this case the Assyrians – see H.W.F. Saggs, "Assyrian prisoners of war and the right to live", in *Vorträge gehalten auf der 28. Rencontre Assyriologique Internationale in Wien 6.-10. Juli 1981*, AfO Beiheft 19 (Horn: Ferdinand Berger & Söhne, 1982).

6 This is by far the most common purpose of the "ethics of the Old Testament". See, for example, the works by B.C. Birch (*Let Justice Roll Down: The Old Testament, Ethics, and Christian Life* [Louisville, Ky.: Westminster John Knox, 1988]); J.W. Rogerson (*Theory and Practice in Old Testament Ethics*, edited by M.D. Carroll R., JSOTSup 405 [London: T&T Clark, 2004]); J.G. Millar (*Now Choose Life: Theology and Ethics in Deuteronomy*, NSBT 6 [Leicester: Apollos, 1998]); W.C. Kaiser Jr. (*Toward Old Testament Ethics* [Grand Rapids, Mich.: Academie Books, 1983]); M.J. Harris (*Divine Command Ethics: Jewish and Christian Perspectives*, Philosophical Ideas in Debate [London: RoutledgeCurzon, 2003]); G.J. Wenham (*Story as Torah: Reading the Old Testament Ethically*, OTS [Edinburgh: T&T Clark, 2000]) and C.J.H. Wright (*Old Testament Ethics for the People of God* [Leicester: Inter-Varsity, 2004]); even *The Bible in Ethics: The Second Sheffield Colloquium* is primarily concerned with modern application (edited by M.D. Carroll R., M. Davies and J.W. Rogerson, JSOTSup 207 [Sheffield: Sheffield Academic Press, 1995]).

national level actually reflected internal differences, stemming from and connected to social and economic class. This particular observation we will pursue in more detail below. First, however, a return to the extant literature.

In the last century there have been a number of attempts to address the nature of the ethical content of the Hebrew Bible.[7] Of these, the majority are of limited use for the present study, as they are decades out of date and hampered by the state of the field in their time (H.G. Mitchell and J.M.P. Smith), unabashedly Christian in orientation and therefore almost wholly ahistorical in approach (W.C. Kaiser and B.C. Birch), or addressing questions largely irrelevant to the question at hand (W. Janzen). Even the most recent study, E. Otto's *Theologische Ethik des Alten Testaments*, which does attempt to relate the biblical texts to relevant ancient Near Eastern material, is limited by its exclusive reliance on the explicitly didactic texts of law and wisdom; this omission limits it especially in our case, as neither of these plays a significant role in the study of warfare.[8] Though the upswing in articles and essays on ethics in the Hebrew Bible which has occurred in English-speaking scholarship over the last two decades suggests that the field is growing, the restriction of most of these to brief and largely theoretical forays indicates that the field is still very much in its infancy.[9]

As already noted, many of the attempts made thus far have also been from a Christian perspective, attempting to articulate the relevance of Old Testament ethics for Christian ethics today rather than addressing the historical question of the nature of ethical thought and behaviour in Israel and Judah in the first millennium. As a result, much of the previous scholarship on Hebrew Bible ethics has taken little pains to articulate the relationship between the beliefs espoused by the biblical texts and the beliefs of the entire historical community(ies) which produced the texts, having taken as their starting place a radi-

---

7 H.G. Mitchell (*The Ethics of the Old Testament*, University of Chicago Publications in Religious Education, Handbooks of Ethics and Religion [Cambridge: Cambridge University Press, 1912]), J.M.P. Smith (*The Moral Life of the Hebrews* [London: Cambridge University Press, 1923]), J. Hempel (*Das Ethos des Alten Testaments*, BZAW 68 [Berlin: A. Töpelmann, 1938]), H. van Oyen (*Ethik des Alten Testaments*, GE 2 [Gütersloh: Gütersloher Verlagshaus, 1967]), Kaiser (*Toward Old Testament Ethics*), Birch (*Let Justice Roll Down*), W. Janzen (*Old Testament Ethics: A Paradigmatic Approach* [Louisville, Ky.: Westminster John Knox, 1994]), E. Otto (*Theologische Ethik des Alten Testaments*, TW 3.2 [Berlin: W. Kohlhammer, 1994]).

8 With the exception of Dt. 20, on which see Chapter 10.

9 E.g., *The Bible in Ethics: The Second Sheffield Colloquium* and the dedicated *Semeia* volume, both from 1995. Excepting Otto, recent German scholarship has largely ignored ethics.

cally different point of view than that required by the historical type of study attempted here.

Only a few scholars have advocated such a historically-based study of ethics in ancient Israel and Judah, and their suggestions have as yet been largely on the theoretical level.[10] The most important contribution of this methodological work has been the recognition that to make no distinction between the ethical community as described in the Hebrew Bible and the ethical community as lived and breathed in the Levant in the first millennium BCE is highly problematic.[11] As J. Barton emphasises in one such discussion,

> the Old Testament is evidence for, not coterminous with, the life and thought of ancient Israel; Old Testament writers may at times state or imply positions which were the common currency of ancient Israelites, but they may also propound novel, or controversial, or minority positions.[12]

Given the limited nature of historically-based attempts at Hebrew Bible ethics, there is little literature to which we may refer as a successful application of this point. One of the few attempts to address an essentially ethical issue historically, in fact, does not recognise this point, and as a result fails in its historical objectives: this is M. Zehnder's *Umgang mit Fremden in Israel und Assyrien*.[13] Because Zehnder's subject matter relates so closely to the topic taken as the focus for this study, its shortcomings will be discussed in more detail below and in Chapter 4. For the moment it may suffice to mention that Zehnder's conclusions are ill-effected by his decision to take the biblical texts as straightforwardly reflective of "Israel", without making any distinction between the viewpoint(s) put forth by the biblical texts and the viewpoint(s) of the living community(ies) behind the texts.

---

10 See, e.g., R.R. Wilson, "Approaches to Old Testament ethics", in *Canon, Theology, and Old Testament Interpretation: Essays in Honor of Brevard S. Childs*, edited by G.M. Tucker, D.L. Petersen and R.R. Wilson (Philadelphia, Pa.: Fortress, 1988); "Ethics in conflict: sociological aspects of ancient Israelite ethics", in *Text and Tradition: The Hebrew Bible and Folklore*, edited by S. Niditch, SS (Atlanta, Ga.: Scholars, 1990); "Sources and methods in the study of ancient Israelite ethics", *Semeia* 66 (1995): 55-63; Barton, *Ethics and the Old Testament* (London: SCM, 1998); *Understanding Old Testament Ethics: Approaches and Explorations* (Louisville, Ky.: Westminster John Knox, 2003). An application of the method is Barton's *Amos's Oracles Against the Nations: A Study of Amos 1.3-2.5*, SOTSMS 6 (Cambridge: Cambridge University Press, 1980).

11 This point is, of course, made readily by scholars such as with regard to historical research on Israel and Judah generally, but seems to have been only slowly picked up by those interested in the sub-section of social history which ethics comprises.

12 Barton, *Understanding*, 17.

13 M. Zehnder, *Umgang mit Fremden in Israel und Assyrien: Ein Beitrag zur Anthropologie des »Fremden« im Licht antiker Quellen*, BWANT 168 (Stuttgart: Kohlhammer, 2005).

These bracketed plurals draw our attention to one of the two principal methodological contributions which the present study makes to the study of Hebrew Bible and ancient Near Eastern ethics, namely the fundamental importance of recognising the social origin of texts and other materials employed in the historical endeavour.[14] Some beliefs may be held by most, if not all members of a society, but many others are held only by certain segments of it. The difficulty, if not impossibility, of speaking of the ethics of an entire society must be recognised in any attempt to describe the ethical thinking of ancient communities. It is essential to identify the origin of the "informant" (in terminology adopted from M. Liverani), in order to properly locate it in its social matrix.[15]

This is essential particularly in the comparative endeavour. Until now, however, the comparison of biblical texts to ancient Near Eastern materials has been done with little, if any, recognition that the social matrices of the biblical informant(s) are radically different from the social matrix of most other known ancient Near Eastern informants. Rather than recognising that most of the ancient Near Eastern material derives from a royal or similarly élite social background while a significant proportion of the biblical informants do not, scholars have taken each side as a sufficiently accurate reflection of its society as a whole as to merit the wholesale comparison between the one and the other. As this has tended to buttress that hoped-for conclusion of biblical uniqueness, it has been carried on almost without objection. In the case of *Umgang mit Fremden in Israel und Assyrien*, the problems which arose from glossing over the distinctions among biblical texts were compounded by Zehnder's uncritical comparison of this composite "Israel" to Assyrian materials of essentially royal social provenance. Comparing the élite perspective of the Assyrian material with the entire swathe of biblical material obscures the internal differences in ethical thinking which arise from the key role of social context in the formation of ethics, and portrays these as differences between the societies as a whole instead. For various historical reasons, the biblical texts are not congruous in social origin to the majority of the other texts and materials pre-

14 Barton has hinted at this in his emphasis on the importance of distinguishing between statements such as "all or most Israelites held that X" and "certain Old Testament authors held that X" (*Understanding*, 16). In light of the following remarks, we would emphasise that "some Israelites (or Judahites), in particular those with affinities to Y social group, held that X".

15 M. Liverani, "Memorandum on the approach to historiographic texts", *Or* 42 (1973): 178-194.

served from the ancient Near East, and this must be taken into account in any attempt to compare the biblical texts to those materials.

Here the recognition of informant origins will be fully recognised, and the consequences for the study's conclusions will be clear. I have made a point of making assertions on the ethical thought of the ancient Near East with regard to warfare only insofar as concomitant assertions could be made with regard to the social background of the informant text, bearing in mind, of course, the many uncertainties which are attendant upon such assertions. The texts are not made, as far as possible, to speak beyond their natural limits: those which appear to derive from the section of society which we will call the élite are considered reflective of the practices of the same; those which appear to derive from elsewhere are considered separately.

An important corollary to this methodological point is that ethics must be contextualised and understood in their own intellectual framework. Ethics do not exist in an intellectual vacuum, but are closely connected to and indeed dependent upon what we will here call ideology. The content of the intellectual framework relevant for understanding a given ethical belief is intimately related to the social context of the belief.

The tendency in biblical scholarship (and even ancient Near Eastern scholarship, in which the personal attachment tends to be less) to recoil in disgust at the more violent descriptions of war has usually aborted prematurely any attempt to explain or understand these acts in their own context. Where warfare is concerned, scholars seem to have observed reports of violence with total disregard for context, apparently presuming that ancient peoples engaged in violent practices despite consciously and knowingly considering them immoral.[16]

The second methodological contribution of this study arises from the first, namely, that in addition to distinguishing between social backgrounds (and ideologies) in analysing ethical thinking in the ancient Near East, it is equally necessary to consider the influence of historical circumstances. The interaction between history, society and ideology provides the essential source material for ethical thought. Historical events affect the reality of society, and changes in society are reflected in changes in its ideas about what is or is not appropriate behaviour.[17]

---

16 The most attention that is usually paid to context is limited to apologetic references to the necessities of nation-building during the biblical conquest and similar.

17 The one study in which the importance of historical context for ethics has been recognised is A. Mein's *Ezekiel and the Ethics of Exile*, OTM (Oxford: Oxford University Press, 2001). Here we will expand this recognition to an examination of the

We thus note the importance of being aware of several elements of "context" in the study of ancient Near Eastern ethics: the immediate cultural (i.e. national) context of the society in question, as defined further by chronological parameters; the "sub-contexts" of various subgroups within that culture; and the "macro-context(s)" of the wider, international atmosphere of which the single national context is itself a sub-context.

Though these assertions of the importance of context in ethics may seem obvious, it is nonetheless the case that, particularly in the field of Hebrew Bible ethics, the extent to which context is acknowledged as a factor affecting social norms has been remarkably less than one might expect. The implicit or explicit concerns of scholars to apply Hebrew Bible ethics to modern Christian ethics has tended to obscure the importance of their historical context in favour of transcendent ideals transferable to modern ethical thought. All of these attempts have been further impeded by attempts to incorporate the entirety of biblical history into one synthetic whole, preventing the possibility of properly detailed analysis of intellectual and ideological factors affecting Hebrew Bible ethics over time, as well as obscuring the simultaneous coexistence of multiple social strata in Israelite society. Previous studies have also, with rare exception, been hardly conscious of the wider ancient Near Eastern context of Hebrew Bible ethics. Despite the ever-increasing availability of ancient Near Eastern materials for providing a broader context for Hebrew Bible ethics, there still seems to be an overwhelming emphasis instead upon the isolation of the latter from their distinct social situation as comprised by the broader ancient Near East. Attempts to consider the wider ancient Near Eastern context of the ethics of the Hebrew Bible and of ancient Israel and ancient Judah have as yet been minimal, especially in English-speaking scholarship (German scholarship, primarily in the guise of Otto, is somewhat improved), and have been essentially confined to the much narrower category of legal material, instead of more broadly drawn upon for ethics in general. This ignoring of the ancient Near Eastern context in particular seems a gross omission, and an attempt to rectify it is one of the primary aims of this study.

The question addressed by this study, while pertaining to the subset of thought known as ethics, is for these reasons an essentially historical question. The interest of other scholars in the relevance of the Hebrew Bible for modern ethics is not the focus of this study – though I

---

changes in ethical thinking about warfare which arose as a result of nearly two centuries of political and social developments in Assyria and Judah.

would contend that such endeavours cannot properly be carried out without due attention to historical considerations.

In order to enable an appropriately historical approach to the question at hand, this study could not conduct a systematic review of every ancient Near Eastern culture; to do so would have led to the significant details of each being lost to overly-broad depictions. Bearing in mind the depth of research necessary to undertake a project of this kind, the study had to be restricted to only a few cultures. The primary foci of investigation have therefore been limited to the nations of Israel, Judah and Assyria. In deciding which cultures to examine, the practical fact that it is these three nations for which contemporaneous primary evidence is in the largest supply was a significant factor. For Israel and Judah we are in possession of biblical texts, despite the difficulties they pose for historical research as secondary rather than primary sources, and the royal archives of the neo-Assyrian empire are extensive and increasingly available for scholarly study. Evidence for most of the other cultures of the ancient Near East is either very limited (e.g. other small Levantine states) or chronologically far-flung (Ugarit, Mari). The only significant exception to this is Egypt, which has been excluded in part due to the limitations of a project of this size and in part due to the fact that Israel and Judah tend to exhibit closer (though by no means exclusive) cultural relationships with other Semitic cultures than with Egypt.

The heavy emphasis laid on contextual factors by this study also strongly discouraged the indiscriminate use of chronologically far-flung materials. As Malul noted, increasing the variations in chronology and geography between the subjects of comparison correlates to a decrease in the ability of the observer to make comparisons of any significance. Hence it was considered preferable to limit the study to nations of contemporary existence; their separation being thereby limited to (the inevitable) geography. The variations observed within even a single society over relatively short periods of time further confirmed the validity of the concern that a broad chronological net would have obscured the important nuances of historical and social context: if such change were possible even within a relatively short space of time and within a single culture, the increase of chronological distance could hardly have resulted in anything but increased differences within the culture itself, thereby making the indiscriminate comparison of its features to other cultures decreasingly valid.

Having limited the scope of the investigation to three nations, and bearing the concern for chronological contemporaneity in mind, the chronological parameters were set at approximately the beginning of the eighth and the end of the seventh centuries BCE. This contained on the Assyrian side the final resurgence of the Neo-Assyrian empire, as well as a half century before this. Eventually the earlier material was abandoned, in part due to limited evidence, but also due to changes in the behaviour evidenced in the two periods: a shift worthy of study in and of itself but beyond the scope of this study. The Assyrian material, then, was ultimately limited to that pertaining to the final imperial Neo-Assyrian (hereafter Assyrian) period, beginning with the accession of Tiglath-pileser III in 745 BCE and continuing through his descendants and successors until the fall of the Assyrian empire in 612.[18] In the case of Judah and Israel, the chronological parameters were also designed to restrict the study to a time period for which some historical knowledge might be more or less reasonably asserted; the further into the early days of these nations the project ventured, the more time would have had to be spent on purely historiographical issues, and the less certain would any assertions about the reliability of the available texts' information have been, about either history or ethics.[19] The end dates for Assyria and Israel were naturally set by their demises in 612 and 721, respectively. Judah ceased as a (semi-)independent political entity with its destruction by the Babylonians in 587, but in this case the continuation of national identity, albeit in a modified form, offered the option of extending the investigation beyond the political destruction of one of the nations. However, the choice of warfare as the project's case study and the central role which this phenomenon played in the nation's destruction suggested that to do so might be problematic, insofar as an event of such significant impact on the culture and identity of the people might be expected to affect not only its theology but also its ethics. An initial review of exilic and post-exilic texts suggested that there was in fact an observable shift in moral thinking at this time, at least with regard to war ethics, and as a result the end date for Judah was set at the time of its political demise, as were those for Israel and Assyria. The nature of the biblical evidence has in some cases worked against the possibility of a total division between pre- and post-exilic material and thought, but to the extent possible this distinction has been maintained.

---

18 All dates are hereafter BCE unless otherwise noted.

19 Foray into the pre-monarchic period, it hardly need be mentioned, suffers from this problem in the extreme, as well as involving a social form of an entirely different nature. It has thus, along with the earlier monarchic period, been put aside for the purposes of this project, though the narratives about these periods may be thought pertinent for those periods in which they were compiled and edited (but on which see Chapter 6.2).

Our case study therefore proceeds as follows.

Part I, "Ideology, cosmology and ethics", addresses the intellectual background of ethical thought in the societies in question. First, there is a general chapter on the function of ideology in societies and its relevance to military encounters (Chapter 2), followed by chapters detailing its specific royal manifestations in Assyria (Chapter 3) and Judah and Israel (Chapter 4).

With this groundwork laid we proceed to Part II, "Ethics and society", which constitutes an application of our first methodological point – variability according to the social context of an informant. Chapter 5 describes the deployment of royal ideology in the legitimation of military actions in the early Assyrian period, and this is followed by a parallel chapter with regard to Judah and Israel (Chapter 6). Part III concludes with a chapter addressing the appearance of an alternative social perspective in *Amos* (Chapter 7).

Part III, "Ethics and history", applies the second of our methodological points to the warfare case study, with Chapter 8 examining the changes in the use of royal military ideology across the reigns of Sennacherib, Esarhaddon and Assurbanipal. Chapter 9 examines this principle with regard to the prophets Isaiah of Jerusalem and Nahum, and Chapter 10 suggests an interpretation of the practice of *ḥērem* according to this model of ethical development over time.

One ought, before embarking on any project, to be quite clear about the terminology and concepts employed within it, and this is no less – and probably especially – the case with a study on the subject of ethics and morality. Here then, let us immediately state that these two terms will be employed essentially interchangeably. None of our sources constitute a philosophical disquisition on the subject at hand, and to impose on these texts the finer distinctions of terminology adopted by modern philosophical discussions would be inappropriate and anachronistic. The terms are therefore used here in their common meanings, and no great weight ought to be attached to the use of the one or the other in a given phrase.

Both terms refer to those principles of conduct which govern human behaviour, and therefore relate to both an individual's or society's beliefs about actions which are desirable or undesirable, as well as those wider social factors which affect these beliefs.

Finally, this is also perhaps an opportune moment to iterate that this study will, insofar as is reasonably possible, avoid making evaluative assessment of the acts and beliefs of the societies in question. Rather, this is an attempt to articulate the specific moral parameters of one aspect of ancient societies and the overarching ideological and ethical framework which gave rise to those parameters. The essential role of ideology in determining ethics demands that the topic be approached with a full appreciation of the total social context of ethics, and, as will be elaborated in more detail in the following discussion of ideology and sociology, this approach implies, if not requires, a certain moral abstinence on the part of the scholar attempting to describe and elucidate it.

Part I

Ideology, cosmology and ethics

2. Ideology and the confrontation of cultures

Developing a theoretical framework which facilitates the cross-cultural aspects of this study has relied heavily on theories of the purposes and function of ideology in society, broadly categorised academically as the sociology of knowledge. The works of K. Mannheim, P.L. Berger and C. Geertz have been particularly influential in this field and the two latter have proven especially useful.[1] Taking into account the appropriate cautionary warnings often made by biblical scholars when it comes to the use of sociological models in biblical studies, the work done by these sociologists on ideology, religion and related topics are employed for their usefulness in articulating theoretically what has been observed practically in Israel, Judah and Assyria.[2]

Ideology, or sociology of knowledge, originated with Mannheim's *Ideologie und Utopie*, in which Mannheim distinguished between ideology as a conscious distortion of reality – the derogative sense in which it is still frequently employed in common parlance – and ideology as comprising "the characteristics and composition of the total structure of the mind of this epoch or of this group".[3] Mannheim himself favoured the latter definition, in which ideology essentially comprises the entire world view of a given individual. The key element of this definition is the notion that ideology is the product of concrete historical circumstances: with Mannheim originated the recognition that a person's socio-historical background affects his or her way of looking at the world and interacting with it.

Insofar as we have described ethics as including not only actual acts but also the reasons behind beliefs about right and wrong acts, this concept of ideology contains a crucial element for understanding ethi-

---

1 K. Mannheim, *Ideology and Utopia: An Introduction to the Sociology of Knowledge*, ILP, translated by L. Wirth and E. Shils (New York, N.Y.: Harcourt, Brace & Co, 1936); P.L. Berger, *The Sacred Canopy: Elements of a Sociological Theory of Religion* (Garden City, N.Y.: Doubleday, 1969), reprinted as *The Social Reality of Religion* (Norwich: Penguin, 1973); C. Geertz, *The Interpretation of Cultures: Selected Essays* (London: Fontana, 1973).

2 See C.S. Rodd, "On applying a sociological theory to biblical studies", in *Social-Scientific Old Testament Criticism*, edited by D.J. Chalcraft, BS 47 (Sheffield: Sheffield Academic Press, 1997), reprinted from *JSOT* 19 (1981): 95-106; G.A. Herion, "The impact of modern and social science assumptions in the reconstruction of Israelite history", in *Social-Scientific Old Testament Criticism*, edited by D.J. Chalcraft, BS 47 (Sheffield: Sheffield Academic Press, 1997), reprinted from *JSOT* 34 (1986): 3-33.

3 Mannheim, 55-56.

cal beliefs. Ideology affects – indeed defines – a person's entire outlook on reality, including what is or is not acceptable behaviour for the members of his or her community. The norm is for the ethical to cohere with the ideological framework:

> deeper insight into the [moral] problem is reached if we are able to show that morality and ethics themselves are conditioned by certain definite situations, and that such fundamental concepts as duty, transgression, and sin have not always existed but have made their appearance as correlatives of distinct social situations.[4]

Taken to the extreme, the effect of ideology may even be taken to deny the possibility of moral consciousness, due to the impossibility of being conscious of one's own ideology. Mannheim argued that

> nothing can be more wrong than to describe the real attitude of the individual when enjoying a work of art quite unreflectively, or when acting according to ethical patterns inculcated in him since childhood, in terms of conscious choice between values.[5]

As Mannheim himself recognised, however, ideology is constantly evolving, and its changes and flexibility imply that those who share in a given ideology do have the power to affect the moral dictates arising from it. We thus recognise the importance of ideology, which acts as the overarching framework in which ethical decisions are made, while maintaining that ideology does not render conscious ethical thought impossible.

If Mannheim defined ideology as the overarching framework according to which the members of a given society see the world, Berger and Geertz developed Mannheim's ideas further on two points: describing the role which religion plays in buttressing ideology and describing what happens when the ideology of one society is confronted by that of another. Their work has proved highly effective in articulating the socio-ethical phenomena observed with regard to military encounters in Israel, Judah and Assyria.

The most relevant aspect of Berger's work for our purposes is his theory of socialisation; that is, the means by which the intellectual construct of human society is created. Human society, he argues, cannot exist without structure – "to live in the social world is to live an ordered and meaningful life" – and the process of socialisation is the means by which social structure is developed and perpetuated.[6] The process itself is threefold: first, human beings project themselves onto

4 Mannheim, 81.
5 Mannheim, 82.
6 Berger, 21.

the world (externalisation); second, the product of this externalisation confronts its producers as something external to and other than themselves (objectification); and, finally, the objectified product is reappropriated (internalisation).[7] The entire process results in something which was originally a product of the human mind being objectified and re-appropriated as having an independent existence, thereby gaining in authority.

The implications of Berger's theory of socialisation may now be apparent. Insofar as socialisation dictates the structure of human relationships, socialisation is the process by which a society's ethical framework is created. The extent to which this socialisation process is unconscious is especially crucial in understanding the place and function of ethics in society. When successful, socialisation effectively obscures its own existence: rather than being a conscious structuring of human relationships, socialisation is an unconscious process, one of which humans are hardly aware. Indeed,

> socialization achieves success to the degree that this taken-for-granted quality is internalized. It is not enough that the individual look upon the key meanings of the social order as useful, desirable, or right. It is much better (better, that is, in terms of social stability) if he looks upon them as inevitable, as part and parcel of the universal "nature of things."[8]

The process of socialisation is wholly internalised, to the point that the framework it produces is seen as entirely "natural". The ultimate in social stability is achieved when a society's members cannot even conceive of a different way of doing things. In such a society, the given social order is one and the same as the natural world: "society" as such does not exist independently of "nature". Various aspects of society – institutions, behaviours, relationships – are organised in the current way not only because they are meant to be that way, but because there is no other conceivable system according to which they could be organised. By being objectified, ideas attain an aura of authority and inevitability. As a result, alternative social systems are perceived as not merely alternative but as actually unnatural: since there cannot be more than one natural social order, and the one to which the subject belongs constitutes that natural order, any other social system must be unnatural. As the language of "natural order" and "deviation" suggests, the social order acquires the trappings of moral order through its identification with natural order.

7 Berger, 4-6.
8 Berger, 24.

When the role of religion in socialisation is made clear, the influence of ideology on ethics is made ever more evident. While religion is not a necessary element of socialisation (or of ethics, for that matter), it is a common element because of its ability to cope with the persistent aspects of reality which threaten to undermine a society's ideology. Such threats tend to cluster around what Berger calls "marginal situations" (e.g. death), and the plausibility of a social order depends on its ability to explain such threats as part of the existing order – to "legitimate" them, in Berger's terms. Religion, as it happens, is especially good at doing this – mainly because it can, when all else fails, appeal to vague divine mysteries to explain incongruencies.[9] Through its ability to appeal to the divine as the source of the world order, religion lets people believe

> that, in acting out the institutional programs that have been imposed upon them, they are but realizing the deepest aspirations of their own being and putting themselves in harmony with the fundamental order of the universe.[10]

Religion's success as socialiser is based on its ability to create the ultimately convincing "aura of factuality" to the "general order of existence": its ability to create not only the social order, or "cosmos", but a "sacred cosmos".[11] In other words, religion bolsters society by providing an ultimate, irrefutable answer to the question of why society is ordered as it is.

In the political sphere, for example, theology can legitimate a social order such as monarchy by making human society a microcosm of the divine cosmos. Thus

> the political authority is conceived of as the agent of the gods, or ideally even as a divine incarnation. Human power, government, and punishment thus become sacramental phenomena, that is, channels by which divine forces are made to impinge upon the lives of men. The ruler speaks for the gods, or *is* a god, and to obey him is to be in a right relationship with the world of the gods.[12]

As will be detailed in the next chapter, the Assyrian king is very clearly conceived as the earthly counterpart of the god when he embarks on

9 The role of social legitimator is fundamental to Geertz's definition of religion itself; a religion is "*(1) a system of symbols which acts to (2) establish powerful, pervasive, and long-lasting moods and motivations in men by (3) formulating conceptions of a general order of existence and (4) clothe these conceptions with such an aura of factuality that (5) the moods and motivations seem uniquely realistic*" (Geertz, 90; italics in original).

10 Berger, 32-33.

11 Berger, 25.

12 Berger, 34.

military endeavours, and his actions are legitimated by his participation in the divine struggle for order and against chaos. Interestingly, however, Berger asserted that in Israel (and Judah) this scheme was broken through an emphasis on God's direct activity in history, circumventing the need for a royal human agent; human institutions were thought of in terms of revealed divine imperatives rather than as mirrors of divine institutions.[13] While social structure was still religiously legitimated, it took a different format in Israel. As will become clear in Chapter 4 and the rest of the study, this is the kind of conclusion reached through uncritical comparison of biblical and ancient Near Eastern material.

Coming back to this notion of the "sacred cosmos", we have observed the growing nexus of language surrounding (social) order, the natural order (the cosmos) and the moral order, and now see this language of order set against its opposite, chaos.

> Just as religious legitimation interprets the order of society in terms of an all-embracing sacred order of the universe, so it relates the disorder that is the antithesis of all socially constructed *nomos* to that yawning abyss of chaos that is the oldest antagonist of the sacred.[14]

On the one hand there is a cognitive nexus surrounding a (religiously-legitimated) social order (the cosmos) which, thanks to its identification with the natural order, takes on moral implications; on the other there is the opposite, in which that which does not conform to the "natural" order is expressed as anti-order, that is, chaos. Yet order is necessary to human existence:

> man depends on symbols and symbol systems with a dependence so great as to be decisive for his creaturely viability and, as a result, his sensitivity to even the remote indication that they may prove unable to cope with one or another aspect of experience raises within him the gravest sort of anxiety: "[Man] can adapt himself somehow to anything his image can cope with; but he cannot deal with chaos..."[15]

This human inability to cope with chaos is thought to be one of the instigating factors in the development of ideology (religious or otherwise). The precise nature of this process is unclear, but there are two primary theories. In one, "ideological pronouncements are seen against the background of a universal struggle for advantage"; in the other, ideology is the result of a "chronic effort to correct sociopsychological disequilibrium" (the disjunct between what ought to happen and what

---

13 Berger, 35.

14 Berger, 40.

15 Geertz, 99, quoting S.K.K. Langer, *Philosophy in a New Key* (Boston: Harvard University Press, 1942), 287.

does happen). "In the one, men may pursue power; in the other, they flee anxiety."[16]

While ideology may well arise from both at once, and while the former certainly plays a significant role in understanding the royal ideology of ancient Near Eastern societies in particular, it is the latter to which we will pay further attention here, because it is the role of ideology in mediating "sociopsychological disequilibrium" which proves particularly useful in describing how ancient Near Eastern societies responded intellectually when they came into contact with each other on the battlefield.

What happens when the social order (cosmos) of one society – the "indigenous" order – which has been normalised by the process of socialisation and legitimated internally by religion, comes into contact with the social order of an external group? We have already had reason to note that successful socialisation has the effect of articulating all alternative social systems as "unnatural". When a social order is confronted by such an alternative, "unnatural" social order, it threatens the "indigenous" order by calling into question its "natural" basis. It therefore becomes a cognitive necessity to eliminate this threat.

In the sphere of international politics, the cognitive effect of the encounter between an imperial power and the enemy residing at or beyond the borders of imperial hegemony fits precisely this model. Though the encounter is at first glance strictly physical, involving the actual engagement of two armies on the battlefield, with concrete – that is, political and economic – explanations and implications and strictly practical rationale behind what is permissible treatment of the enemy, the interaction has its ultimate explanation on the level of ideology. Though the opponent may be human, he represents a serious threat to ordered existence because he is the embodiment of an alternative social order – chaos opposed to the indigenous order. Lest his chaos overcome that order, he must be destroyed.

As will be observed in the texts which follow, this resembles the way in which each ancient Near Eastern culture articulates its internal social order as opposed to that of its opponents. The nexus observed in the ancient literature between moral good and the indigenous order, as opposed to moral evil and "foreign" chaos, ought thus to be understood in sociological terms.

16 Geertz, 201.

3. Assyrian cosmology

This ideological polarisation of indigenous order over and against enemy chaos is germane to our understanding of Assyrian foreign affairs. Helpfully, the nature and content of Assyrian ideology has been considered on several occasions by Liverani, who has particularly emphasised the supporting role of Assyrian religion.[1] Though he does not employ the sociological theorisation of ideology which we find so useful, he does use language of order versus chaos which is easily incorporated into the more theoretical articulation.

In his own work on the Assyrian manifestation of the sociological struggle between order and chaos, Liverani speaks of an Assyrian centre representing order and a non-Assyrian periphery which, by being non-Assyrian, is identified as chaos. The universe as a whole is correctly ordered when its entirety is orientated toward the centre, which in the Assyrian case comprises the Assyrian heartland and its capital cities.[2] This ideological geography pervades Assyrian thought. Those who are outside the boundaries of and fail to conform to the (Assyrian) idea of order are called *nakru* – a term whose semantic range includes anyone who is "strange" or "foreign", either of language, city, or people; it denotes a "hostile person", an "enemy".[3] The use of the term is enlightening: it is through his strangeness, his lack of conformity, that the *nakru* poses a challenge to Assyrian order; because of his strangeness he is an enemy. In the language of Berger and Geertz, the *nakru*'s deviation from the known social order identifies him as chaos. Chaos being that which is opposed to order, he must be destroyed. In Liverani's words:

> the interaction of two such different human types (one "correct" and one "strange") must lead to the elimination of the "strange" type. This occurs either by its being assimilated by the "correct" type, or by its physical elimination or by its disappearance from the scene. ... The diversity thus becomes guilt and aberration: the enemy is abnormal, unnatural – we must

---

1 M. Liverani, "The ideology of the Assyrian empire", in *Power and Propaganda: A Symposium on Ancient Empires*, edited by M.T. Larsen, Mesopotamia 7 (Copenhagen: Akademisk Forlag, 1979), 301.

2 Liverani, "Memorandum", 189.

3 Liverani, "Ideology", 310.

eliminate him. He is wicked (*nākiru limnu, ēpiš limutti*, etc.) – we do well to kill him, it is his fault if we must kill him.[4]

The easy movement here from the idea of order arrayed against the threat of chaos to language of moral good against evil reiterates our earlier equation of the social, natural and moral order.

The confrontation of this centralised order with a chaotic periphery was inevitable as long as Assyrian hegemony did not extend universally, but such confrontation was made all the more inevitable by the Assyrians' pursuit of actively imperialistic policies from the mid-eighth century on – policies themselves intimately connected to, indeed derived from, the ideological dichotomy of order versus chaos. The order-chaos dichotomy was a self-perpetuating phenomenon: as a result of the alignment of the Assyrian centre with order and the periphery with chaos, combined with the ideological necessity of eradicating the threat of chaos to order, imperialistic expansion became not a matter of voluntary political expansion but a matter of existence itself. Military violence was a necessity. As for the enemy, this characterisation of warfare as an act against chaos correlates to a depiction of conquest as being in the interests of the conquered, who, through defeat, are rescued from chaos. Indeed, two Assyrian oracles go so far as to characterise their descriptions of the god's violent acts against Assyria's enemies as oracles of "peace" or "well-being" (*šulmu*).[5] As Liverani puts it, "the imperialistic expansion of the central kingdom [becomes] the prevailing of cosmos over the surrounding chaos, it is an enterprise that brings order and civilization."[6] And, crucially, the equation of the natural and social order with the moral order turns this enterprise into a moral one.

The opposition of order to chaos, however, is only the most general articulation of the ideological phenomenon. There will be further opportunity to observe the consequences of such a worldview in the specific texts considered in Chapters 5 and 8, but to fully understand the implications of this dichotomy for warfare it is essential that the specifically ancient Near Eastern articulation of this general phenomenon is addressed. This context is first and foremost the mythological narratives of creation.[7]

---

4 Liverani, "Ideology", 311 (Akkadian as in original).

5 SAA 9 3.2, 3.3 (Nissinen, Seow and Ritner nos. 85, 86). To aid the reader, texts appearing in more than one well-known publication are cited to all such publications.

6 Liverani, "Ideology", 306-307.

7 The impetus for using *Enūma eliš* as the benchmark for the Assyrian royal military ideology derives from the work of E. Weissert on the inscriptions of Sennacherib's battle at Halulê ("Creating a political climate: literary allusions to *Enūma Eliš* in Sennacherib's account of the battle of Halule", in *Assyrien im Wandel der Zeiten: XXXIXe Rencontre Assyriologique Internationale, Heidelberg 6.-10. Juli 1992*, edited by H.

The cosmological tradition of Assyria is best known in the form of *Enūma eliš*, sometimes called the Babylonian Epic of Creation or the Glorification of Marduk.[8] In the version current in eighth and seventh century Assyria the epic includes an account of the creation of the world in which one god, Marduk, is commissioned by the other gods to go forth and fight against the goddess Tiamat, who threatens to destroy the universe. Marduk's victory over Tiamat prevents the dissolution of the universe into chaos, and secures its ordered existence. As a reward for his victory, Marduk is crowned king of the gods.

This depiction of the struggle between order and chaos on a cosmic scale provides us with a significant window into the Assyrians' intellectual universe. In it, it is through the defeat of chaos, embodied by Tiamat, that order reigns and the universe survives. Even more significant for the matter of human warfare, however, is the group of concepts which are incorporated as part of this cosmology.

First, it is specifically through warfare that the victory of order over chaos is achieved. Marduk defeats Tiamat after a violent battle which employs both conventional weaponry (e.g. bow and arrows) and the forces of nature (e.g. flood and storm):

> He fashioned a bow, designated it as his weapon,
> Feathered the arrow, set it in the string.
> He lifted up a mace and carried it in his right hand,
> Slung the bow and quiver at his side,
> Put lightning in front of him,
> His body was filled with an ever-blazing flame.
> He made a net to encircle Tiamat within it,
> Guarded the four winds so that none of her could escape:
> South Wind, North Wind, East Wind, West Wind,
> He kept them close to the net at his side, the gift of his father Anu.
> He created the evil *imḫullu*-wind, the storm, the dust storm,
> The Four Winds, the Seven Winds, the whirlwind, the unfaceable wind.
> He sent out the winds which he had created, seven of them.
> They advanced behind him to make turmoil inside Tiamat.

Waetzoldt and H. Hauptmann, HSAO 6 [Heidelberg: Heidelberger Orientverlag, 1997]). His work will be discussed in greater detail in Chapter 8.

8 As the alternative name indicates, *Enūma eliš* is Babylonian in origin, but the myth represents a long tradition adopted by Assyrian culture (it was found in multiple copies in the Assyrian royal libraries). Given the developments in Assyrian military ideology which arise because of the cosmology's Babylonian origins, a separate study of the use of the myth in its Babylonian context would be highly valuable, but is beyond the scope of what is undertaken here.

The lord raised the flood-weapon, his great weapon,
And mounted the frightful, unfaceable storm-chariot. ...[9]

Second, it is as a direct consequence of this military victory that Marduk is declared king of the gods. The result is an association between kingship and warfare on the highest possible level – that of the gods – at the most significant possible moment – that of creation – and in the most vital act of creation: the defeat of chaos which enables creation, which is itself the establishment of order.

Though interesting, all this mythological talk of kings, war and order on the cosmic, divine scale would be of little use in explaining the behaviour of human warriors if the activities of the gods and the activities of humans existed in mutually exclusive spheres of morality and reality. The narrative of Marduk the warrior establishing order in the face of Tiamat's chaos is ethically irrelevant unless a clear connection between gods and humans can be established.

This brings us then, to the question of the nature of the relationship between the acts of the gods and the acts of men.

The key link in the establishment of a connection between divine and human acts is the institution of kingship. It is specifically as a result of his military triumph that Marduk is declared king of the gods. In this conceptual nexus, war is a function of kingship, and kingship itself becomes defined by war.

The centrality of warfare to royal identity has been emphasised by S.M. Maul, referring to a number of mythological and inscriptional texts of Sumerian and Akkadian origin: his discussions speak in generalised terms of similar motifs attributed to both warrior gods and warrior kings.[10] Detailing the extent of the similarities between the human

---

9 En.el. IV 35-49 (*ib-šim* GIŠ.BAN GIŠ.TUKUL-*šu ú-ad-di mul-mul-lum uš-tar-ki-ba ú-kin-ši mat-nu iš-ši-ma miṭ-ṭi im-na-š ú-šá-ḫi-iz* GIŠ.BAN *u iš-pa-tum i-du-uš-šu i-lul iš-kun* NIM.GÍR *i-na pa-ni-šu nab-la muš-taḫ-me-ṭu zu-mur-šu um-tal-li i-pu-uš-ma sa-pa-ra šul-mu-ú qer-biš ti-amat er-bet-ti šá-a-ri uš-te-eṣ-bi-ta la a-ṣe-e mim-mi-šá* IM.U$_{18}$.LU IM.SI.SÁ IM.KUR.RA IM.MAR.TU *i-du-uš sa-pa-ra uš-taq-ri-ba qí-iš-ti* AD-*šú* ^{d}*a-num ib-ni im-ḫul-la* IM *lem-na me-ḫa-a a-šam-šu-tum* IM.LÍMMU.BA IM.IMIN.BI IM.SÙḪ IM.SÁ.A.NU.SÁ.A *ú-še-ṣa-am-ma* IM.MEŠ *šá ib-nu-ú si-bit-ti-šú-un qer-biš ti-amat šu-ud-lu-ḫu te-bu-ú* EGIR-*šú iš-ši-ma be-lum a-bu-ba* GIŠ.TUKUL-*šú* GAL-*a* GIŠ.GIGIR UD-*mu la maḫ-ri ga-lit-ta ir-kab*). Transliterations of *Enūma eliš* are taken from P. Talon, *Enūma Eliš: The Standard Babylonian Creation Myth*, SAACT 4 (Helsinki: Neo-Assyrian Text Corpus Project, 2005); translations are after S. Dalley, *Myths from Mesopotamia: Creation, The Flood, Gilgamesh, and Others* (Oxford: Oxford University Press, 2000), and Talon. All transliterations follow the formatting of the edition cited.

10 S.M. Maul, "'Wenn der Held (zum Kampfe) auszeiht...' Ein Ninurta-Eršemma", *Or* 60 (1991): 312-334; S.M. Maul, "Der assyrische König – Hüter der Weltordnung", in *Gerechtigkeit: Richten und Retten in der abendländischen Tradition und ihrer*

king's actions in the field of warfare and those of the gods was subsequently undertaken by K.-P. Adam in *Der Königliche Held*.[11] Both Adam and Maul in fact make relatively little reference to *Enūma eliš*, instead basing their discussion on a myth of the creation of humans as detailed in W.R. Mayer's edition.[12] From this myth it is apparent that it is the function of the human king as military leader which distinguishes him from other humans; his kingship is characterised first and foremost by his capacity for war.[13] The human king symbolically receives the divine commission to go to war by receiving the weapons of the gods:

> They gave the king the battle of the [great] gods,
> Anu gave him his crown, Ellil ga[ve him his throne],
> Nergal gave him his weapons,
> Ninurta g[ave him his shining splendour],
> Bēlet-ilī gave [him his beautiful app]earance...[14]

Adam concludes "ohne Umschweife nennt dieser Text die entscheidende Aufgabe des Königs im Alten Orient: Der *König muß Kriege führen*".[15] The name Adam gives this idea is that of his title: "der königliche Held". With this phrase he emphasises that it is not merely a characteristic of the human king to wage war, but rather war is a mutual obligation of both the divine and the human king; the requirement that they go to war is a concept independent of yet adopted by both because it is perceived as an inherent function of the kingship embodied by each:

> daß der Kampf Aufgabe des Königs ist, gilt dabei auf *beiden Ebenen* des Königtums, für die königliche Gottheit und den historischen König. Wie

---

altorientalischen Ursprüngen, edited by J. Assmann, B. Janowski and M. Welker (Munich: Wilhelm Fink Verlag, 1998).

11 K.-P. Adam, *Der Königliche Held: Die Entsprechung von kämpfendem Gott und kämpfendem König in Psalm 18*, WMANT 91 (Neukirchen-Vluyn: Neukirchner Verlag, 2001).

12 W.R. Mayer, "Ein Mythos von der Erschaffung des Menschen und des Königs", *Or* 56 (1987): 55-68.

13 Maul, "König", 71; Adam, 1.

14 Mayer, "Mythos", 56:37′-40′ (*id-*⌜*di*⌝*-nu-ma a-na* LUGAL *ta-ḫa-za* DINGIR.ME[Š GAL.MEŠ] ᵈ*A-nù it-ta-din a-gu-ú*(Text: PA)*-šú* ᵈEN.LÍL *it-*[*ta-din kussâ-šú*] ᵈU.GUR *it-ta-din* ⌞ᴳᴵˢTUKUL⌟.MEŠ*-šú* ᵈMAŠ *i*[*t-ta-din šá-lum-mat-su*] ᵈ*Be-let-*DINGIR.MEŠ *it-ta-din bu-un*[*-na-ni-šú*]; "Es gaben dem König den Kampf die [großen] Götter, Anu gab ihm die Krone, Ellil ga[b ihm den Thron], Nergal gab ihm die Waffen, Ninurta g[ab ihm gließenden Glanze], Bēlet-ilī gab [ihm ein schönes Aus]sehen..."). As Mayer points out, the possessive suffix in these lines can refer to either the god or the king; on the basis of the last he considers the latter more likely (Mayer, "Mythos", 61). Either way the weapons come from the gods and their use with an implicit divine blessing.

15 Adam, 2.

der irdische König das Land im Kampf gegen die Feinde verteidigt, so verteidigt die königliche Gottheit das bedrohte Gemeinwesen der Götter im Kampf gegen die feindlichen Mächte.[16]

Both are engaged toward the same purpose and employ the same means.[17]

Of additional importance is Adam's observation that "die Gottheit tritt in der Rolle des königlichen Helden immer in *historischen Zusammenhängen* auf."[18] This reiterates the connection between divine and human actions against chaos, the enemy: just as the human king's actions are seen as part of the cosmic struggle against chaos – a struggle instigated at creation by the gods – the gods' battle against chaos is simultaneously seen in historical terms.[19] While on the one hand the god and the human king mirror each other in their roles as royal warriors, their actions are both directed towards the destruction of chaotic forces in favour of the creation of order. The divine-human synergy has a single object.

This brings us to our final point regarding the coordinated actions of gods and kings, namely, that such a historical conception of the divine warrior inherently implies a synchronised historical, human agent. In discussions of war in the Hebrew Bible in particular, scholars tend to gloss over human moral responsibility by emphasising that the named agent is frequently (one cannot by any means say always) a divine one. This is an evasive manoeuvre which this study must emphasise as absolutely eliminated. Not only are the acts of divine and human agent so frequently overlapping as to make such a distinction superficial, the nature of ancient Near Eastern belief in divine action in history presumes some sort of effective human agency: statues do not arise with spear in hand, and battles are therefore not fought between armies of statues but armies of men. Supposedly divine acts must, in historical reality, employ human agents. Thus, if a god's claim to have slaughtered the enemy, flayed their soldiers and impaled their commanders is not to be taken as mere imagination but as an expression of the god's contribution to the historical victory of one king and his army over

16 Adam, 13.

17 Note that Adam's identification of god and human king is identification in parallel, not an ontological identification; we are not considering the deification of a human king. The paralleling also does not extend to a complete mirroring of gods and kings, but is limited to certain defined aspects of reality – of which war is the first and foremost.

18 Adam, 26.

19 A similar point was made more generally by B. Albrektson in *History and the Gods: An Essay on the Idea of Historical Events as Divine Manifestation in the Ancient Near East and in Israel*, CBOT 1 (Lund: CWK Gleerup, 1967).

another, it is that real king and army who must slaughter, flay and impale.

Suffice it to suggest that the role of the divine agent in the historical realm is spoken of in language of metaphor; the god "does" X because the god enables a human to do X. Taken to extreme, one might try to argue that such divine oversight of the historical stage effectively eradicated human autonomy – the human actor merely follows the strings pulled by a divine puppeteer – but it is also clear that divine support of human endeavour, perceived in its success, was considered a sign of approval. Divine imitation of human reality ultimately affirms the legitimacy of the acts. The king's actions in war were supported and mirrored by the gods because they were right, and his success reflected both divine support and divine approbation. The intimate relationship between divine and human action did not absolve human beings of moral responsibility.

Warfare, kingship, order. The significance of this conceptual conglomeration for the Assyrian understanding of the act of war can hardly be overestimated. Not only is interaction with the enemy a sociologically comprehensible confrontation with an alternative social order, characterised as chaos, but it is, as expressed through Assyrian cosmology, explicitly articulated on the cosmic plane. Religion is playing its special role as socialiser; the actions of the human king against his human enemy are part of the ultimate and ongoing struggle for order against chaos. To destroy the chaotic enemy is not only a matter of the preservation of Assyrian order, but part of a much wider existential struggle for the preservation of the universe itself. The king's (and by implication his army's) acts mirror and are in harmony with those of the gods; the king acts as the earthly agent, mediating the intentions of the gods through his own actions.

The ethical implications of this paralleling of human and divine have already been touched upon, but may now be made more explicit. That the articulation of the Assyrian military endeavour in terms of and as part of a cosmological struggle for order and against chaos, in which the gods themselves were involved on both a cosmic and historical plane, was fundamental in framing the Assyrian imperial and military project can hardly be disputed. The king's actions on the historical plane are identified and merged with the militarism of the gods on the cosmic plane: his violent dispatch of his enemies is not merely a matter of historical politics, but a matter of life or death, order or chaos, on a cosmic scale. The specific deployment of this concept will be examined in greater detail with respect to individual texts, but for now it is sufficient to say that, in such an understanding of the role of Assyria and its military actions, obtaining the submission of the chaotic enemy was not merely a matter of moral tolerability but a matter of moral imperative.

4. Judahite and Israelite cosmology

The military ideology which pits the king as the defender of cosmic order by means of military action against the chaotic enemy was closely paralleled in Israel and Judah. As in Assyria, the human king's role as defender of order on earth is connected to the god's defence of order at creation.

As above, a strong initial argument for this phenomenon has been made by Adam, who marshals the evidence to contend that the mirrored activities of Yahweh and the human king reflect parallel pursuits of the model of the royal hero (*der königliche Held*):

> das Entsprechungsverhältnis zwischen JHWH als königlicher Gottheit und dem irdischen König als Held [konnte] nur deswegen so eng gefaßt werden ... weil beide dieselbe Handlungsrolle einnehmen: Wie JHWH als Held im Kampf eingreift, kann auch der irdische König eingreifen.[1]

He goes on to discuss the phenomenon in detail with respect to Ps. 18 in particular, evincing a number of parallels in the language and imagery used on the one hand of Yahweh and on the other of the earthly king.

It is not coincidental that the sphere in which this mirroring of activity is most strongly attested is that of military action. As we saw in the Assyrian material, the conglomeration of divine and human royal activity occurs most explicitly in warfare, with the distinguishing aspect of kingship being the conduct of war. This was particularly symbolised by the receipt of the divine weaponry by the human king, but was ultimately connected to a cosmological framework in which the human king perpetuates the struggle against chaos and for order which was begun by the god at creation.[2] Military engagement and victory is thereby the key act which facilitates the creation of an ordered universe.

While Adam certainly alludes to the role of the king and the god in fighting against chaos on the Mesopotamian side, it is curious that he

---

1 Adam, 29.

2 For a discussion of the shared weaponry of divine and human kings, see N. Wyatt, "Degrees of divinity: some mythical and ritual aspects of West Semitic kingship", in *'There's Such Divinity Doth Hedge a King': Selected Essays of Nicholas Wyatt on Royal Ideology in Ugaritic and Old Testament Literature*, SOTSMS (Aldershot: Ashgate, 2005).

does not pursue the Israelite and Judahite parallel. This may be in part due to the fact that his predecessors, W.R. Mayer and Maul, do not explicitly connect the phenomenon to *Enūma eliš*, though, even if they had, it is still possible that Adam would not have pursued it from the biblical perspective, given the lack of an explicit account of a divine struggle for creation in the Hebrew Bible: Gen. 1 has been deliberately stripped of such a battle, while Gen. 2-3 knows nothing of it.

That such a tradition was well-known in Israel and Judah, however, has already been convincingly established by J. Day, in *God's Conflict with the Dragon and the Sea.*[3] Though deliberately obscured in the priestly account of creation, it is certain that Israel and Judah knew of a cosmological account in which it was Yahweh's victory over the forces of chaos, embodied as watery sea creatures, which enabled the establishment of an ordered world. The strongest evidence for this tradition occurs, unsurprisingly, in *Psalms*, which are the biblical literature with a social provenance most closely mirroring the provenance of the royal Assyrian material.[4]

Equally essential, however, is the fact that this motif of Yahweh's battle against chaotic forces at creation appears repeatedly in conjunction with Yahweh's characterisation as divine king. This occurs most clearly in Ps. 93, in which the proclamation that יהוה מלך is followed by strongly cosmological language alluding to the creation and a divine battle with the sea.[5]

In Psalm 89, in which Day also identifies a strong cosmological motif, the theme of the battle against chaos at creation is likewise immediately preceded by language suggesting Yahweh's kingship over other gods:

> For who in the skies can be compared to Yahweh?
> Who among the heavenly beings is like Yahweh,
> A god feared in the council of the holy ones,
> Great and awesome above all around him? (89.7-8)[6]

Similarly, in Ps. 24 the psalm opens with a declaration of Yahweh's role as creator:

> The earth is Yahweh's and all that is in it,
> The world and those who live in it;

---

3 J. Day, *God's Conflict with the Dragon and the Sea: Echoes of a Canaanite Myth in the Old Testament*, COP 35 (Cambridge: Cambridge University Press, 1985).

4 On which see Chapter 6.1.

5 Day notes this connection, suggesting that the idea of Yahweh's kingship may here also be extended to Yahweh's rule over the nations (Day, *Conflict*, 35-36). Given the convergence of these ideas elsewhere, this is highly probable (see Chapter 6).

6 כי מי בשחק יערך ליהוה ידמה ליהוה בבני אלים: אל נערץ בסוד קדשים רבה ונורא על־כל־סביביו:

For he has founded it on the seas
And established it on the rivers (24.1-2).[7]

Though he considers it an uncertain case, Day concludes that this passage, in conjunction with the reference in 24.8 to Yahweh in military terms, most probably does refer to a battle with the sea.[8] The likelihood of this is reinforced by the inclusion in the psalm of repeated references to Yahweh as king (24.7, 8, 9, 10): without falling into circular arguments, it is more than coincidence that these three motifs appear together.

Last but not least is Ps. 18, but as Adam has discussed at length the royal characterisation of Yahweh in this psalm it is only necessary to note the language suggestive of Yahweh's creative role as cosmic victor (89.11-16); these will be discussed in greater detail below (Chapter 6).

In Israel and Judah as well as Assyria, then, there was a tradition linking the motifs of war, kingship and the establishment of order at creation.[9] Though the limitations of the sources mean that the Hebrew version is more difficult to flesh out than the Akkadian, its presence in the texts of royal provenance confirms our suspicion that the Israelite and Judahite élites shared with their Assyrian counterparts the intellectual location of warfare in a cosmological context of battle against chaos.[10]

Remarkably, however, the similarity in the Assyrian, Judahite and Israelite ideologies of warfare was explicitly denied by Zehnder in his *Umgang mit Fremden in Israel und Assyrien*. In his conclusions he writes:

> die relative Grausamkeit Assyriens auf der einen und die relative Milde Israels auf der anderen Seite hängen mit den oben genannten ideologischen Grundlagen zusammen: Die Qualifizierung von Gegnern als Nicht-Menschen, wie sie in Assyrien vorkommt, erleichtert die grausame Behandlung des Gegners; umgekehrt schiebt der Gedanke einer schöpfungstheologisch begründeten Einheit des Menschengeschlechts, wie er in Israel entwickelt wird, enthemmtem Töten einen Riegel [vor].[11]

---

7 ליהוה הארץ ומלואה תבל וישבי בה: כי־הוא על־ימים יסדה ועל־נהרות יכוננה:

8 Day, *Conflict*, 37-38.

9 Some have attempted to distinguish the Israelite and Judahite tradition of kingship by drawing attention to the emphasis on the god's (Yahweh's) kingship, over and against the human king. That the Assyrians also considered the god to be the "real" king, however, is clear from the enthronement ritual of Assurbanipal, in which it is Aššur who is proclaimed king, and Assurbanipal as his agent (SAA 3 11; see Maul, "König", 75).

10 For further evidence for these ideas among the élites see Chapters 6 and 9.

11 Zehnder, 554.

However, as we have just seen, the biblical texts do contain clear evidence of an ideological framework in Judah and in Israel which closely mirrors that observed in Assyrian texts.

The clearest explanation for Zehnder's conclusion is his explicit decision to take the biblical texts canonically, without giving due recognition to the diverse origins of the texts contained within the Hebrew Bible and without recognising the significantly different origins of the biblical texts when compared to the Assyrian texts he discusses. A similar decision, with similar consequences, was made by Otto in his *Theologische Ethik des Alten Testaments*: by taking the biblical texts essentially canonically, Otto allows the canonical dominance of non-royal material to preclude those texts in which a chaotic struggle appears and affect his judgment in his assessment of such texts.[12]

In those texts which are most approximately equivalent in social origin and background to that which dominates the Assyrian material, however, evidence is readily forthcoming for the same basic cosmology and ideology in Israel and Judah.

12 Otto, *Ethik*, 92-9. In particular Otto contends that the concept of humanity as a positive contributor in the struggle against chaos was absent in Israel; this arises on the one hand from a primary comparison to Egyptian materials and on the other from a blurring of texts' social origins.

Part II

Ethics and society

5. Ethics of the Assyrian élite

The first third of the Neo-Assyrian empire's resurgence, dominated by the reigns of Tiglath-pileser III and Sargon II, is characterised by general allusions to the creation struggle and relatively moderate levels of violence. These kings' actions set the standard for the period and are indicative of the levels of violence which the Assyrian élites tolerated in conjunction within the broad ideological framework described in Chapter 3.

5.1. Method

Before beginning the analysis proper, a few preliminary remarks with regard to the use of these sources for the discernment of ethical thinking are required. First, as its historical orientation indicates, this study supposes that some information about the actual historical conduct of warfare is obtainable from the primary materials available, even if that information is inevitably incomplete. Second, there are two basic categories into which deviations from historical reality in these sources may fall: those of addition and those of omission. Insofar as ethics is in large part a matter of ideas of what *ought* to be done, rather than necessarily what *is* done, such additions and omissions are as informative for our purposes as would be a purely factual history: while the latter would tell us what has happened, the former tells us what ought to have happened.

The absence of certain activities from an account suggests, from an ethical perspective, one of two things: either that such activities were viewed as ethically suspect, such that, even if they were done, they were expunged from the record from embarrassment or disgust; or that they were so repugnant that they were in fact not engaged upon at all.

This only holds, of course, in those instances in which the author(s) intends to cast a positive light on the historical subject(s) in question. In the case of the Assyrian literature, the royal provenance of the material and the material's role as royal propaganda makes the assumption of such an intent relatively straightforward.[1]

5.2. Tiglath-pileser III (745-727)

Tiglath-pileser III sets the stage for the era. The descriptions of his campaigns speak of destruction in largely general terms, with only limited references to more extreme forms of interaction with the defeated enemy. Correlating to this are occasional but not frequent allusions to the creation myth, indicating that the king was seen as the god's counterpart on earth but which do not press the point.

5.2.1. Cosmology

The allusions indicate that behind Tiglath-pileser's engagement in military activities is the idea that the king in battle is the earthly counterpart of the god, conquering the chaotic forces and thereby enabling the ordered existence of the universe. This is done primarily through allu-

---

1 On this see M. Liverani ("Propaganda", in volume 5 of *Anchor Bible Dictionary*, edited by D.N. Freedman (London: Doubleday, 1992). Propaganda is the means by which this explanation is disseminated and reinforced, particularly to those who to some greater or lesser degree resist its explanatory power: "the deliberate (albeit most dissimulated) spreading of ideas, information, rumors, etc. in order to support one's own political (or religious) cause, to acquire more proselytes, and in the last analysis to gain more power" (474). Note also the distinction between propaganda and ideology; ideology is that which is effectively taken for granted as the natural and only explanation of social reality, while propaganda is ideology's more active cousin. For further discussions of the use of the Assyrian inscriptions for the reconstruction of history, see e.g., A.K. Grayson, "Assyrian royal inscriptions: literary characteristics", in *Assyrian Royal Inscriptions: New Horizons in Literary, Ideological, and Historical Analysis: Papers of a Symposium held in Cetona (Siena), June 26-28, 1980*, edited by F.M. Fales, OAC 17 (Rome: Isituto per l'Oriente, 1981); L.D. Levine, "Preliminary remarks on the historical inscriptions of Sennacherib", in *History, Historiography and Interpretation: Studies in Biblical and Cuneiform Literatures*, edited by H. Tadmor and M. Weinfeld (Leiden: Brill, 1984); Liverani, "Memorandum"; M. De Odorico, *The Use of Numbers and Quantifications in the Assyrian Royal Inscriptions*, SAAS 3 (Helsinki: Neo-Assyrian Text Corpus Project, 1995); A.L. Oppenheim, *Ancient Mesopotamia: Portrait of a Dead Civilization*, second edition, completed by E. Reiner (London: University of Chicago Press, 1977); and J. Renger, "Neuassyrische Königsinschriften als Genre der Keilschriftliteratur – zum Stil und zur Kompositionstechnik der Inschriften Sargons II. von Assyrien", in *Keilschriftliche Literaturen: Assyriologique Internationale Münster, 8-12.7.1985*, edited by K. Hecker and W. Sommerfield (Berlin: Dietrich Reimer, 1986).

sive language, particularly with regards to weaponry: Tiglath-pileser's effects on his enemies are described as like the effects wrought by the weapons of the god at creation, namely the flood (*abūbu*) and the net (*sapāru*).[2] The former not being an especially natural weapon of war, it is unlikely to be used by chance; it is more probable that the reference to it in Tiglath-pileser's inscriptions is deliberately employed to connect the king's actions against his enemies as in accord with the god's against chaos.

The clearest allusion to the role of Tiglath-pileser as the earthly opponent of chaos occurs in the titulary, which serves as a summary of the king's perception of his role. There Tiglath-pileser is described as the one who "smashed like pots all the unsubmissive, swept over them like the flood, made them as powerless ghosts".[3] We note in particular that it is specifically those who do not submit to Tiglath-pileser (*lā māgirišu*) who are destroyed by means of flood; it is their refusal to become part of the Assyrian world system which identifies them as chaotic and in need of destruction.

Allusive language occurs at three further points in Tiglath-pileser's inscriptions. The capital of Bit-Shilani is "laid waste as though ruined by the flood".[4] He is also said to overwhelm the Bit-Kapsi, Bit-Sangi

---

2 *Enūma eliš* also refers to less distinctive weapons such as the bow (*qaštu*) and arrow (*mulmullu*). Lightning (*nablu*) and wind (*šāru, meḫû*) are also named, but not alluded to by Tiglath-pileser.

3 H. Tadmor, *The Inscriptions of Tiglath-Pileser III King of Assyria: Critical Edition, with Introductions, Translations and Commentary* (Jerusalem: The Israel Academy of Sciences and Humanities, 1994), Summ. 11:2 (*kul-lat la ma-gi-ri-šu kīma haṣ-bat-ti ú-daq-qi-qu a-bu-biš is-pu-nu-ma zi-qi-qiš im-nu-u*; cf. Summ. 7:2). Dalley argues that this type of sweeping language originates in lament forms, where they are prefatory to language of restoration (see S. Dalley, "The language of destruction and its interpretation", *BM* 36 (2005): 275-285). We agree that the lament language draws upon similar imagery, and suggest that the laments' use of the language also draws upon the concept of (Assyrian) warfare as the means by which order is established (or restored). The submission of foreign peoples and nations reinforces the cosmic order personified by the king; their resistance threatens this cosmic order. It is necessary to destroy the enemy, so that the cosmically destabilising elements which they represent may also be destroyed (see also M. Rivaroli and L. Verderame, "To be a non-Assyrian", in *Ethnicity in Ancient Mesopotamia: Papers Read at the 48th Rencontre Assyriologique Internationale,* edited by W.H. van Soldt, UNHAIL 102 [Leiden: Nederlands Instituut voor het Nabije Oosten, 2005]). The case of the laments is informative in that it suggests that destruction may be perceived as a route to order, much in keeping with the conception of the Assyrian king's military conquests as facilitating his role as a just and righteous shepherd over all lands.

4 Tadmor, *Inscriptions*, Summ. 1:9 (*kīma til a-bu-bi ú-ab-bit*); the phrase is also made to refer to the entirety of Bit-Shilani, Bit-Amukkani and Bit-Sha'alli (Tadmor, *Inscriptions*, Summ. 7:25).

and Bit-Urzakki "like a net", and to sweep down on the Puqudu "like a net". [5] The fact that these allusions occur in the context of general descriptions of military destruction suggests that they are employed to reflect merely the broadly parallel actions of the king and the god, rather than to being aimed specifically at any particular act in need of legitimation. The lack of specificity in these allusions suggests that few if any of the actions undertaken during Tiglath-pileser's campaigns were perceived as morally problematic and consequently in need of special attention.

5.2.2. Practice

As for the acts undertaken, the Tiglath-pileser materials supply a range of evidence. First, there are indications to suggest that large numbers of enemy dead were perceived positively. Tiglath-pileser claims, for instance, that "their [warriors] I killed (and) I filled the mountain gorges (with their corpses",[6] and "I filled [the plain] with the bodies of their warriors [like gras]s".[7] One fragmentary passage refers to Tiglath-pileser making the Sinzi river "as red as dyed wool" with blood.[8]

Similarly expansive are the frequent reports to the effect of "I destroyed, devastated and set on fire."[9] This or similar language is used to describe consequences for enemy cities or territories in almost every encounter recorded. Twice the destruction of orchards or other agricultural resources (an act thought to imply that a siege had been unsuccessful, and be designed to minimise the opponent's future capacity for resistance) are mentioned explicitly, but usually the texts resort to general, stereotyped language, frequently using verbs such as *abātu* (to destroy completely), *ḫarābu* (to devastate), *napālu* (to demolish) and *naqāru* (to demolish).[10] The most specific act which occurs frequently is

5 Tadmor, *Inscriptions*, Ann. 11:6, Summ. 7:13 (*kīma sa-pa-ri as-hu-up*).

6 Tadmor, *Inscriptions*, Ann. 17:7′ (*...]-⸢šú⸣-nu ⸢a⸣-duk hur-ri na-at-bak šadî*^{i} *ú-mal-li-šú-nu-ti*).

7 Tadmor, *Inscriptions*, Summ. 8:10′ (*...kīma ur]-qí-ti pagrē*^{meš} ^{lú}*mun-<dah>-ṣe-e-šú-nu ú-mal-la-a* [*ṣēri...*).

8 Tadmor, *Inscriptions*, Summ. 7:48 (^{íd}*Si-in-zi nārtu*(ÍD)^{tu} *ki-ma na-ba-si*).

9 *ap-pul aq-qur i-na išāti áš-ru-up.*

10 Tadmor, *Inscriptions*, Ann. 23:11′-12′, Summ. 7:24. The economic destruction wrought by Assyrian forces in this and subsequent periods was not random, but a means of reducing the enemy's will and ability to resist – thus supporting the ultimate object of the opponent's rapid incorporation into the Assyrian system. I. Eph'al argues that Assyria's ruling class was, in proportion to its general population, relatively small, as was its military in proportion to its territory, and so, with a relatively

burning (*šarāpu*). This emphasis on physical destruction may be understood as an expression of the eradication of the enemy threat.

The emphasis on the extensive numbers of enemy dead and widespread general destruction indicates that such acts (and reports of them) did not trigger concern regarding high levels of violence in warfare. Interpreted morally, the clear purpose of these texts was to extol the king.[11] The texts would have failed in their goals if the acts in which the king is portrayed are incompatible with the audience's ethical-ideological framework. In other words, successful praise demands moral approval: the monarch will not build an enviable reputation unless his acts align with the values of the audience. For a king to boast regarding the extent of the enemy army devastated by his campaigns indicates that such acts form a coherent part of his and his audience's ethical world view. Similar language occurs throughout subsequent inscriptions and indicates that the violent and aggressive acts endemic to warfare were not in and of themselves morally problematic.

That said, the violent acts portrayed by the inscriptions are not indiscriminate. Under Tiglath-pileser (and, as will be seen, throughout the inscriptions), violence enacted against enemy persons is at its most extreme and its most explicit in the descriptions of the treatment(s) of opposition leaders and their followers.

The most extreme such act under Tiglath-pileser is the impalement of enemy leaders on stakes. In his thirteenth campaign, which included an attack on Rezin of Damascus, Tiglath-pileser's annals report that, Rezin himself having fled, "his chief ministers I impaled alive and had his country behold them."[12] The king of Bit-Shilani, who did not flee, was similarly treated: "Nabû-ušabši, their king, I impaled before the

---

small army responsible for defending the entirety of the empire, the ability to defeat an enemy with speed became a valued skill, and one of the quickest means of doing this was to ruin the economic potential of a country and thereby minimise its ability to maintain its belligerent stance ("On warfare and military control in the ancient near eastern empires: a research outline", in *History, Historiography and Interpretation: Studies in Biblical and Cuneiform Literatures*, edited by H. Tadmor and M. Weinfeld [Leiden: E.J. Brill, 1983], 96-97). At the same time, the vassalage system demanded an annual tribute from vassal nations, providing a further, economic reason to limit the destruction to relatively short term damage. The combination of these factors makes it unsurprising that in cases of ready conquest the destruction was relatively superficial, while those territories which resisted had their economic livelihoods destroyed – the better to reduce their ability to resist when the Assyrians returned.

11 See Liverani, "Propaganda".

12 Tadmor, *Inscriptions*, Ann. 23:9′-10′ ([lú]*ašarēdūti*[meš]*-šú bal-ṭu-us-su-nu* [*a-na*] *za-qi-pa-a-ni ú-še-li-ma ú-šad-gi-la māt-su*).

gate of his city and exposed him to the gaze of his countrymen."[13] The warriors of several cities were impaled during the second campaign, and those who survived had their hands amputated.[14] Though these treatments were violent, they were limited to enemy leadership, sometimes including the wider army, but not the general population. This indicates an awareness of moral nuance in the types of treatment appropriate to certain classes of enemy, and quenches the common belief that Assyrian military violence was mindless brutality inflicted on any available target.[15]

The limitation of such treatment to the leadership, or at most the fighting men, of the enemy population further indicates that its purpose was not indiscriminate torment. As both B. Oded and H.W.F. Saggs have suggested, there is a strong component of psychological warfare involved in such actions, as well as being means of communi-

---

13 Tadmor, *Inscriptions*, Summ. 1:9-10 (^{md}*Nabû-ú-šab-ši šarra-šú-nu mé-eh-ret abul āli-šú a-na* ^{giš}*za-qi-pi ú-še-li-˹ma˺ <ú-šad-gi-la> māt-su*), cf. Summ. 7:15-16. In the first summary inscription version this statement is preceded by the description of the rest of the city in cosmic language: "Sarrabanu, their great royal city, I laid waste as though ruined by the flood, and I despoiled it" (^{uru}*Sa-ar-ra-ba-a-nu āl šarru-ti-šú-nu rabâ*^{a} *kīma tíl a-bu-bi ú-ab-bit-ma* [*šal*]*-la-su áš-lu-la*; Summ. 1:8-9).

14 Tadmor, *Inscriptions*, Ann. 11:7.

15 One scene among Tiglath-pileser's reliefs depicts the practice of impalement. In it, three figures are shown hung on stakes, directly outside the city walls, leading S. Smith to describe their location as designed to allow the staked bodies to "serve as a warning to the defenders" (*Assyrian Sculptures in the British Museum from Shalmaneser III to Sennacherib* [London: British Museum, 1938], Pl. XIV; *ASBM*, 10). Such an intention is in line with the discussion of staking and other practices in the inscriptions, but in this particular relief the armies are still engaged in furious combat, and the only person who appears to have noticed the impaled figures is a woman weeping on the nearest rampart. In the inscriptions bodily maltreatment appeared to target almost exclusively the leading players of an opposing city or state, rather than the general public, and impalement in particular was only mentioned with respect to leaders (not common soldiers). If, however, the defenders of this particular city are still engaged in combat with the Assyrians, those impaled are probably not the leaders, who would have been critical, if not absolutely necessary, to ongoing resistance. Furthermore, impalement and other public maltreatment were supposed to have been deliberately designed as deterrents. Here almost no one has noticed the impaled figures. Punishment also occurs more appropriately after the city has been conquered, problematising this schema. The scene has three possible implications. First and most probably, the image has been forced to deal awkwardly with a desire to depict multiple stages of a battle on a single relief. Alternatively, the relief may suggest that impalement, contrary to the explicit evidence of the inscriptions, was not a practice reserved for leaders alone. Finally, the city may have fought on without its leaders (though how the leaders might have been tempted out of the city into such a position as to end up impaled, while the rest of the force remained sufficiently protected as to warrant further resistance, is unclear).

cating a warning to anyone considering resisting Assyrian dominance in the future: "the aim of this brutality was probably to strike terror in the heart of the enemy."[16] The explicitly public nature of the impaling of Rezin's chief ministers and of Nabû-ušabši confirms this intention: exposure of the impaled bodies in the sight of the general population demonstrated the consequences of resisting Assyrian power and acted as a public warning to anyone tempted to imitate them.

What might at first seem pure cruelty thus has a specific imperial function, namely to discourage future opposition to Assyrian dominance. Saggs accordingly argues against any assertion that the primary purpose of these acts involved infliction of pain or punishment.[17] In this Saggs is almost certainly overly general, though the early stage of empire in which Tiglath-pileser's acts find their context minimises the emphasis on the punitive element. That it was already present, however, is clear from the language used in the one convincing instance of Tiglath-pileser's ignoring his usual policy of correlating higher levels of destruction to accusations of rebellion (on which see below).[18]

Both versions of the event are fragmentary, and the identity of the enemy is unclear. The country is said to have been rebelling, but after extensive killing and plundering its people pleaded for mercy and Tiglath-pileser granted it: "I accepted their plea to [forgive] their rebellion (lit. sin) and s[pared] their country."[19] The language of sin and forgiveness indicates that Tiglath-pileser saw his initial destruction as the response consequent on insubordination on the part of an opponent: punitive indeed.

Also significant ideologically is that the granting of forgiveness is correlated to full submission to Assyrian dominance. As long as an opponent persisted in resisting Assyrian power, they were fully identified as chaotic elements in need of elimination. This passage is in fact the only known instance of acknowledged mercy to a rebellious vassal state by Tiglath-pileser. His reaction is remarkable, given that the other known instances of vassals rebelling under his reign led to the mass deportation of those countries' inhabitants and punishment of their leaders. It is therefore significant that the recounting of the plea for

16 B. Oded, "'The command of the god' as a reason for going to war in the Assyrian royal inscriptions", in *Ah, Assyria...Studies in Assyrian History and Ancient Near Eastern Historiography Presented to Hayim Tadmor*, edited by M. Cogan and I. Eph'al, SH 33 (Jerusalem: Magnes, 1991), 226n37; see also H.W.F. Saggs, "Assyrian warfare in the Sargonid period", *Iraq* 25 (1963): 148-149.

17 Saggs, "Warfare", 149-150.

18 Tadmor, *Inscriptions*, Summ. 4, Summ. 8.

19 Tadmor, *Inscriptions*, Summ. 8:13′ (...*mi*]-⸢*iš*⸣ *hi-ṭi-šú-nu am-hur-šu-nu-ti-ma māt-su-nu ú-*⸢*bal*⸣-[*li-iṭ*]).

forgiveness uses plural suffixes, indicating that it was the people as a whole making the request, rather than their leader, who, if identified as the Hanunu in the following line, had fled to Egypt. The disappearance of the rebel leader, in combination with the popular request for "mercy", appears to have entailed a level of voluntary submission sufficient for bringing the people under the reach of the Assyrian cosmic system.[20] A more detailed analysis of the circumstances and Tiglath-pileser's response awaits a less fragmentary record of the incident.

Corroborating evidence that the defacement and public exposure of enemy bodies was considered punitive as well as propagandic is also indicated by the terminology of rebellion used elsewhere in Tiglath-pileser's inscriptions. There does not, however, seem to have been a fixed "punishment" for such leaders at this time. Of the two leaders specified rebellious, one "forfeited his life"[21] while the other was deported to Assyria in fetters (no indication is given as to his subsequent fate).[22]

The question of whether Assyrian acts of war involved the deliberate infliction of pain will be discussed further below, but ideologically speaking it is worth noting that the willingness to mutilate the human body for purposes of publicity suggests a particular attitude toward the human body – or at least to the enemy body – which allowed it to be used as a billboard for Assyrian domination. This ability was probably

---

20 N. Na'aman offers an alternate hypothesis, suggesting that the phrase "within his palace" in the same episode refers to the death of the Israelite king Pekah, and thereby indicates that the leader of the rebellious country was appropriately punished (or otherwise removed from the scene) and allowing the incorporation of the general population into the Assyrian system without further punishment ("Historical and Chronological Notes on the Kingdoms of Israel and Judah in the Eighth Century B.C.", *VT* 36 [1986]: 72-73).

21 Tadmor, *Inscriptions*, Ann. 25:3'.

22 Tadmor, *Inscriptions*, Summ. 7:19-20. Referring to the reliefs and texts of Sargon and Esarhaddon indicating that only men of rank or status were bound as captives, Oded suggests that again the purpose of such bonds was primarily a matter of humiliation and punishment, in addition to means of preventing escape (*Mass Deportations and Deportees in the Neo-Assyrian Empire* [Wiesbaden: Dr. Ludvig Reichert Verlag, 1979], 35). On two occasions leaders' families were taken captive or deported, but in neither occurrence was rebelliousness a factor (Tadmor, *Inscriptions*, Summ. 1:11-13, Summ. 7:14-17, Summ. 8:15'-16'). It has been suggested that the deportation of family members was an initial step in Assyrian practice, aimed at securing a king's future cooperation, but the instances under Tiglath-pileser involve the family of Hanunu of Gaza, who had evidently disappeared, and the family of Nabû-ušabši of Bit-Shilani, who was himself impaled. Captive families in such cases would have been of little use as collateral unless the original kings' replacements were of the same royal family.

connected to the ideological and moral alienation of the enemy, which we have described in general terms in Chapters 2 and 3.

Like the inscriptions, Tiglath-pileser's reliefs are not repelled by depictions of enemy dead, nor do they shy away from depicting Assyrian soldiers in the act of ensuring that there would be such dead.[23] More ethically interesting than scenes of general battlefield carnage, however, are scenes of activities beyond that which might be considered militarily necessary, such as decapitation. Decapitated heads are depicted twice: one head is presented to a eunuch, and one is presented to the king along with a prisoner dragged along by the beard.[24] J.E. Curtis and J.E. Reade suppose that the decapitations were for the purpose of estimating the number of enemy dead, but, unlike in later reliefs, the small number of examples in the reliefs of Tiglath-pileser suggests rather that the heads shown are of enemy leaders, whose deaths are confirmed by the bodily evidence. This suggestion is supported by the fact that the decapitated heads appear only in post-battle scenes, indicating that the killing of enemy soldiers by decapitation specifically was not a matter of simple battlefield expedience – an interpretation corroborated by the practical tedium of the practice.[25]

Other than the instances of impalement and decapitation, there is little to suggest especially widespread or especially violent treatment of conquered enemies at either the general or leadership level. One of the reliefs depicts an individual, probably an official or other prominent figure, being trodden on during his appearance before the king – probably a symbolic gesture emphasising the man's subordination.[26] It may also be another allusion to creation; treading upon the neck of the defeated Tiamat is mentioned as a sign of her total defeat.[27]

As for the more general population, the remaining élites of that population were sometimes also faced with deportation. Again, this tactic appears to have been designed to disrupt the native political

23 Dead enemies: R.D. Barnett and M. Falkner, *The Sculptures of Aššur-naṣir-apli II (883-859 B.C.) Tiglath-pileser III (745-727 B.C.) Esarhaddon (681-669 B.C.) from the Central and South-West Palaces at Nimrud* (London: British Museum, 1962), Pl. XXXI=XXXII, Pl. LVIII. Assyrian soldiers in the act of killing enemy soldiers: Layard, Pl. 63 (*ASBM*, Pl. XIII; J.E. Curtis and J.E. Reade, editors, *Art and Empire: Treasures from Assyria in the British Museum* [London: British Museum, 1995], No. 11); also Barnett and Falkner, Pl. LVIII. Publication of the reliefs has been unsystematic, so to aid the reader references are made to the location of the relief in multiple principle publications.

24 Barnett and Falkner, Pl. XLVIII=XLIX; Barnett and Falkner, Pl. LIX.

25 Barnett and Falkner, Pl. XXXIII=XXXIV.

26 *ASBM*, Pl. VIII; cf. Ps. 110.1.

27 En.el. II 146 (*ki-ša-ad ti-amat ur-ru-ḫi-iš ta-kab-ba-as at-ta*).

structure to an extent which minimised the chances of later rebellion. Oded writes that

> although the deportations were only partial, the carrying away of leading citizens and high-ranking civil and military officials, as well as skilled workers...sufficed to convulse the structure of a defeated state, to fragment and weaken the people, and greatly reduced the likelihood of a fresh uprising against Assyria.[28]

Such was the fate of the Damascenes, the people of Bit-Shilani and Bit-Sha'alli and other Aramaean tribes.[29] Several of these reports are unclear about whether the enemy was a rebellious vassal or a previously independent state, but the instances of deportation in which the status is evident are always reported as rebellious. It may be tentatively surmised that deportation was considered appropriate under Tiglath-pileser in cases of previously subordinate and now rebellious vassal states, but that deportation was not so controversial as to demand the clear and unambiguous identification of deportees as rebels.

The practicalities of deportation have been examined in detail already by Oded and Zehnder and need not be repeated here.[30] Both argue that the treatment of deportees was generally good, aside from the initial forced removal from the native land, and deportations may thus have been employed as an acceptable means of fending off potential problems without resorting to mass executions. More theoretically, Liverani describes deportation as part of a universal orientation toward Assyria as the cosmic (and economic) centre; as a result, the movement of materials and people from outlying areas to the centre is perceived as a positive good:

> deportation, as presented from the viewpoint of the deporters (a viewpoint which we know from the Assyrian annals) is a positive fact, since it is a contribution to world order. The zones from which the deportees come gain from the situation, since they shall be re-structured, repopulated and thus gained to cosmos from chaos; the deportees themselves gain from the displacement, since they come closer to the center and so are in the part of the world which works correctly.[31]

Through the process of deportation the élites of a conquered territory were reorientated – economically, politically, geographically – towards an Assyrian centre. When employed to punish rebellion specifically, this effect is heightened; those who refuse to reorientate voluntarily are

---

28 Oded, *Deportations*, 44.

29 Tadmor, *Inscriptions*, Ann. 23:14'-15'; Summ. 1:11-13; Summ. 2:15; Summ. 7:14-18, 21-22; Summ. 11:16.

30 Oded, *Deportations*; Zehnder.

31 Liverani, "Memorandum", 191.

reorientated forcibly. The incorporation of these people into the Assyrian system is ultimately completed through their integration into Assyrian society.[32]

Thus it is not surprising that royal correspondence attests to a consistent concern with deportee welfare and resettlement. Many deportees would have become wards of the state; two letters of Tiglath-pileser address the welfare of these persons in some detail and are therefore quoted at length.

> On the matter on which the king my lord sent me a message, saying: "Feed 6,000 prisoners as your responsibility." How long (*till the lives of*) the 6,000 prisoners *come to an end*? All the magnates *on hearing* the staunch words of the king my lord sent a message (about it). I said: "There is no grain ration." The king my lord gave me an order. He said: "You have indeed received (sufficient). He has delivered to you 40,000 units of grain rations." *But surely* the king knows that there are not corn rations enough for 6,000 (prisoners). Let him deliver 3,000 (prisoners) to me (and) 3,000 to Shamash-bunaya. May this be fitting for the king my lord. As to the message the king my lord sent me, saying: "I will deliver subsequent prisoners to them," (rather) let them share these (present ones) with me, (and) let me for my part share subsequent ones with them.[33]

> Royal Command to Ashur-rimanni (and) to Nabu-bel-ahheshu the Scribe: The prisoners, until you have brought them and settled (them), are your responsibility. Your [cattle] and sheep (are) at your disposal for you to settle....Seven times over you shall not be careless; for that you would die. If there is anyone sick amongst the prisoners whom they bring to you, you shall *gather* (*them*) *together* from amongst (the group). However many there are, they shall transport (them), (and) place them in your presence until they are fit.[34]

32 On which see Zehnder.

33 H.W.F. Saggs, *The Nimrud Letters, 1952*, volume 5 of *Cuneiform Texts from Nimrud* (Trowbridge: British School of Archaeology in Iraq, 2001), ND 2634:16-39 (*ša šarru b*[*e*]*-lí iš-p*[*u-r*]*a-ni ma-a* VI LIM ^{amēl}*hu-ub-tu ina pa-ni-ka ša-ki-il a-du ma-ti* VI LIM *lìb-li-ú*: [*l*]*u* ^{amēl}GAL.MEŠ *gab-bu a-mat tak-la-a-te šarri-e b*[*e*]*-lí-ía* AŠ MU [I]M? *x* ⸢*i*⸣?-[*sa*]*p*?-*ru mu-uk* Š[E.P]AD *la-áš-šú šarru* [*b*]*e-*[*l*]*i iq-ṭi-bi-ia-a ma-a lu-u ta-*[*h*]*u-r*[*a*]*-ni* XL LIM Š[E.P]AD.[M]EŠ *i*[*t*?-*t*]*i*?-*di-na-ka* [*l*]*u-*⸢*ú*⸣ [*ša*]*rru ú-da-a ki-i* ŠE.PAD^{i}: *la-áš-šu-ni a-du ma-ti* VI LIM: III LIM *lid-di-nu-ni* I⸢II⸣ [L]IM-*ma* ⸢*a*⸣-*na* $^{m.d}$*šamas-būn*(DÙ)*-a-a lid-di-*[*na*] *an-ni-ú a-na šarri b*[*e*]??-*l*[*í*]??-[*i*]*a* [*l*]*i-ta-har ša šarru be-lí iš-pu-ra-ni ma-a* ^{amēl}*hu-ub-*[*t*]*u* [*a*]*r-ki-ia-ú a-da-*[*n*]*a-šú-nu an-ni-ia-ú ís-s*[*i*]*-e-a lu-ša-an-ši-lu u*[*r-k*]*i-ia-ú a-na-ku i-s*[*i*]*-i-šú-nu lu-ša-an-ši-il*).

34 Saggs, *Nimrud*, ND 2735:1-6, 7′-13′ (*a-bat šarri a-na* ^{m}*aš-šur-rím-an-ni a-na* $^{m.d}$*nabû*$_{3}$*-bēl-ahhē*$_{2}$^{meš}*-šú* [L]Ú.A.BA *hu-ub-tu am-mar a-di na-ṣa-ni tu-šá-aṣ-bit-u-ni* ^{amēl}*pāhati-ka ši* ... *a-di* VII-*šú* [*l*]*a ta-ši-a-ṭa ina muh-hi ta-mu-at šum-mu* ^{amēl}*marṣu*(GIG) *ina* ^{amēl}*hu-ub-ti ša ú-še-ba-l*[*a*]*-kan-ni issu lìb-bi tal-k*[*i*]*-di lìb-bi ma-de-e i-ba-ši i-ma-ta-hu-ú-ni ina pa-ni-ka i-kar-ru-ru-šu*).

There is little reason to expect exaggeration in an epistolary text of this kind, and the extent of state expenditure on such numbers is noteworthy – as is the degree of forward planning aimed at ensuring minimal difficulties for future groups of deportees.[35] Both texts attest to a high degree of concern for the welfare of defeated persons, even at the royal level. The latter text especially indicates that this concern could extend beyond the basic provision of essential foodstuffs and shelter to extra care for those who have become ill, perhaps suggesting a conscious awareness of the strenuous nature of the deportation process and an effort to mitigate its debilitating effects.[36] Without doubt part of this concern was self-serving, in that ill, disabled or dead deportees were of no use as a labour force (physical or intellectual, given the élite composition of most deportation groups). Nonetheless, the repeated emphasis on responsibility for these people gives evidence against an attitude of dehumanisation of the enemy, once they have been defeated.

One of the most brutal tactics employed by ancient armies and the one which involved the least differentiation between civilians and military personnel was siege. Modern descriptions of the use of siege warfare by the Assyrians are negative to the point of condemnatory; J.W. Wevers describes it as designed to be both physically and morally destructive, while M. Walzer declares that its object "is surrender; and the means is not the defeat of the enemy army, but the fearful spectacle of the civilian dead."[37]

Such an assessment, however, is based at least in part on more modern siege warfare. The inscriptions suggest that sieges frequently did not last very long, so many of the more gruesome consequences may have been averted. More importantly, sieges were the last line of offence, employed only when surrender could not be obtained in some other way. As would be expected of a ideological framework aimed at eliminating chaos, that is, cultures not part of (and therefore opposed

35 A high number of prisoners also seems attested in a letter reporting 200 such persons taken from a town; while it is impossible to know the size of the town, 200 individuals seems likely to have been a relatively high percentage of its population (Saggs, *Nimrud*, ND 2381). There are corroborating numbers in some administrative texts, though these are not usually over 1,000 persons, and the highly fragmentary and abbreviated nature of the texts makes definitive conclusions about the extent of deportation impossible. See SAA 11; also De Odorico on the accuracy of numbers in the royal inscriptions.

36 On the provision of foodstuffs see also Saggs, *Nimrud*, ND 2470.

37 J.W. Wevers, "War, Methods of", in volume 4 of *Interpreter's Dictionary of the Bible*, edited by G.A. Buttrick (New York, N.Y.: Abingdon, 1962), 804; M. Walzer, *Just and Unjust Wars: A Moral Argument with Historical Illustrations* (New York, N.Y.: Penguin Books, 1977), 161.

to) the Assyrian system of order, the primary object of warfare is not the destruction of the enemy but the destruction of it as opposed to Assyria. If an opponent could be relieved of its identification with chaos via a non-violent transfer of affiliation, this was sufficient to satisfy the Assyrian ideological requirements.

Supportive of such an approach are the records in Tiglath-pileser's correspondence regarding attempts at negotiation as a means of resolving the Babylonian rebellion of Mukin-zer.[38] The Assyrian officials do not seem to be having much success with the citizens of Babylon (who are said to be harbouring Mukin-zer), on account of them not believing that the Assyrian king would back up his assertions with military force, but they do nonetheless indicate an initial inclination on the part of Tiglath-pileser to attempt negotiation with an opponent rather than a policy of immediate military intervention, even if the negotiations ultimately failed. The episode also makes clear that there is still the possibility that the Babylonians may turn themselves around, voluntarily submit to Assyrian authority, and thereby avoid the association with chaos (that which is anti-Assyrian) which demands (punitive) military engagement. In other words, the Babylonians are not inherently wicked, but are characterised according to their actions. The pivot on which such characterisation turns is of course an Assyria-centric idea of cosmic order, but there is nonetheless a sense of autonomy in the process.

If a siege is eventually laid, it blurs the lines between military personnel and civilians in a way that battlefield encounters do not; a siege treats all inhabitants as uniformly deserving of, or at least uniformly liable for, military assault. As the Babylonian negotiations just referred to reveal, however, this communal guilt seems to have been arrived at by offering an opportunity for the citizens to reject those who resist Assyrian power: the Assyrian officials "spoke to the citizens of Babylon in these terms: 'Why are you hostile to us for their [the rebels] sake?'".[39] If the opportunity was rebuffed, their guilt was confirmed.[40]

If a city succumbed to a siege by force, its walls were generally broken and the city burned: Bit-Agusi is described as "ravaged" (*ḫepû*) and

38 Saggs, *Nimrud*, ND 2632.

39 Saggs, *Nimrud*, ND 2632:11-13 (*i-za-zu a-ni-ni k*[*i*] *an-ni-ni a-na mārē babili*$^{ki.meš}$ *ni-iq-ṭí-bi* [sic] *ma-a m*[*i-n*]*i ina muh-hi-*[*š*]*u-nu t*[*a*]*-na*[*k-ka*]*-ra-na-ši*).

40 The reliefs of the siege of Lachish by Sennacherib also indicate that civilians were sometimes allowed to leave a besieged city in peace, suggesting perhaps an implicit rationale that those who did not leave were remaining in the city to assist the military.

Sarrabanu is "laid waste as though ruined by the flood".[41] By contrast, if the city capitulated before a siege was necessary then they paid tribute, sometimes providing hostages.[42] The object of both outcomes is the eradication of a foreign threat to the Assyrian system, in the one case through political subordination and in the other by (ostensibly) total destruction.

5.3. Sargon II (724-705)

There are notable differences between the records of Sargon II and those of Tiglath-pileser, though there is also significant continuity.

5.3.1. Cosmology

Like Tiglath-pileser, Sargon uses imagery from creation mythology: references to flood (*abūbu*) and net (*sapāru*) continue and are joined by references to fog (*imbaru*) and storm (*meḫû*).[43] The latter is another of the weapons explicitly employed by Marduk against Tiamat. Though *imbaru* is not one of Marduk's initial weapons in his battle with Tiamat, it is (in an unfortunately fragmentary passage of *Enūma eliš*) described as made by him out of her spittle.[44] The association of Sargon with the deeds of the god at creation is reiterated accordingly.

---

41 Tadmor, *Inscriptions*, Summ. 1:9, Summ. 9:24′. For transliteration, see above.

42 Wevers, "War", 805.

43 D.D. Luckenbill, *Historical Records of Assyria from the Earliest Times to Sargon*, volume 1 of *Ancient Records of Assyria and Babylonia* (Chicago, Ill.: University of Chicago Press, 1926-1927), §33; A. Fuchs, *Die Inschriften Sargons II. aus Khorsabad* (Göttingen: Cuvillier, 1994), Ann. 296 (*kima tīb meḫê*); *ARAB*, §39; Fuchs, Ann. 373 (*kima tīl abubi*). The latter phrase occurs twice in the *Letter to Aššur* with regard to cities in Urarṭu (*ARAB*, §§152, 158). Sargon overpowers various districts of Urarṭu "as with a net" in the *Letter to Aššur* (*ḫu-ḫa-reš*; *ARAB*, §159; W.R. Mayer, "Sargons Feldzug gegen Urartu – 714 v. Chr.: Text und Übersetzung", *MDOG* 115 (1983): 88:194); similarly, ^{uru}*Ši-nu-uḫ-tu āl*(uru) *šarru*(lugal)-*ti-šú im-ba-riš as-ḫup* (*ARAB*, §7; Fuchs, Ann. 69); also in the *Letter to Aššur* (*ki-ma im-ba-r[i*; *ARAB*, §161; Mayer, "Sargons", 90:215). Some but not all of the inscriptions first translated in Luckenbill have been re-edited by Fuchs; for ease of reference, citations are made to both volumes where relevant, and to Luckenbill alone where no more recent edition exists.

44 En.el. V 51.

Allusions may also include the phrase "at the command of the great lord Marduk I set my chariots in order"[45] and two references to the New Year festival after the conquest of Babylon.[46] Sargon also repeatedly emphasises that he was "without rival" in battle and combat, which may allude to the beginning passage of the recitation of the fifty names of Marduk, the climax of *Enūma eliš*, in which Marduk is declared to be without rival.[47] Finally, Marduk-apla-iddina (Merodach-baladan) is also said to flood Babylon's environs "as with the mighty waves (of the sea)", foreshadowing the more direct identification of Assyria's enemies with the forces of chaos which occurs in subsequent periods (see also below).[48]

An important clarification of the Assyrian use of *Enūma eliš* occurs in Sargon's *Letter to Aššur*. The text refers to the creation narrative when it declares that Marduk has, from the beginning, given the gods of the world (that is, their territories) to Aššur, in order to honour him.[49] This circumlocution puts the Assyrian king in the role of Marduk – the Assyrian king's conquests likewise subordinate the foreign gods and their territories to Aššur's power – and clarifies how the Assyrians perceived their assumption of the Marduk-centred *Enūma eliš*, despite identifying their own head of pantheon as Aššur. With this elucidated, the inscrip-

45 *ARAB*, §31; Fuchs, Ann. 264 (*ṣindu*), cf. En.el. IV 50 (GIŠ.GIGIR, *narkabtu*). In his *Letter to Aššur*, Sargon refers to the "armies of Šamaš and Marduk" as well as the "yoke of Nergal and Adad" (*ARAB*, §142).

46 *ARAB*, §38; Fuchs, Ann. 321; *ARAB*, §184.

47 *ARAB*, §54; Fuchs, Prunk. 13 (*ga-ba-ra-a-a ul ib-ši-ma ina e-peš qabli*(murub4) *u tāḫazi*(mè) *ul a-mu-ra mu-ni-ḫu*); *ARAB*, §104; Fuchs, R.9-10 (*ga-ba-ra-šu la ib-šu-ma i-na qab-li ù ta-ḫa-zi la e-mu-ru mu-ni-ḫu*); *ARAB*, §107; Fuchs, Bro. 18-19 (*ga-ba-ra-a-šú la ib-šu-ma i-na qab-lu ù ta-ḫa-zi* [*l*]*a e-mu-ru mu-ni-ḫu*). Cf. En.el. VI 106.

48 *ARAB*, §31; Fuchs, Ann. 270 (*kima mīl kiššati*). This has been variably construed, and highlights the frequent difficulty of distinguishing between metaphorical and literal depictions of an event; for an argument that this refers to an actual defensive moat, see M.A. Powell ("Merodach-baladan at Dur-Jakin: a note on the defense of Babylonian cities", *JCS* 34 [1982]: 59-61). However, as he admits, such an obstacle would have taken several thousand men more than three months to construct, perhaps tending to support a metaphorical interpretation (61).

49 "...Assur, father of the gods, lord of lands, king of the whole of heaven and earth, begetter of all, lord of lords, to whom, from eternity, the Enlil (lord) of the gods, Marduk, has given the gods of land and mountain of the four quarters (of the world) to honor him, not one escaping, bringing them to Eḫursaggalkukurra with their treasures" (d*A-šur a-bu* DINGIR.MEŠ *be-el ma-ta-a-ti šàr kiš-šat* AN-*e* KI-*tim a-lid* <*gim-re*> EN EN.EN *ša ul-tu u4-um sa-a-ti* DINGIR.MEŠ KUR ù KUR-*i ša kib-rat 4-i a-na šu-tuq-qu-ri-šu la na-par-šu-de ma-na-ma it-ti i-šit-ti-šu-nu kit-mur-ti a-na šu-ru-ub* É.ḪUR.SAG.GAL.KUR.KUR.RA *iš-ru-ku-uš* dEN.LÍL.LÁ DINGIR.MEŠ dAMAR.UTU; *ARAB*, §170; Mayer, "Sargons", 100:314-317). The passage goes on to refer to "Šamaš the warrior", not an insignificant statement in light of the above.

tions' declarations that the king's campaigns are on behalf of and at the command of Aššur reiterate the king's identification as the earthly counterpart of Marduk.

Sargon's references to nets, which, as has been seen, are most convincingly understood as allusions to the creation myth, reflect a development in Sargon's allusive language. Unlike the references in Tiglath-pileser's inscriptions, however, Sargon's inscriptions do not use *sapāru* alone, but also use the term *ḫuḫāru*.[50] This choice of vocabulary is intriguing as the term *ḫuḫāru* is normally a symbol of Šamaš – who is in fact regularly mentioned in Sargon's inscriptions. Given the role of Šamaš as the god of justice, it seems likely that, in using this term and making these references, Sargon is supporting his actions by simultaneously referring to *Enūma eliš* and identifying himself with the god of justice. This is in keeping with the cosmic framework of warfare characteristic of all the Assyrian kings as well as with Sargon's special interest in justice.

The emphasis on justice becomes clearer under his son and successor, Sennacherib, but is evident already in Sargon's persistent description of his enemies as having rebelled against Assyrian rule. This emphasis may be attributed to multiple factors. First, the imperial activities of Tiglath-pileser meant that Sargon had inherited an empire which then needed to be maintained; there were a greater number of subordinate populations to control, and consequently a greater number of conflicts arising as a result of maintaining the empire. At the same time, this emphasis on the rebelliousness of the opponent appears to reflect an increased concern with the conduct of these wars, or, more specifically, a greater interest in rationalising them. According to the inscriptions, the level of violence required to maintain the empire was greater than that which had been required to expand it in the first place (see below). Changes in the language used to describe this violence indicate that these increased levels of violence required a concomitant increase in moral rationalisation. Though the violence itself resulted from historical circumstances, historical circumstances alone do not appear to have been sufficient to legitimate it. Rather, the legitimation of these acts was achieved through the conflation of the political with the ethical. In order for the acts pursued by the Assyrian king to be morally acceptable, the acts of his enemies were conceived in more explicitly ethical terms.

50 *ARAB*, §10; Fuchs, Ann. 86; *ARAB*, §47; Fuchs, Ann. 421; *ARAB*, §159; Mayer, "Sargons", 88:194.

We already saw the beginning of this emphasis on justice in Tiglath-pileser's references to his enemies' sin, reflecting a concept of warfare as in some way punitive. The term for a sinful person (*ḫīṭu*) being the same term as the word for a rebellious person, the inscriptions of Sargon take this to a higher level, and in combination with the continuation of cosmic language reiterate the ideological underpinnings of Sargon's campaigns. Rebellion can never be a merely political act because there is no word to describe such an act independently of the ethical (and religious) language of sinfulness. The equation of the political with the ethical is reiterated by the terms used for "enemy" (*lemnu, bēl lemutti*): these terms simultaneously denote both the "enemy" and one who is "wicked, evil".[51] Oded has discussed this phenomenon in general terms in his monograph on the justification of war in the inscriptions, arguing that the portrayal of the enemy as synonymous with evil allows the audience to see war "as motivated by moral and ethical reasons, and by the quest for justice, rather than by the desire to gain political and economic advantages."[52] The use of such terminology to describe the enemy is an important means of legitimating the use of military force against them.

It is crucial, however, that the "sin" or "wickedness" of the Assyrians' enemies is not perceived in a purely abstract sense – that is, that by originating outside of the geographical bounds of Assyria, a person is always and inherently evil – nor as something invented as and when convenient, for the sake of political expediency. Rather, the enemy's characterisation as wicked is tied to the enemy's own acts: above all else, the response which he has made with regard to "order". The enemy's identification as an enemy, as "wicked", as "sinful", is contingent precisely on his refusal to be incorporated into the cosmic order: by rejecting order, he identifies himself with chaos.

Order is, of course, the order personified and perpetuated by Assyria, on behalf of and in concert with Aššur and Marduk, but it is the place of warfare within this cosmic system which shifts an opponent's relationship to Assyria from the purely political sphere into the cosmic sphere. An opponent's rejection of Assyrian hegemony has cosmic implications, insofar as the rejection of Assyria is rejection of order itself, and anyone who rejects Assyria's political power thus constitutes a threat to the ordered existence of the universe. To eliminate the chaotic threat is to (re)integrate the opponent into the system of order – and the necessity obtained from the cosmic nature of the situation means that

51 Compare Chapter 6, below.

52 B. Oded, *War, Peace and Empire: Justifications for War in Assyrian Royal Inscriptions* (Weisbaden: Dr Ludwig Reichert Verlag, 1992), 38.

this may be done by force if required. Sargon's inscriptions' emphatic description of his opponents as wicked, as sinful, is an articulation of the enemies' rejection of and consequent threat to the cosmic order. It is because they are such a threat that they must be eliminated and the violence which his inscriptions describe necessitated.

In application: the peoples of Sukka, Bala and Abitikna are deported "because of the sin which they had committed", while I'au-bi'di and Mutallum are both called wicked/evil.[53] Sargon's *Letter to Aššur* describes Sargon's prayer that he "might bring about his [Ursâ's] defeat in battle, turn his insolent words against himself, and make him bear his sin/punishment".[54] The inscriptions hardly needed to state explicitly that these enemies were acting against the will of the gods and against the moral order by rebelling against Assyrian authority, because the language used to describe such acts already contained this concept.

5.3.2. Practice

In terms of acts of war Sargon was much like Tiglath-pileser, making liberal use of deportations, destruction, plundering and burning. "I destroyed, I devastated, I burned with fire" is typical.

Only a few enemy leaders were killed immediately, either in combat or afterwards. Two are flayed, and the body of one is put on public display.[55] Again we see the calculated use of punitive acts for the purpose of discouraging future resistance to Assyrian authority. That this could be a successful means of deterring such resistance is indicated explicitly in one of the episodes of flaying, in which the flaying is said to have provoked pleas for mercy from another leader (Ullusunu). That the display of living captives could serve a similar purpose may also be suggested by a letter from Sargon to Nabû-duru-uṣur, one of his officials in Urarṭu, in which a group of captives are mobilised in concert with the arrival of Urarṭian emissaries. The captives appear to be being put on display as a tacit threat to the emissaries, aimed at ensuring their compliance with Sargon's wishes.

The limitation of these more extreme forms of punishment to enemy leaders is reiterated in Sargon's reliefs.[56] The reliefs preserve a

---

53 *ARAB*, §6; Fuchs, Ann. 67 (*i-na ḫi-iṭ-ṭi iḫ-ṭu-ú*).

54 *ARAB*, §153; Mayer, "Sargons", 80:124 (*i-na qé-reb tam-ḫa-ri si-kip-ta-šu <ana> šá-ka-ni ù i-re-eḫ pi-i-šu* UGU-*šu tu-ur-rim-ma an-na-šu šu-uš-ši-i*).

55 *ARAB*, §§10, 55, 56.

56 J.E. Reade identifies the room in which the following examples were located as Sargon's receiving room, and contends that it is heavy on propagandistic images de-

single scene of a man being flayed; the slab is badly damaged, but the nude victim is spread-eagled in the manner of the flayings depicted in later reliefs, and the Assyrian soldier appears to be holding some type of scraping tool in his right hand and applying it to the victim's arm.[57] It is possible that the victim has been pegged at the ankles and wrists, though the two-dimensionality of the image – he appears to be suspended in mid-air, supported only lightly by the Assyrian soldier – makes it difficult to tell.

In the same room were also two near-identical reliefs, each depicting the king engaged with three captives. The first is damaged, but it is reasonably clear that the king has the three men on leashes which have been run either through their tongues or through their lips.[58] One is kneeling and seems about to have his eye(s) poked out by the king, who wields a spear. All three figures extend their hands toward the king in a gesture of supplication: the image has the effect of casting Sargon as a merciless king.[59] The second relief is very similar, though much less well preserved.[60] The direct responsibility of the king for the treatment of his conquered enemies is especially evident in these scenes.

The punishments recorded by the inscriptions for leaders accused of rebellion is variable, but public humiliation similar to this is frequent. Thus Mutallu, a usurper to the throne of Gurgum, was publicly humiliated: "I bound his hands, made him unclean(?) and exposed him [to the public gaze(?)]."[61] Urzana of Urarṭu was made to sit before his city gate.[62] All of these examples indicate that public forms of punish-

---

liberately designed to make an impression on visitors ("Ideology and propaganda in Assyrian art", in *Power and Propaganda: A Symposium on Ancient Empires*, edited by M.T. Larsen, Mesopotamia 7 [Copenhagen: Akademisk Forlag, 1979], 338). It is notable, in light of the subsequent changes in royal policy with regard to the treatment of defeated leaders, that at this time it would have been only through the second-hand experience of these reliefs that the majority of Assyrians would have been exposed to these activities.

57 E. Flandin, *Monument de Ninive*, volume 2 [Paris: Imprimerie Nationale, 1849], Pl. 120.

58 Flandin V, 154.

59 Flandin V, 153.

60 Flandin II, Pl. 116.

61 *ARAB*, §29. The nature of the humiliation is unclear, though its character as humiliation is reasonably evident. Lie has "he had done to his hands I caused to ? , and I let (him) see the light (?)" (*-šú e-pu-*[š]*u qâtê*$^{II.meš}$*-šú ú-šat(?)-me ú-kal-li-ma* [*nu-u-ru(?)*]; 38:4); A.T. Olmstead collates the versions and comes up with *na- -ti - ?-šu e-pu-*⸢*šu*⸣, but makes no attempt at translation ("The text of Sargon's annals", *AJSL* 47 (1931): 269).

62 *ARAB*, §172.

ment were employed by Sargon in much the same way as his predecessor: to make public examples of those who resisted Assyrian hegemony and to encourage conformity in future.

In the reliefs there is also one impalement scene, in which fourteen impaled enemies are depicted outside a besieged, flaming city.[63] All resistance seems to have collapsed; Assyrians are scaling the walls as defenders throw up their arms in surrender. The issue of the identity of the impaled, noted with regard to a similar scene under Tiglath-pileser, remains, although their identification as the city's leadership is in this case more certain given the attendant surrender of the city.[64] Images of decapitated heads again appear only twice, though, unlike the attestations of Tiglath-pileser, neither of these can be identified as leaders.[65] They may thus signal a trend which develops in earnest in later reliefs: the general decapitation of enemy soldiers.

That said, there are also a number of reliefs which depict decapitated bodies, with the heads absent. In later reliefs, there is a clearer purpose for the detachment of enemies' heads from their bodies: delivery to a scribal contingent for tally. In Sargon's images this purpose is not evident, and the disembodied heads are never themselves depicted. It is unclear whether historians are to presume such a function under Sargon, but the plethora of headless bodies indicates that Assyrian soldiers were probably frequently engaged in decapitation of the dead. Also, the lack of apparent reason for the practice may itself be significant, since, were decapitation of the enemy a novel development, one

63 Flandin I, Pl. 55.

64 There is, however, the added concern of the number of bodies; a leadership of fourteen seems high in the context of the reliefs, but the annals' ambiguities do imply that widespread staking may not have been unknown. The citadel itself is apparently inhabited by no more than a dozen individuals, which may also suggest that details such as number and size have been loosely interpreted by the designer(s). This itself may indicate that such a high number of individuals staked was an improvement.

Another issue reiterated from Tiglath-pileser's period is the ability of the reliefs to depict the sequence of events in which sequence would matter for moral purposes. Thus some of Sargon's reliefs show citadels in which there are significant numbers of apparently surrendering soldiers under attack (Flandin I, Pls. 55, 68, 70; though contra Flandin II, Pls. 93, 147). Typically the citadel's top range of soldiers is still armed, while the inner ranks are unarmed and have their arms raised in what appears to be a pose of surrender. It is somewhat difficult to know whether the images are attempting to depict multiple stages of a battle at once, or whether they are actually depicting surrendering soldiers which the Assyrians are continuing to attack (there are some citadels where this juxtaposition of surrendering enemy and attacking Assyrian is not evident).

65 Flandin II, Pls. 90, 145.

would expect that the reliefs would have felt a need to depict its purpose. That the heads were then at a later date depicted as in use for accounting purposes may either indicate a simple, amoral change in practical practice, or an increased sensitivity for the justification of the disfigurement of enemies' bodies.

A potential factor in these scenes is the identity of the soldiers engaged in the decapitation. Flandin, on the basis of the soldiers' attire in one of the Sargon images, supposes one of the soldiers depicted in this act to have been a member of the auxiliary troops.[66] While there do not seem to be any qualms elsewhere about depicting Assyrian soldiers engaged in this behaviour, the earlier occurrences under Tiglath-pileser probably depict the executions of leaders rather than general soldiers. If the soldier in the other Sargon relief is also non-Assyrian, the reliefs may suggest that in this period acceptance of the practice of decapitation of general soldiers was not yet widespread, or that there was a difference between what was considered acceptable behaviour for Assyrian soldiers and what was tolerated of auxiliary troops. Given that Assyrians are certainly portrayed engaged in such acts at a later stage, one might surmise that the moral tolerance of this type of act increased over the period in question, which allowed Assyrians to be depicted engaged in it at the later stage. Such an attempt to draw this type of distinction between the ethics of native Assyrians and the ethics of assimilated Assyrians, however, is problematised by the ongoing assertion of the annals that, upon the annexation of a country to the empire, its people were "counted as Assyrians" (see below). In that context there seems to be no need to maintain a distinction between native and assimilated Assyrians, and the maintenance of a moral distinction in the reliefs may be inconsistent with this.

The Ullusunu incident (above) is a rare occurrence of what might be identified as merciful behaviour on the part of Sargon. This act of forgiveness is particularly remarkable because Ullusunu (an Assyrian puppet over the Manneans) is said to have instigated the rebelliousness of others. The language used by the inscriptions to describe the incident make clear the moral aspects of the situation, as perceived from the Assyrian point of view: "I forgave his innumerable transgressions, forgot his crimes, had mercy upon him and placed him (once more) on the throne of his kingdom."[67] The phenomena observed thus far indicate that Ullusunu had somehow managed to reinstate his place within the

66 Flandin V, 162.

67 H. Winckler, *Die Keilschrifttexte Sargons* (Leipzig: Eduard Pfeiffer, 1888), 106:51; *ARAB*, §56 (ḫi-iṭ-ṭi-šu la mi-na a-bu-uk ma a-mi-iš ḫab-la(t)-su ri-í-ma ar-ši-šu ma i-na (iṣu) kussû šarrû-ti-šu u-ší-šib-šu).

Assyrian order. The means by which this occurred was payment of tribute: such payment was an acknowledgement of Assyrian authority, and brought the subordinate state into the sphere of Assyrian hegemony.

The tribute, combined with Ullusunu and his nobles "crawling on all fours like dogs" – another sign of subordination – succeeded in re-establishing the Manneans' orientation toward the hegemonic Assyrian centre.[68] Accordingly, Sargon "took pity on them and received their petition, I listened to their words of supplication, and spoke their pardon."[69] Instead of the Manneans' anti-Assyrian orientation requiring attack with the object of elimination, the Manneans now constituted part of the Assyrian order, and Sargon accordingly pledged to defend the area against invaders. Similarly, though recounted in less detail, more than thirty other foreign leaders offer tribute in the same campaign and are correspondingly not attacked.[70] The consequences for the people of Zikirtu, who did not submit to the Assyrian order – as symbolised by refusing tribute – are typical of those not thus assimilated: "I destroyed their walls, I set fire to the houses inside them, I destroyed them like a flood, I battered them into heaps of ruins".[71]

That such (re)integration could occur even at a late stage is indicated by the distinctions made among the allies of Marduk-apla-iddina (Merodach-baladan) in Babylon: a number of the chieftains paid tribute, while those who remained in league with Marduk-apla-iddina suffered the appropriate consequences.[72] This demonstration of the consequences of resistance provoked several other cities to subsequently submit.

These reports suggest that the key determining factor for Sargon's treatment of enemy cities and groups was their willingness to submit to his rule; the "rebelliousness" of the inscriptions seems to have been as much a description of resistance to any attempt to impose Assyrian order as a matter of rebellion in the specific sense of throwing off previous political allegiances.

The correspondence preserved from Sargon's period corroborates this interest in obtaining submissiveness as opposed to inflicting indiscriminate violence. These texts show a preference for negotiating tactics

68 *ARAB*, §148; Mayer, "Sargons", 72:58 (UGU *er-bé rit-ti-šu-nu ip-taš-ši-lu ki-ma kal-bi*).

69 *ARAB*, §148; Mayer, "Sargons", 72:59 (*re-e-ma ar*<-ši>*-šu-nu-ti-ma ut-nen-ni-šu-nu al-qe at-mu-šu-nu ša te-nin-ti áš-mé-ma aq-bi-šu-nu a-ḫu-lap*).

70 *ARAB*, §§145-149.

71 *ARAB*, §151; Mayer, "Sargons", 76:90 (BÀD.MEŠ-*šú-nu ap-pu-ul* É.MEŠ *qer-bi-šú-nu* ^{d}BIL.GI *ú-šá-aṣ-bit-ma ki-ma ša a-bu-bu ú-ab-bi-tu* DUL-*niš ú-kám-mer*).

72 *ARAB*, §32.

in lieu of immediate and direct military action. In a case in which the Urarṭians are said to have captured a half dozen Assyrian soldiers, the palace herald reports to the king that he has instructed the major-domo to hold off on forcibly retrieving the men, recommending instead that he write enquiring "Why have you seized our men?"[73] Another alternative response is attested in a letter in which Sargon is said to have ordered a governor on the Šubrian frontier to gain negotiating leverage by capturing enemy men in equal number and holding them until the Assyrians were released.[74] Negotiation as an option in the case of insubordination – as opposed to immediate military retaliation – is also attested when the governor of Halzi-atbar (also on the Šubrian frontier) writes to the king enquiring whether negotiations ought to be pursued with unsubmissive Mumaeans or if the king has other orders.[75]

The extent of the violence described in Sargon's extant correspondence is low. This is as expected of texts discussing events in which the king was not directly involved, thereby precluding most of the major military exercises of the expanding empire. The affairs of which his governors wrote were most likely relatively minor skirmishes, with the opponents not (yet) constituting a level of threat to which a dramatic and violent response was justified. Thus areas previously unsubmissive to Assyrian power seem to have been treated relatively lightly: the letter which advocates negotiation in the first instance also reports that the Ušhaean and Qudaean "towns which were not submissive" were merely obliged to provide labour or "king's men" (perhaps implying that this made them submissive, precluding further hostilities).[76] With reference to this particular incident especially, G.B. Lanfranchi writes:

> naturally, problems had occasionally to be solved by force... Use of force, however, was not mandatory. The Assyrian approach to local problems may rather be perceived as generally cautious – a picture which decidedly contrasts with the stereotyped image of Assyrian cruelty and violence.[77]

That said, the governor then queries: "Shall I relea[se] the troops at my disposal, or should they (continue to) keep the watch?"[78] In another letter the term "release" (Dt *ramû*) may refer to troops released from their active battle duty for the purposes of unrestrained plundering.[79] It

73 SAA 5 115:r.1-2 ([*m*]*a a-ta-a* LÚ*.ERIM.MEŠ-*ni tu-ṣa-bi-ta*).

74 SAA 5 33.

75 SAA 5 78.

76 SAA 5 78.

77 SAA 5 xxiv.

78 LÚ*.*e-mu-qi* [*šu-n*]*u ša ina* IGI-*ia lu-ra-*[*mi-š*]*ú-nu ú-la-a ma-*˹*ṣar*˺*-tú* [0] *li-ṣu-ur* [0!] (SAA 5 78: r.7-10).

79 SAA 15 118.

is possible that the term is used similarly here. If that is the case, it might explain the apparently minimalist punishment otherwise inflicted on these resistant towns. It could also be that the light touch reported in many letters is merely the early stages of what would subsequently become the type of punitive treatment better known from the annals, which do not appear in the correspondence because they involved the king directly. At these relatively early stages, however, nothing more extreme than general plundering seems to have been deemed appropriate. Indirectly, therefore, they confirm a prevailing ethic of proportionality in Assyrian military practice under Sargon.

With regard to the general population of territories defeated by Sargon, there is a greater emphasis on the totality of destruction than there was in the inscriptions of Tiglath-pileser. This may be seen in phrases such as "I cut them down with the sword" and "great or small, not one escaped; they cut (them) down with the sword".[80] Likewise some unknown coastal people: "I brought them down to the sea(shore) and slew them, great and small, with the sword."[81] That Sargon's campaigns may have sometimes included a more expansive infliction of violence on the general population than was evident in Tiglath-pileser's inscriptions is suggested by a phrase peculiar to Sargon's inscriptions: "I bespattered his people with the venom of death". It occurs twice regarding the Babylonians and twice regarding the people of Zikirtu and Andia, in the Urarṭu campaign (see below).[82] On the other hand, that these reports include an element of rhetorical exaggeration is suggested by the Sargon correspondence which refers to relatively small numbers of deportees.[83]

Sargon had not, in any case, abandoned Tiglath-pileser's ability to discriminate among opponents. In addition to the recognition of an

---

80 *ARAB*, §23; Lie, 28:167-168; Olmstead, 267 (*i-na* ^{i}[^{s}*kakki*] *ú-šam-qit-šu-nu-ti*); *ARAB*, §37; Lie, 56:383-384; Olmstead, 267 (*ṣi-ḫir ra-bi la ip-par-ši-du i-na-ru i-na kak-ki ik-šu-dam-ma*).

81 *ARAB*, §16; Lie, 20:119 (*a-na tam-di ú-ri-da-áš-šú-nu-ti-ma ṣi-ḫir ra-bi* [*i-na*]^{iš}*kakki ú-šam-qit*).

82 Lie, 60:413; *ARAB*, §§39, 67, 118, 155 (*mê*]^{meš} [*i*]*-mat mu-ti as-lu-ḫa nišê*^{meš}*-šú*).

83 When deportee numbers are reported under Sargon, they are much fewer than claimed by the inscriptions, e.g., a mere 160 persons (SAA 1 257). More generally, larger groups of deportees are attested by other administrative texts, but the level of care which the same correspondence attests raises the question of the general probability of large scale deportations, given the inevitably limited ability of the state to provision – never mind control – them (see below). Were the deportees regularly in groups of the high hundreds or even thousands, they would have had a higher potential of becoming difficult to control, as well as constituting a substantial burden on the resources of the state (see also De Odorico on the reliability of accounting in the inscriptions).

opponent's entrance into the Assyrian system upon payment of tribute, the case of the usurper Mutallu of Gurgum indicates that the people of Gurgum were not punished for the usurper's "crimes".[84] Despite using language of pardoning – suggesting that he still saw the people as guilty – the passage indicates that Sargon was able to distinguish between self-incurred guilt (people rebelling in conjunction with their leaders) and guilt by association.

A similarly diverse response occurred in his dealings with the Babylonians. Despite especially violent language describing his treatment of the rebels, there is a clear distinction between the people who resisted and those who did not. Twice the inscription specifies that it was only the rebellious who were killed or deported. Equally enlightening is the description of numerous cities as having been liberated: "the citizens of Sippar, Nippur, Babylon and Borsippa, who were imprisoned therein for no crime (*or*, detained against their will) I set free and let them see the light (of day)."[85] This is consistent with a worldview in which submission to and incorporation in the Assyrian system is in the best interests of the subordinated: the dual role of the king as warrior and shepherd coming together.

The differentiation of varying degrees of culpability militates against arguments such as those of F.M. Fales, who has contended that the Assyrians viewed their enemies as merely many manifestations of a single enemy.[86] Contrary to such a sweeping statement, the passages just described indicate that Sargon was able to and did make distinctions among various players within the enemy state, especially once that state or city had succumbed to Assyrian power. Reflecting this ability is the common formula "I counted them as Assyrians".[87] One of the positive results of Zehnder's work on the treatment of foreigners in Assyria is the collation of evidence which shows a high level of incorporation of conquered peoples into "Assyria", affirming that the offensiveness of foreigners was not so much their (ethnic) foreignness as their politically independent existence. This is confirmed by the distinc-

84 *ARAB*, §§29, 61.

85 Winckler, 122:135; *ARAB*, §69 (aplî Sippara Nippuru Babilu u Barsippa ša i-na la an-ni-šu-nu i-na kir-bi-šu ka-mu-u ṣi-bit-ta-šu-nn [sic] a-pu-ud-ma u-kal-lim-šu-nu-ti nu-ru); cf. *ARAB*, §78.

86 F.M. Fales, "The enemy in Assyrian royal inscriptions: 'the moral judgement'", in volume 2 of *Mesopotamien und seine Nachbarn: politische und kulturelle Wechselbeziehungen im Alten Vorderasien vom 4. bis 1. Jahrtausend v. Chr. XXV. Rencontre assyriologique internationale Berlin, 3. bis 7. Juli 1978*, edited by H.-J. Nissen and J. Renger, BBVO 1 (Berlin: Dietrich Reimer Verlag, 1982), 425.

87 E.g., *ARAB*, §30; Lie, 40:262 (*it-ti nišê*^{meš} ^{mât}*Aš-šur*^{ki} *am-nu-šu-nu-ti*).

tions made even among the conquered, who at that point had begun their transition into the Assyrian ideological system.

Like his predecessor, Sargon engaged in the deportation of defeated populations. Enemy leaders were frequently deported, often in chains, and sometimes alongside their families. Both Mutallu and his family were considered war spoil, as were Tarhunazi the Melidian and the king of Ashdod, who had both withheld tribute.[88] The families of Mutallum, Ursâ and Urzana also bore the consequences for their relatives' insubordination.[89] A number of leaders are deported in chains as the consequence for political insubordination.[90] Oded's study of deportation tactics suggest that the use of chains is almost always on leaders or other high-ranking officials of the conquered nation, and he likewise suggests that it was aimed at discouraging future rebellion.[91]

Alongside the deportation of such high-ranking figures, however, was the general deportation of defeated populations. Sargon's correspondence deals extensively with the treatment of captives and deportees after defeat, and provides an important counter-balance to the more dramatic interests of the inscriptions.

For the most part, these indicate a remarkable level of interest at the royal level in the welfare and health of these people, similar to that demonstrated by Tiglath-pileser's correspondence. Išmanni-Aššur reports that

> the harvest of the deportee[s ...] had come out well; they brought along all the *food* they had. The deportees and the pack animals are eating stored grain [...] like the king's servants. The deportees and the pack animals are [well]; the king my lord [can be] pleased.[92]

Though the deportees consume their own food, the text suggests that they would not have been left to starve had their supplies not met a minimum standard. Several texts indicate such a general level of provision; they are given shelter, food, water and protection.[93] One letter indicates the possible provision of oil as well, though the writer seems to find this beyond normal protocol.[94] On the basis of texts like these Lanfranchi concludes that "deportees and POWs appear to have been

---

88 *ARAB*, §§29-30, 60-62.

89 *ARAB*, §§22, 45, 56, 64.

90 *ARAB*, §§8, 25, 26.

91 Oded, *Deportations*, 35.

92 SAA 1 219:10-16 (LÚ*.-*šag-lu-*[*te x x x*] ŠE.*e-bu-ru-šú-nu i-di-mi*[!]-*i*[*q*[!] *a-dan-niš*] ⸢NINDA?⸣.MEŠ *am-mar ina* [IGI]-*šú-nu i-ta-ṣ*[*u*]-*ni* LÚ*.*šag-lu-te* ANŠE.*ṣap-pu* ŠE.*tab*[!]-*ku*[!] KÚ [*x*]*x* ⸢*a*[!]*ki*[!]⸣ LÚ*.ARAD.MEŠ-*ni ša* LUGAL [*x x x*]-*a a-na* LÚ*.*šag-lu-te* [*x x x*] *a-na a-ṣap-pi* [ŠÀ-*bu ša*] LUGAL EN-*ia lu* DÙG.GA).

93 SAA 1 10, 126, 247, 257, 260; SAA 5 80, 242; SAA 15 12.

94 SAA 1 257.

inspected at regular intervals and provided with food, drink and other necessities – a 'humanitarian' feature not included in the usual image of Assyrian war conduct."[95]

The letters also attest to the dangers of deportation. The governor of Harran reports that "nobody has died or escaped since I reviewed them"[96]; the treasurer of Dur-Šarrukin reports having received and checked a number of people and oxen, only to find that some were missing.[97] In another letter the governor of Naṣibina reports bringing captives into four cities; "the exhausted ones I made enter Naṣibina on the 23rd."[98] It is unclear whether this is meant to refer to all the captives, or whether there was some special consideration given to the pace enforced upon those particularly spent by the journey. The same letter also attests to the ill-effects of the deportation process: "The people are ve[ry] we[ak]; *weather* has eaten up [their] *loo[ks]* and the mountains have crushed them. They are coming *ague-stricken*."[99] The letters nonetheless indicate that these facts are conveyed due to concern for deportee welfare at the highest level; immediately following this description is the admonition that "[the ki]ng, our lord, should know (this)."[100] Whatever the provisions, it is clear that deportation was an undesirable fate and one feared by Assyria's enemies – indeed one employed deliberately for that purpose, according to one letter: "We must deport [the house of Ilumma-tak]lak, and we must also deport [...], so they will fear [the king...".[101]

All of these activities appear to have been considered acceptable according to the established norms of the time, and did not require further, specialised attempts to justify them. Though the language of sin and rebellion is stronger and more persistent in Sargon's inscriptions than in Tiglath-pileser's, this is unsurprising in the reign of a king

---

95 SAA 5 xxvii.

96 SAA 1 195:r.1-2 (LÚ-*ma la* ÚŠ LÚ-*ma la* ZÁH TA* É *a-na-ku a-šur-ú-šá-nu-ni*).

97 SAA 1 128.

98 SAA 1 247:9′-r.1 (*na-ga-ma-ru-u-te* UD-23-KAM *ina* URU.*na-ṣib-na ú-se-ri-ib*). *nagmuru* is derived from a verb meaning something to the effect of completed, annihilated, fully used up (*CAD* G, 24-32).

99 SAA 5 156:r.1-7 (UN.MEŠ *e-ta-[an-šú] a-dan-[niš]* ⸢*šá*?⸣-*ár*!-*bu la*[*m*?-*šú-nu*] *e-ta-kal* KUR.⸢MEŠ⸣-[*ni*] [*i*]*m*!-*tar-qu-šú-nu qu-ba-te-šú-nu il-la-ku-u-ni*).

100 SAA 5 156:r.8 ([L]UGAL EN-*ni lu ú-da*).

101 SAA 15 40:2′-4′ ([É mDINGIR-*ma-tak*]-⸢*lak*⸣ *nu-šag-la* [*x x x*] *nu-šag-la-a-ma* [LUGAL] *i-pa-lu-hu*); cf. SAA 15 221. The Puqudaeans had good reason to fear Sargon: in the first part of his campaign "the Assyrians had devastated their territory and starved them out in their hiding places in the swamps of the Uqnû river (the eastern branch of the Tigris) until their sheikhs had given up" (SAA 15 xxi).

whose military activities were aimed much more at preserving an established empire than building one up from scratch.

The characterisation of the enemy as rebellious in Sargon's inscriptions is in fact so persistent that its absence is exceptional. There are very few opponents who are not labelled rebellious or described as having somehow provoked Assyrian attack, and it is particularly interesting to note that all but two of the exceptions appear in the *Letter to Aššur* – which in fact *never* describes an enemy as rebellious. In terms of legitimating Assyrian military activities, it is significant that it is in the *Letter to Aššur* that a number of the clearest allusions to *Enūma eliš* occur, and there that the relative roles of Aššur and Marduk are enumerated.

As has already been established, Sargon, like Tiglath-pileser, was comfortable employing strong language to describe the violence inflicted on his enemies and with describing himself in violent terms, but it is in the *Letter to Aššur* that the most vivid examples of this occur. For instance:

> I killed large numbers of his (troops), the bodies of his warriors I cut down like millet, filling the mountain valleys (with them). I made their blood run down the ravines and precipices like a river, dyeing plain, countryside and highlands red like anenome. His warriors, the mainstay of his army, bearers of bow and lance, I slaughtered about his feet like lambs, I cut off their heads. His noblemen, counsellors (and) his courtiers, I shattered their weapons in battle and took them and their horses prisoner.[102]

The nature of the *Letter to Aššur* has been considered in detail by A.L. Oppenheim, who rightly observed that the text is unusual in the effort to which it goes in order to legitimate Sargon's acts in this particular campaign. "In some way", he suggests,

> the destruction and plundering of the famous temple in Muṣaṣir seems to have been an event of considerable importance outside of Urarṭu, as well as a sacrilege that shocked many people, quite different from the continuous raids of the Assyrians on their neighbours and the habitual spoliation of their temples and palaces.[103]

102 *ARAB*, §154; Mayer, "Sargons", 80:134-137 (*di-ik-ta-šu ma-'a-at-tu a-du-uk-ma* LÚ.ÚŠ.MEŠ *qu-ra-di-šu ki-ma* ^{še}BULUG$_4$ *áš-ṭi-ma sa-pan-ni* KUR-*e ú-mal-li* ÚŠ.MEŠ-*šú-nu ḫur-ri na-at-ba-ki* ÍD-*eš ú-šar-di-ma ṣe-e-ri ki-i-di ba-ma-a-te aṣ-ru-ba il-lu-reš* ^{lú}*mun-daḫ-ṣi-šu tu-kul-ti um-ma-ni-šu na-áš* ^{giš}BAN *as-ma-re-e pa-an* GÌR^{II}-*šu ki-ma as-li ú-ṭa-bi-iḫ-ma* SAG.DU.MEŠ-*šú-nu ú-nak-kis* SAG.KAL.MEŠ-*šú ma-li-ki man-za-az pa-ni-šu i-na qé-reb tu-šá-ri* ^{giš}TUKUL.MEŠ-*šú-nu ú-šab-bir-ma a-di* ANŠE.KUR<.RA>.MEŠ-*šú-nu al-qa-šu-nu-ti*).

103 A.L. Oppenheim, "The city of Assur in 714 B.C.", *JNES* 19 (1960): 137.

Oppenheim suggests that the Assyrians were taking revenge for some similar desecration of an Assyrian temple, but admits that there is no evidence for this in the Assyrian sources. If this were the rationale, one might have also expected a reference to it in the *Letter to Aššur*, but there is none. What does appear, as Oppenheim notes, is a series of three specific divine signs: the first Oppenheim calls a legal argument: a reference to the right of Aššur, given by Marduk, to bring the images and treasures of the gods into his sanctuary. We have already cited this passage, with a slightly different interpretation, above. Signs from the moon god Sîn and from Šamaš follow.

Oppenheim describes the first sign, with regard to the relationship between Aššur, Marduk and conquest, as an "elsewhere unheard-of divine regulation which made it Sargon's religious duty, so to speak, to pillage the temple of Ḫaldia [the principal god of Urarṭu] in Muṣaṣir and to bring his and his consort's images to Assyria".[104] As our earlier interpretation of this passage indicated, however, the imperative to which Sargon's letter refers is not unheard of so much as hitherto not elaborated explicitly: as we have already seen, scattered references to *Enūma eliš* occur throughout the inscriptions of Tiglath-pileser as well as those of Sargon. It is only in the *Letter to Aššur*, however, that the cosmological framework in which the king and Marduk act in concert to combat the forces of chaos and to win over ever-more extensive territories for the order of Aššur is explicitly referred to. Oppenheim is certainly right to suspect that the extent to which divine legitimation of Sargon's actions is made explicit in the *Letter* is reflective of some fairly high level of concern in Assyria as to their legitimacy: the event "must have been considered outrageous...Sargon felt compelled to convince the citizens of Assur of the appropriateness of his behaviour".[105] It is not surprising that the descriptions of the punishments inflicted on Urarṭu are more extreme than any others recorded for Tiglath-pileser or Sargon.

Two of the most significant actions of Sargon, however, are inflicted on both the Urarṭians and the Babylonians. Both are described as "bespattered with the venom of death", and it is only the Urarṭians and the Babylonians whose agricultural resources are attacked. The similarities between these are not coincidental, for the only other episode under Sargon which exhibits such strong allusions to the creation nar-

---

104 Oppenheim, "City", 136.

105 A.L. Oppenheim, "Neo-Assyrian and Neo-Babylonian empires", in *The Symbolic Instrument in Early Times*, volume 1 of *Propaganda and Communication in World History*, edited by H.D. Lasswell, D. Lerner and H. Speier (Honolulu, Hawaii: University Press of Hawaii, 1979), 125.

rative is that relating to Marduk-apla-iddina and the Babylonians. Like the *Letter to Aššur*'s references to the role of Marduk in the extension of the ordered territory of Aššur, the language referring to Marduk-apla-iddina as flooding Babylon's environs "as with the mighty waves (of the sea)" is an instance of the use of explicitly cosmological language to justify more extreme behaviour under the rule of Sargon. Also confirming this suspicion is the description of Marduk-apla-iddina as the "likeness of a *gallû*-demon": precisely one of the minions of Tiamat in *Enūma eliš*.[106]

At first glance, the most distinctive element of the treatment of the Urarṭians, and the one which required the special treatment of a *Letter to Aššur* while that accorded the Babylonians did not, was the plundering of the temple of the god Ḫaldia and the deportation of his and his consort's statues.[107] Alternately and more probably, in light of the subsequent and ongoing increase in extremity in Assyrian warfare, the *Letter to Aššur* regarding the Urarṭians succeeded in its attempt to legitimate the episode and, more specifically, the acts engaged upon during it. As a result, the subsequent engagement with Marduk-apla-iddina could allude to the same ideas as means of legitimating similar actions.

This phenomenon, in which a king's inscriptions legitimate an increased level of violence against a given enemy by making more explicit the connection between the role of the king in warfare and the role of the god at creation, foreshadows the increasingly direct identification of Assyria's enemies with the forces of chaos which occurs in subsequent periods. The use of such allusions in their historical contexts will comprise the focus of Chapter 8.

---

106 Fuchs, Prunk. 122 (*ḫi-ri-iṣ gallî*(gal$_5$.lá!) *lem-ni*).

107 *ARAB*, §172-173. This of course presumes that a similar letter with regard to the Babylonian episode did not also exist at some point.

6. Ethics of the Judahite and Israelite élite

Two principle groups of texts reveal Judahite and Israelite usage of the cosmological framework in legitimating military activities. One group, the psalms, is useful primarily in its reference to the theoretical aspects of the framework; the other group, the books of *Kings* and *Chronicles,* reveals details of its practical enactment.

6.1. Psalms

The psalms of the Hebrew Bible offer one of the nearest parallels to the Assyrian literature with regard to their original social location, as the psalms which the psalter has preserved from the pre-exilic period are likely to have been largely derived from the official cult.

6.1.1. Method

Yet these texts are not unproblematic: the psalms have come through a long and often unclear history of transmission, and the psalter does not preserve its hymns or prayers as they were originally used. Rather, the pertinent pre-exilic material survives only through the filter of later worshippers' preferences, and sometimes it is only through a process of weeding out later additions and subtractions to the psalms that something approximating an older text may be guessed at.

In a historical endeavour of this kind, dating is one of the most significant issues to be addressed before using a text as a record of pre-exilic monarchic thinking. In addition to eliminating psalms of exilic or post-exilic provenance, we must also account for the fact that, of psalms which may be dated with some certainty to the pre-exilic monarchic period, there are many which contain passages and themes of even older origin. This is a significant difficulty in the use of the psalms for this study's particular purposes, as the precise dating of any psalm into the eighth or seventh centuries is nearly if not actually impossible. In addition to the perpetual redevelopment of older materials in new psalms, the texts are never so detailed as to assure the scholar of a precise date or event from which they derive.

For the purposes of this study, those psalms which are decidedly exilic or post-exilic have been disregarded, for obvious reasons. Those which are supposed to show signs of a very early date have been used only with extreme caution – on the principle that their preservation may indicate an ongoing adherence to the ideas reflected therein – or not used at all. In the majority of instances, however, there are no grounds on which to make judgments of date, other than very broadly designating a psalm pre- or post-exilic (and often not even this is generally agreed upon). Unlike Assyrian texts, whose specificity allows for the tracing of historical developments within the royal ideological and ethical framework, the psalms may only be employed to illuminate these areas in general terms.

Given our attempts to distinguish also between Israelite and Judahite material, at least in principle, it is also necessary to note the psalms' geographical ambiguity. It is generally supposed that the majority, by nature of Israelite and Judahite history, are of southern provenance, though there are arguments for some northern psalms. The following observations are therefore most probably only directly relevant to the southern kingdom of Judah and its official cult. As with temporal specificity, however, there is a great deal of geographical imprecision in these texts, and many have no particularly clear indication of southern provenance beyond the general probability of transmission history.

Attending the matter strictly at hand, the lack of specificity so generally observable also translates into a lack of historical detail with regard to acts of war. Unlike prose, in which a certain amount of factual description is required, the psalms are clearly liberated from the need to impart the particularities of the situation (or situations) to which they refer. Thus while there are numerous psalms which more or less clearly refer to war, concrete details border on non-existent. The poetic character of the texts also lends itself to the liberal use of metaphorical and allusive language, often making the distinction between psalms uttered by individuals (with regards to personal enemies) and those uttered on a national stage (with regards to foreign enemies) quite difficult, as both employ metaphors more literally relevant to the other.

Part of the problem is the identity of the speaker, which is frequently ambiguous. Psalms spoken by or on behalf of the community at large are the most likely sources for information on war and ethics, as, generally speaking, war is a matter of national and not individual concern. Also especially relevant are psalms spoken by or on behalf of the king, who in his role as representative of the people to Yahweh (and of Yahweh to the people) would have been particularly poised to supplicate on the nation's behalf with regard to war.

The identification of the speaker in the psalms (and of their consequent subject) has traditionally been undertaken using form criticism, with those spoken in a communal plural or in the singular but with clearly royal overtones being considered to refer to enemies of a national character.[1] This form-critical distinction is effectively set aside, however, by scholars who include large numbers of the individual prayers and individual thanksgivings among the royal psalms, and argue that many of the psalms spoken by individuals may have been said on behalf of the nation by a representative individual, such as the king or a high priest.[2] J.H. Eaton's methodology has undergone its share of criticism, but it is difficult to deny his argument that the origins of the psalms and the psalter in the official cult mean that there are almost certainly a number of royal psalms in the psalter unidentified as such. With this in mind, this study has cast its net relatively broadly.

Regardless of the identity of the speaker, there remains the question of whether those psalms which clearly refer to war were composed with actual battles in mind or if they were written for some sort of ritual context. A great deal has been written about the nature of New Year and kingship rituals in Judah, and it is hardly implausible to suppose that Judah's cult included some dramatic staging of a Judahite victory over its enemies.[3] Certainly the themes of the creation narrative, which may be frequently identified in the psalter, and which was associated in Mesopotamia with the New Year celebration, tend to suggest such a context in Judah. Such a ritual context would also explain the lack of details in the psalms, since a ritualised enemy would have been sketched in general cosmological terms rather than in specific historical ones.

Alternative and also plausible is that the psalms were actually used as prayers and pleas before or in the midst of battle, or as thanks and praise afterwards.[4] In this case the cosmological language of the psalms would even more clearly associate the earthly enemy of the king with chaos and the king himself with the god at creation. For this study,

---

1 H.-J. Kraus, *Psalms 1-59: A Commentary*, translated by H.C. Oswald (Minneapolis, Minn.: Augsburg, 1988), 95.

2 E.g., J.H. Eaton, *Kingship and the Psalms*, SBT(SS) 32 (London: SCM, 1976); see also Kraus, *Psalms*, 95-96 and S. Mowinckel, *The Psalms in Israel's Worship*, translated by D.R. Ap-Thomas. (Oxford: Basil Blackwell, 1962), 1:207.

3 Beginning especially with I. Engnell, *Studies in Divine Kingship in the Ancient Near East* (Uppsala: Almqvist & Wiksell, 1943).

4 E. Haglund, *Historical Motifs in the Psalms*, CBOT 23 (Stockholm: CWK Gleerup, 1984), 126; Mowinckel, *Psalms*, 1:220-221.

however, it may not greatly matter whether the psalms were written for a cultic battle or an actual one. In either instance the theological premise is that the god, in concert with the king, acts to ensure the destruction of the chaotic enemy threat. A cultic enactment is a symbolic manifestation of Yahweh and the king's concerted activity to that end, while recitation as part of the preparations for or part of the culmination of war itself is a means of reiterating the respective roles of the figures involved. The one element which might be expected to fade or disappear in the cultic rendition would be the particularities of an enemy's offences, which render them chaotic forces to be put down; these may be equally absent from psalms spoken prior to the actual clash of armies on the battlefield.

6.1.2. Analysis

6.1.2.1. Cosmology

Given the provenance of the psalms, it comes as no surprise that they reveal an ideology of intimate synergy between Yahweh and the king. The most extensive examination to date of the psalms' expression of this synergy is Adam's *Der Königliche Held*, which is a detailed study of the language and imagery used of Yahweh and of the king in Ps. 18.[5] Adam was able to adduce an extensive range of evidence for the paralleling of Yahweh and the human king, ranging from mutual depiction with royal military iconography to the use of specific terms and phrases. All of the king's military abilities are ascribed divine origin (cf. the Assyrian mythology of the origins of kingship), while descriptions of Yahweh's acts frame the description of the king's exploits. On the basis of these correspondences, Adam writes: "Den wörtlichen Parallelen liegt eine *sachliche Entsprechung* zwischen irdischem König und JHWH zugrunde: Beide üben die königliche Handlungsrolle des Helden aus."[6]

---

5 The depiction of Yahweh as a warrior is of course well-attested. Yahweh is said to draw the sword, the spear and the javelin (7.13; 35.3) and to have strung the bow (7.13-14), an especially royal image, as noted. Psalm 60 describes Ephraim and Judah as Yahweh's helmet and sceptre (60.9). Yahweh is described as the psalmists' shield (18.3, 31; 28.7; 33.20; 59.12; 144.2), saving refuge (28.8), fortress (18.3; 31.3, 4; 59.10, 17, 18; 62.3, 6; 71.3; 144.2) or stronghold (18.3), and as a strong tower against the enemy (61.4).

6 Adam, 125.

Pertinent to the observation of this phenomenon elsewhere in the psalms are several specific components of Adam's overall conclusion. First, the terminology used: a number of verbs typically associated with Yahweh's military activities are used by Ps. 18 to correlate Yahweh with the king (especially מחץ, צמת). Military imagery of bow and arrow (קשת, חץ) and shield (מגן) are common to both Yahweh and the king, both as equipment used by them and as epithets for Yahweh; also such phrases as to be "girded with strength", which is associated with Yahweh's enthronement (אזר *pi*). The emphasis on Yahweh as the military tutor to the king also emphasises "die besondere Nähe zwischen Gottheit und König im Kampf".[7] The same idea occurs in Ps. 144.1; as in the Assyrian mythology of the origins of kingship, the king is understood as having received the conduct of war from the god(s). Also worth noting, particularly given the tendency for the depiction of Yahweh's involvement to somewhat overpower that of the human king, is Adam's point that the use of verbs such as ישע and עזר, which tend to emphasise Yahweh's role, are not used in an attempt to claim that it is *only* Yahweh who takes an active role in military for victory, but that these verbs are used of "JHWHs Eingreifen in den Kampf und damit das intendierte Zusammenwirken JHWHs mit dem König im Kampf."[8] ישע in particular is connected to Yahweh's intervention "als königlicher Held" in all its appearances throughout the Hebrew Bible.

It is unfortunate, of course, that we do not have a specifically Hebrew rendering of the battle at creation, as the existence of such a text would make the identification of allusions to it much clearer. However, despite this impediment, cosmological overtones may be recognised in the imagery of Ps. 18. Thus the first half of the psalm, in which Yahweh's own actions are described, speaks of Yahweh's weapons in meteorological terms: hail, thundering, lightning, coals of fire (ברד, רעם *hi*, ברק [with the Septuagint, 2 Sam. 22.15], גחלי אש; 18.11-15). His chariot is the wind and he is clothed in clouds (רוח, עב). Yahweh's actions culminate with "then the channels of the sea were seen, and the foundations of the world were laid bare" (18.16). Yahweh then proceeds in the subsequent verses to convey the knowledge of warfare to the king. As already argued in Chapter 4, this association of cosmological creation motifs and both human and divine kingship provide strong evidence in favour of the proposal that the Judahite royal ideology of warfare was founded on a similar cosmological basis to that which is evident in more detail in the Assyrian material.

---

7 Adam, 206.

8 Adam, 209.

The synergy of Yahweh and the king in warfare also occurs in a number of other psalms. As Adam does note, this phenomenon is particularly strong in the first three books of *Psalms*, as would be expected of a royal and thus pre-exilic motif.[9] The psalter commences with what is probably a royal coronation psalm emphasising exactly this theme.[10] There have also been suggestions that this psalm should be seen as part of rites of ritual combat, perhaps at the New Year festival, and it seems more than coincidence that these two *Sitze im Leben* are in contention.

Part of the identification of the king with the god is his description as the god's son, and Ps. 2 is one of the clearest statements of this idea in the Hebrew Bible. It is clear that in neither Assyria nor Israel nor Judah was this sonship thought to be of the literal biological type, nor of any type which led to the divinisation of the king, but that this "sonship" is a metaphorical means of expressing the intimate relationship and unified objectives of god and king. In Ps. 2, the oracular announcement of the king's status as the son of Yahweh is, not insignificantly, followed immediately by an expression of its consequences, namely, that Yahweh's acts coincide with the desires of the king for military success.

> Ask of me, and I will make the nations your heritage,
> and the ends of the earth your possession.
> You shall break them with a rod of iron,
> and dash them in pieces like a potter's vessel (2.8-9).[11]

A coronation hymn establishes the paradigm of the king's relationship with the deity for his newly-commenced reign, and the paradigm clearly established by this psalm is that the king's sonship assures a synergy with Yahweh toward his military victory. That this may, in addition to being a straightforward military statement, also allude to the creation narrative is suggested by the verb at the beginning of 2.9. The Masoretic text has תרעם, which has been taken previously as רעע, to break. If taken as רעם to roar, thunder, it would be the same meteorological language used of Yahweh in Ps. 18, here made to refer to the king by Yahweh himself. The only other appearance of the form is at Job 40.9, where it is similarly joined by military and creative language; *Job*, of course, is one of the strongest remaining remnants of Yahweh's

9 See also G.H. Wilson, *The Editing of the Hebrew Psalter*, SBLDS 76 (Chico, Ca.: Scholars Press, 1985) and J.C. McCann, *Shape and Shaping of the Psalter*, JSOTSup 159 (Sheffield: JSOT, 1993).

10 I.e., Ps. 2; on Ps. 1 as part of the late redactional unification of *Psalms*, see G.H. Wilson.

11 שאל ממני ואתנה גוים נחלתך ואחזתך אפסי־ארץ: תרעם בשבט ברזל ככלי יוצר תנפצם:

victory over chaos at creation, and the motif appears immediately on the heels of this passage.

Psalm 21, which is a rare royal thanksgiving, also demonstrates the effective coalescence of the king and Yahweh which we have seen in Pss. 2 and 18. There the description of success ("your hand will find out all your enemies...") in the second person may be read to refer either to the king (as an oracle) or to Yahweh (as praise). The majority of commentators take it to be the king, largely on the basis of the reference to Yahweh in the third person in 21.9, but ultimately it is theologically moot whether it is the king or Yahweh whose agency is referred to, and indeed the ready slippage between a second person which probably addresses the king and a third person reference to Yahweh and back again indicates how the historical, human agent is united with the cosmological divine.

Throughout the psalms there is a tendency to emphasise the divine agent at the expense of the human one, in a manner typical of poetic and hymnic literature. As in Assyrian thought, the intimacy of the divine-human parallel effectively makes aggression against Judah tantamount to aggression against the deity. Judah's enemies are Yahweh's enemies; there is no distinction between the enemy of the king and that of Yahweh (e.g., 2.2, 8, 10; 18.47; 45.5; 72.11; 110.5; 144.2). Psalm 98 (perhaps an enthronement psalm), for example, speaks exclusively in terms of the acts of Yahweh, with no explicit mention of his human agent, the king. Human agency is similarly obscured in Ps. 68, but only at first glance. Bearing in mind that war booty and tribute were divided between king and temple, this is as much a reference to the human as to the divine king. That real, earthly victory is in mind is also clear from references to the division of spoil (68.12) and a victory parade in Jerusalem (68.24-27). Even in such an apparently ahistorical psalm as Ps. 98, however, the opening strophe refers to the house of Israel, while the entire psalm is rife with references to the foreign human audience of "Yahweh's" deeds. It thus implicitly confirms the historical, human plane of the divine activity. That the human counterpart to Yahweh's action is the king himself is confirmed by the affirmation that Yahweh, warrior, is king: it is as king that the god engages in the royal function of warfare.

Returning to Ps. 21, the synergy between divine and human king is, as elsewhere, intent on destruction. The oracle, if it is such, emphasises how "all your enemies" will be consumed and swallowed up; even the enemy's children will be destroyed (21.11). Rather dramatically, the passage concludes: "you will aim at their faces with your bows" (21.13). Rather than aiming to incapacitate, the king will aim to kill.

Psalm 89 closes the pre-exilic collection of psalms and reflects many of the same sentiments as Pss. 2, 18 and 21.[12] It is also one of the clearest texts in which Yahweh's struggle against chaos at creation and king's military engagements are associated. The psalm does not seem to derive from a coronation context, but is clearly connected to the Davidic covenant – perhaps the most decisive biblical expression of the unified purpose and activity of god and king. There are also close parallels between the description of the king and the description of Yahweh. "You have a mighty arm", the psalm says of Yahweh; "strong is your hand, high your right hand" (89.14). "My hand", responds Yahweh, "shall always remain with him [the king]; my arm also shall strengthen him...I will set his hand on the sea and his right hand on the rivers" (89.22, 26).

That this is a direct statement of the synergy between the king's military endeavours and Yahweh's original creative battle against chaos is confirmed by the preceding declaration that

> You [Yahweh] rule the raging of the sea;
> when its waves rise, you still them.
> You crushed Rahab like a carcass;
> you scattered your enemies with your mighty arm (89.11).

The equation of the enemy with chaos is evident from the poetic parallelism, and its application to the king's mortal enemies clear from the repetition of the same terms in 89.23-24:

> The enemy shall not outwit him,
> the wicked shall not humble him.
> I will crush his foes before him
> and strike down those who hate him.

This part of the psalm concludes with a statement of the royal (covenant) relationship between the god and the king, reiterating the convergence of divine and human activity.

Contributing to the identification of the psalm as set against a background of specifically royal military actions is the explicitly royal language used of Yahweh (כסא; 89.15) as well as traditional royal language of righteousness and justice. The king himself is called shield

12 There is no agreement on what, if any, specific context gave rise to Ps. 89, though most commentators seem to lean toward a ritual context rather than a historical one (M.E. Tate, *Psalms 51-100*, WBC 20 [Dallas, Tex.: Word, 1990], 414-415; Eaton, 121-122; C.S. Rodd, "Psalms", in *The Oxford Bible Commentary*, edited by J. Barton and J. Muddiman [Oxford: Oxford University Press, 2001], 391). Whether the final stanzas of the psalm are from an ordinary pre-exilic military context or were added after the final destruction of Jerusalem is also debated; the lack of reference to exile perhaps tends to favour the former.

(מגן) which, as we have already had reason to note, is also language associated with "der königliche Held", and which makes eminently clear the king's engagement in the god's battle against chaos.

In the final verses of the psalm (89.38-51), we also see an aspect of the royal military ideology, a concern with defeat, which is less prevalent in the Assyrian materials, due to a greater frequency of success and therefore less theological concern with defeat. Somehow, it is clear, the assumed synergy of god with king has been disrupted, and earthly success is no longer assured.

There is obviously a close relationship between Ps. 89 and the Nathan oracle in 2 Sam. 7. There, when the king does wrong, Yahweh "will punish him with a rod such as mortals use, with blows inflicted by human beings" (2 Sam. 7.14). This implies that the king's military difficulties imply his moral wrongdoing, yet Ps. 89 strongly protests that Yahweh's abandonment is unfounded (89.38-51). The balance between the two conflicting elements of the oracle is weighed carefully: between the premise that defeat entails culpability, and the supposition that Yahweh will never abandon the king.

That the practical limitations of the Judahite kingdom were not necessarily taken to preclude expansionist or imperial ambition is clear from Ps. 72. Here again the association of the king with the establishment and preservation of justice and righteousness is clear, as is the overlap between the social order ("May he judge your people with righteousness, and your poor with justice"; 72.2) and the natural order ("may the mountains yield prosperity for the people"; 72.3b).

The association of this natural-social order with a cosmic imperial programme comes to the fore with 72.8-11. The passage describes the king's power as universal and complete, with particular emphasis on the subordination of foreign kings through tribute or physical prostration. The geographic realities of the Near East make it impossible to determine for certain whether the phrase "from sea to sea" is meant literally, in which case it is a clear claim to universal dominion, or as a reference to the sea defeated at creation, in which case it is equally cosmic in scope. That perhaps the latter is intended (or both meanings are meant simultaneously) is suggested by the subsequent reference to the river. It is very common in biblical scholarship to assume that references to a universal kingdom of this sort only occur in late eschatological texts, but the strong association of this idea with royal military engagement makes clear that the later eschatology was building on a well-established royal concept.

Similarly ambitious promises for the military successes of the king appear in Ps. 110, also a likely coronation psalm. The divine involvement is clearer than in Ps. 2, though the actions are also more historical in implication. The prophetic "oracle of Yahweh" appears only here in the psalms (110.1), and the psalm may be (or have the form of) an oracular pronouncement during the coronation ritual. The idea that the execution of violent defeat is a matter of the establishment of justice is brought out by 110.5, when these acts are said to be done in the execution of judgment. The destruction – explicitly Yahweh's but implicitly that of his human agent, the king, especially in light of 110.1 – is thorough: the nations are to be full of corpses and shattered heads. Not insignificantly, the first target is the leadership, which is the figurehead of insubordination and opposition.

The language of justice emphasises that the subordination of all creation to the dominion of the Judahite king is perceived as in the interests of the foreign nations.[13] This point of view parallels the Assyrian perception of the *pax Assyriaca* as a system of benign oversight, achieved by liberating peoples from their native oppressors and thereby ensuring their well-being, and is in keeping with a ideological framework in which the indigenous order is the one true order, with all others deviant (cf. also Ps. 98). The primary targets of punishment in these psalms are the king and other leadership figures, in keeping with the Assyrian targeting of leaders and élites – the implicit flip side being the royal shepherd's concern for the general population.

What have sometimes been identified as "pacifist" tendencies in the descriptions of Yahweh are part of this same idea, in which the military triumphs of god and king are depicted as in the interests of the defeated. Thus Ps. 46 declares that Yahweh "makes wars cease to the end of the earth; he breaks the bow, and shatters the spear; he burns the shields with fire" (46.10).[14] This cessation of war is the consequence of universal defeat; on its own the phrase just cited is deceptively pacifist, but it is immediately preceded by a call to "come, behold the works of Yahweh; see what desolations he has brought on the earth" (46.9).

In Ps. 68 Yahweh is called upon to "trample under foot those who lust after tribute; scatter the peoples who delight in war" (68.31b).[15] On the one hand this seems to be a rejection of warfare and those who pursue it wantonly – but the means of ending warfare it is itself violent. It

13 Cf. e.g., Isa. 40-55.

14 משבית מלחמות עד־קצה הארץ קשת ישבר וקצץ חנית עגלות ישרף באש. Adopting the common repointing of "carts, wagons" to "shields".

15 Masoretic text: מתרפס ברצי כסף בזר עמים קרבות יחפצו. The interpretive issues of this psalm are "most difficult" – "almost legendary". The present form of the psalm is probably post-exilic, but it includes older, traditional material and is often dated very early (see Tate, 174).

is not incidental that the same tribute-bearing condemned in 68.31 is acceptable both immediately before and immediately after (68.29, 32). The change is that there the tribute is directed toward Yahweh. In all the psalms which depict the cessation of warfare, the same formulation comes to the fore: war will cease because all nations will be subject to Jerusalem, its king and its god. The reorientation of the nations toward a Judahite centre will be complete.

Part of this conception is the same dual depiction of foreigners as encountered among the Assyrians. On the one hand, foreign peoples are in need of pastoral care and rescue from their corrupt leaders – hence the expectation that a universal Judahite dominion is the only route to "peace". At the same time, they are often characterised as wicked, necessitating opposition (punishment). Again, language of justice and righteousness is rife in the latter instances, with a persistent alignment of Yahweh and the psalmist with the cause of justice and conflation of the nations with the wicked. Thus Ps. 9.15-16 has the parallelism "the nations have sunk in the pit they have made...the wicked are snared", and in a clear reference to military opponents Ps. 68.21 has "his [God's] enemies...those who walk in their guilty ways". Likewise Ps. 144 frames the king's appeals to Yahweh for military assistance in terms of the wickedness of the enemy:

> Rescue me from the cruel sword,
> and deliver me from the hand of aliens,
> whose mouths speak lies,
> and whose right hands are false (144.11).

The extent to which militarily-enacted justice is expected to go is described in Ps. 9.5-6:

> You have rebuked the nations,
> you have destroyed the wicked;
> you have blotted out their name forever and ever.
> The enemies have vanished in everlasting ruins;
> their cities you have rooted out;
> the very memory of them has perished.

Similar to the habit of some of the Assyrian kings of describing their enemies as rebellious and wicked, consequently making military manoeuvres justifiably punitive, these psalms attach the language of wickedness to Judah's enemies in such a way as to cast Judah as engaging in the morally supportable, even morally demanded, suppression of purveyors of unnatural, antisocial, immoral activities. Though it is difficult to surmise without more concrete details, one suspects that – in parallel to the Assyrian approach – the primary issue in the identification of enemies as wicked was their resistance to Judahite hegemony, rather than a belief in the absolute and inherent wickedness of non-Judahites.[16]

6.1.2.2. Practice

Unsurprisingly, these poetic texts do not reveal many details about the practical acts of war, informative though they are with regard to the ideology behind them. Aside from those points already discussed, there are only a few passages worth mentioning. Psalm 68.22-24 is one of the rare explicit moments. As elsewhere, the enemies are called guilty, and their defeat justified as punishment. The actual fate of the punished is obscured by the Masoretic text's awkward statement that the enemies will be brought to Judah for the purposes of shattering (מחץ) the victors' feet in the blood; the versions all suggest "bathe" (רחץ).[17] M.E. Tate attempts to retain the Masoretic text with "shake off", but bathing in blood suits the context, given the disrespectful treatment involving dogs immediately following, and the phrase is paralleled in Ps. 58 in a similar situation. (Psalm 58 does little else, however, beyond affirming the action's association with triumph over an enemy.) The text probably does then refer to bathing feet in enemy blood, though it is unclear whether this was meant literally or as a metaphorical expression for (military) humiliation and defeat. The psalm's subsequent reference to dogs is best taken in its literal sense, alongside other occurrences of similar language (1 Kg. 21.19; 1 Kg. 22.38; 2 Kg. 9.35-37). R.J. Clifford describes the defilement of the enemy corpses in Ps. 68 as symbolic of complete victory; it would have constituted an unmistakable exhibition of power.[18]

Psalm 83's vague references to the fates of various previous enemies which the psalmist wishes Yahweh to re-enact on the current enemies are unusual in that they can be traced in the traditions passed down elsewhere in the Hebrew Bible.[19] All of the traditions mentioned

---

16 As reflected by Zehnder's conclusions, the final form of the Hebrew Bible has frequently obscured this more benevolent attitude toward foreigners. This is, however, a phenomenon connected in large part to the late monarchic and subsequent exilic and post-exilic experiences of the traditions' tradents.

17 Rodd, "Psalms", 385; Tate, 170.

18 R.J. Clifford, *Psalms 1-72*, AOTC (Nashville, Tenn.: Abingdon, 2002), 318.

19 The date of Ps. 83 sees no consensus (E. Zenger supposes post-exilic, Clifford pre-exilic, and Tate gives it up as impossible to tell). The list of nations it gives are historically impossible as a unified assault force, and the fact that they number ten has led more than one scholar to consider the list symbolic (Rodd, "Psalms", 389-390; R.J. Clifford, *Psalms 73-150*, AOTC [Nashville, Tenn.: Abingdon, 2003], 67; Tate, 345). The

are pre-monarchic, but the reiteration of them in this psalm seems to indicate ongoing approval.

The psalm is clear in its assertions of the nations' wickedness (and hence their legitimacy as military targets); the nations are said to have conspired against Israel with the intent of destroying it and commandeering its territories for themselves. That territory is also explicitly identified as belonging to Yahweh, thereby making their crime also a religious one. Sisera and Jabin are the enemies of Judg. 4-5, defeated by Deborah, Barak and Jael. The violent end of Sisera, wrought by Jael, is well-known, but there is little further information in the *Judges* narrative to indicate what, if any, particularities of the battle at the Wadi Kishon were in the mind of the psalmist, other than a general rout. The defeat is in *Judges* specified as "by the sword", but there is no other information regarding method or consequence, other than to claim that there were no survivors save Sisera, temporarily (Judg. 4.16).

The Midianites and Amalekites (Judg. 6-8) are given more of a description both with regard to their ill-treatment of the Israelites, which justifies their destruction, and with regard to the Israelites' retribution. The latter is said to be led by Gideon (Jerubbaal) with only 300 men, in order that the victory be duly credited to Yahweh (Judg. 7.2-8). After the Midianites fled, the Ephraimites captured and decapitated two captains (Oreb and Zeeb, also named in Ps. 83.12) and brought the heads to Gideon (Judg. 7.25).

The fate of the Midianite kings Zebah and Zalmunna (Ps. 83.12) is more convoluted. Though Gideon captures them, they are not immediately killed. This seems to be for one (or both) of two reasons. Gideon first drags the kings back to the people of Succoth, suggesting that (temporary) leniency may have been motivated by the desire to prove his triumph to the officials of Succoth – who are then trampled to death in punishment for their failure to assist Gideon (the men of Penuel are also killed, with similar rationale). The officials, however, had only demanded to see the kings' hands, and the kings hardly needed to be left alive to count as proof of capture. The eventual execution of Zebah and Zalmunna takes on an aspect of spectacle, or public display of power; such demonstrations, aimed at those who do not accept a king's claim to power, will be further examined in Chapter 8. There also seems to be a personal grudge involved in Gideon's actions: had the kings not killed Gideon's brothers, then their lives would have been spared (Judg. 8.18-19). There is no mention of Yahweh in this section.

---

presence of Assyria and absence of Babylon in the list seem to strengthen the argument for a pre-exilic date (Clifford, *Psalms 73-150*, 68).

Returning to Ps. 83, the present enemies are paralleled to these ancient enemies, and the fates of the latter evoked as equally suitable for the former. The psalm makes clear the role of Yahweh in bringing this about. Psalm 83 puts particular emphasis on the element of spectacle, on the humiliation of the enemies and their armies, though this is cast in theological terms: the public displays of power will bring about the enemies' recognition of the power of Yahweh.[20]

Psalm 149 emphasises the punitive role of warfare and the role of humans as agents of divine punishment.[21] The psalm's explicitness is evident especially in the embarrassed apologetics of the commentaries. This imperative and its articulated purpose, however –

> to execute vengeance on the nations
> and punishment on the peoples,
> to bind their kings with fetters
> and their nobles with chains of iron,
> to execute on them the judgment decreed (149.7-9)

– is ultimately little more than a more explicit and more vehement articulation of those sentiments observed elsewhere: that Yahweh's enemies and Judah's enemies are one and the same, that war is motivated by the perceived wickedness of the opposing nations, and that Judah is enacting a just punishment for the sins of its opponents.[22] There is little new here.

The only point of practical note is the reiteration of an apparent battlefield distinction between the opponents as a generic whole and their leaders. The general fate of suffering "vengeance" and "punishment" are decreed for the former, while the latter are more specifically singled out as to be bound – perhaps while being deported, though this is not explicit.

Suggestive of a tendency against standardised mercy in military contexts is the report in Ps. 18 that the enemies "cried for help...they cried to Yahweh, but he did not answer them" (18.42). The text also suggests that a religious motivation cannot be claimed as the sole rationale for the subjugation of the enemy (as might be argued from Ps. 83); these enemies appear to have turned to Yahweh (perhaps upon the

---

20 Cf. Assyrian military successes as displays of the power of Aššur (Chapter 8).

21 Commentators seem agreed on the victorious nature of Ps. 149, but vary widely otherwise; Clifford considers it exilic while Allen and Rodd presuppose a pre-exilic date and disagree as to whether the psalm is for a real victory or a cultic drama (Clifford, *Psalms 73-150*, 315; Rodd, "Psalms", 404; L.C. Allen, *Psalms 101-150*, WBC 21 [Waco, Tex.: Word, 1983], 319).

22 The "democratisation" of the agent may tend to suggest an exilic or post-exilic date; a full study of the effect of the exile on the military ethics of the Hebrew Bible would be required to identify such a phenomenon for certain.

failure of their own gods to deliver them). It is perhaps surprising that Yahweh is said to have ignored them, given that acknowledgement of a foreign god seems to imply some level of submission to the social-cosmic order represented by the attacking army, but evidently this was not at a sufficient level as to equate to submission, and the king's infliction of defeat continues unchecked.

One possible reason for allowing the enemy to live nonetheless appears in Ps. 59, in which Yahweh is asked not to kill the psalmist's enemies (59.12).[23] The apparent purpose of this, which is subsequent to a plea to "spare none of those who treacherously plot evil" (59.6) and is followed by a request to "consume them until they are no more" (59.14), is that the living enemies may serve as a reminder, perhaps of the power of Yahweh.

Other descriptions of the king's actions are similarly inconsistent, as demonstrated by Ps. 18. On the one hand the enemies are consumed, beaten like dust and cast out: language of total destruction. That total destruction was not achieved, however, is evident from the later verses, which even seem to suggest that military action was hardly required to ensure the enemies' submission. A similar supposition occurs in Ps. 48, in which the kings of the nations are assembled to attack Jerusalem, but flee upon seeing the city.[24] The ideal, of total dominance of the king, is evident in the description of the enemies as cringing and trembling before him, but it would seem that language of total destruction is stereotyped and metaphorical, and that practical submissiveness was considered ideologically satisfactory.

6.1.2.3. Conclusions

While lacking in concrete details, the psalms provide key information on the ideological background to Judahite – and probably also Israelite – military practices. The ideological framework of the king and the god converging in warfare to defeat the threatening chaos, as the enemy was perceived, is apparent in numerous passages. The language used in the psalms suggests that this struggle was conceived specifically in a cosmic context, as part of the creation struggle between Yahweh and

23 The psalm is somewhat peculiar in itself, seeming to be an individual lament with strong communal elements, which have led some to identify it as a communal lament and others to identify it as royal (see Kraus, *Psalms*, 277-278; Tate, 94; Rodd, "Psalms", 383).

24 Compare the Assyrian kings' expectation that the enemy would surrender immediately upon sight of the king in all his splendour.

the sea. That the king is engaged in the perpetuation and extension of this same struggle for order is evident from the general affiliations between Yahweh and the king as well as more specific allusions in Pss. 2, 18 and 72.

Yahweh is frequently the agent of the enemies' destruction, though the role of the human king is not wholly obscured; he takes a clear and explicit role in the destruction of his and Yahweh's enemies. Military affront against Judah is interpreted as a theological affront to the sovereignty of Yahweh, and accordingly demanding of punishment. This can be seen in the emphasis on the moral rectitude of this destruction, with language of wickedness and innocence attached to the enemies and the Judahites respectively. Even those psalms in which a hint of a warless ideal comes through depict that ideal as achieved through violent means – legitimated as the necessary route to a universal Judahite dominion. All of these elements indicate that the object of military acts is the incorporation of an ever-increasing territory into the ordered dominion of the god and king, which is itself centred on the homeland (Ps. 68).

Though they generally lack an interest in the specific means of victory, the psalms demonstrate an expectation of victory. That the method employed to obtain it would be violent seems to have been a given, and there is no specific rejection of any military activities, either on the part of the Judahites nor in the general condemnations directed against the enemies in the appeals for Yahweh's intervention.

6.2. *Kings* and *Chronicles*

6.2.1. Method

The "historical books" of the Deuteronomistic History are fraught with controversy over date(s), sources and author(s).[25] Rather than wading

25 See A. de Pury and T. Römer for a recent overview of the research on these issues ("Deuteronomistic Historiography (DH): history of research and debated issues", in *Israel Constructs its History: Deuteronomistic Historiography in Recent Research*, edited by A. de Pury, T. Römer and J.-D. Macchi, JSOTSup 306 [Sheffield: Sheffield University Press, 2000]). The term "author" is used here to include the various individuals and/or groups involved in the production, compilation and preservation of these texts, and is intended to recognise their deliberate shaping of the books' contents. On the use of Hebrew Bible texts for the construction of history, see essays in e.g., H. Tadmor and M. Weinfeld, eds., *History, Historiography and Interpretation: Studies in Biblical and Cuneiform Literatures* (Leiden: Brill, 1983); A. de Pury, T. Römer and

into these tumultuous waters and risk satisfying no one as to the reliability of any given text for the reconstruction of ethical history in the eighth and seventh centuries, this study will confine itself to a few brief remarks on those passages of *Kings* and *Chronicles* which purport to relate events within this historical period. Though the texts of *Joshua, Judges, Samuel* and the earlier chapters of *Kings* can legitimately be supposed to reflect the ethical thinking of their final authors and editors, the severe lack of consensus with regard to the redaction history of these texts makes their deployment for our own historical purposes too complex and too tenuous to be warranted here.[26]

The religious preoccupations of the authors of *Kings* and *Chronicles* have left precious few accounts of military activities, and none of substance later than the reign of Hezekiah. What accounts there are preserve very few details, and the peripheral significance of international affairs for the theological interests of these narratives means that space is not given over to the articulation of the ideological background of the acts which are described.

This disinterest is not wholly unhelpful. Because military history was not the focus of either *Kings* or *Chronicles*, the authors may be presumed to have had a wide scope for the complete omission of those events which disagreed with their own sensibilities and with the portrait they aimed to produce of any given king. By no means do either *Kings* or *Chronicles* purport to be a thorough account of all the doings of the kings of Judah and Israel, and, supposing that their authors did have more thorough, annalistic records available to them, they must have had many incidents which they chose not to include. It may therefore be supposed that the inclusion of an event which does not have a clear judgment made regarding it was at least not incompatible with the overall assessment of the king concerned.[27]

J.-D. Macchi, eds., *Israel Constructs its History: Deuteronomistic Historiography in Recent Research*, JSOTSup 306 (Sheffield: Sheffield University Press, 2000); J. Day, ed., *In Search of Pre-exilic Israel*, JSOTSup 406 (London: T&T Clark, 2004); L. Grabbe, ed. *'Like a Bird in a Cage': The Invasion of Sennacherib in 701 BCE*, JSOTSup 363 (Sheffield: Sheffield Academic Press, 2003); and V.P. Long, *Israel's Past in Present Research: Essays on Ancient Israelite Historiography*, SBTS 7 (Winona Lake, Ind.: Eisenbrauns, 1999).

26 The books of *Chronicles* are of course well outside our historical range for the opinions of their editor(s) to be pertinent, but they, like *Kings*, are employed – with due caution – as a source for the periods they purport to describe.

27 This is obviously of more note when events which would be considered offensive by modern standards are included in the reports for otherwise well-assessed kings; such occurrences act as opportune controls on the moral assumptions of modern scholarship.

This has two repercussions for our study. First, the preserved accounts cannot be taken as a complete record of the types of military acts undertaken by the kings and armies of Israel and Judah. This is a statement of the obvious insofar as the accounts preserved are clearly so limited that they could hardly comprise a complete account of the military offensives engaged upon by these two parties, and is therefore unlikely to fully reflect the range of military activities with which they were comfortable, but it is also worthy of being stated explicitly for the sake of granting due recognition to the ability of the later authors to eliminate any episodes which they saw fit. The latter point brings us to the second repercussion, namely that the ethical sensibilities reflected by the texts as they now stand are those of the authors, and are not necessarily to be considered fully reflective of the sensibilities of their subjects.[28] The absence of certain acts does not tell us that the kings of Israel or Judah did not engage upon them, nor does it tell us that it would have been considered morally offensive if they had. Such an absence rather can only tell us that, if the kings did engage in such acts, the later author(s) did not see fit to recount them – for reasons which may or may not have had to do with their ethical standing.[29] Each stage

---

28 Though note that the deuteronomistic author(s) also sometimes let contradictory texts survive untouched (see e.g., M. Noth, *The Deuteronomistic History*, translated by D.R. Ap-Thomas, J. Barton, J. Doull and M.D. Rutter, JSOTSup 15 [Sheffield: JSOT, 1981], 84; M. Rose, "Deuteronomistic ideology and theology of the Old Testament", in *Israel Constructs its History: Deuteronomistic Historiography in Recent Research*, JSOTSup 306, edited by A. de Pury, T. Römer and J.-D. Macchi [Sheffield: Sheffield University Press, 2000], 438). The difficulty of identifying such texts when the issue in question is not one of the primary interests of the deuteronomist is another reason to avoid using the entirety of the Deuteronomistic History as evidence for the views of a late seventh century writer.

29 The date and context of this later author is the most problematic point for the use of the Deuteronomistic History as a whole in a history of ethics. As followers of this debate will know, there is little agreement as to the nature and extent of pre-exilic sources or versions of the Deuteronomistic History (indeed, its very existence) as well as the extent and significance of exilic and post-exilic redaction. Given the difficulties in delineating the redactional layers of the text, the nature of the author's treatment of and relationship to those sources is equally elusive. This author tends to be persuaded by the arguments for an initial pre-exilic version of the Deuteronomistic History in the late seventh century. If this is the case, then the entire Deuteronomistic History is potentially informative as to the ethical thinking of a late seventh century author, insofar as the author has included accounts of various military activities in the final narrative. Unfortunately, the certainty of at least one exilic or later revision of the narrative, combined with the invariable inconclusiveness of attempts to distinguish between these layers, makes the discernment of a late seventh century version of the Deuteronomistic History far too tentative to merit the consideration of its entirety as reflective of the late seventh century milieu.

of the transmission process will have potentially narrowed the number of incidents recounted (and thereby reduced the range of activities attested to), but events which survived the later authorial process (and which may thereby tell us about that author's ideas) reached that process in the first place only because they were sufficiently morally tolerable as to have occurred (or at least to have been purported to have occurred, which is not entirely the same thing but is nonetheless reflective of moral sensibilities). The accounts which remain may give us only a limited view of the original events, but it seems nonetheless likely to be a relatively accurate portrayal of those activities which are recounted.[30]

6.2.2. Analysis

6.2.2.1. Cosmology

The nature of the source material means that it is unlikely to be revealing as to the ideological rationale behind military activities. This section

30 Supportive of the general accuracy of the reports, as distinguished from their accuracy in reflecting the overall range of activities, is a point made by R.D. Nelson, who seems otherwise to be quite wary of the historical accuracy of the deuteronomist's sources ("the operative principle seems to have been to include whatever supported the theological point being made"): "the historian's oral and written sources would have been at least potentially available to contemporary readers. Therefore, the historian could not ignore or deform these sources out of recognizable shape" (*The Historical Books*, IBT [Nashville, Tenn.: Abingdon, 1998], 28, 25). The difficulties which so many scholars seem to have with the biblical text as history are perhaps not the basic plausibility of most of the events described (most of which are fundamentally rather dull accounts of battles, cult reforms and royal successions), but rather the meaning which the authors and editors of these events ascribed to these events. It is interesting that even a minimalist like N.P. Lemche describes the texts as history, even as he protests the attribution of its driving force to an agent divine rather than human (*The Israelites in History and Tradition*, LAI [London: SPCK, 1998], 93; cf.. J.A. Soggin, *Introduction to the Old Testament: from its Origins to the Closing of the Alexandrian Canon*, translated by J. Bowden [London: SCM, 1980], 163). That the ancients saw Yahweh behind the events of history, however, does not make those events any less historically real. (One might compare the scholarly conception of the fall of an apple pre- and post- I. Newton's articulation of gravity; the human understanding of the cause of the event changed, and was described accordingly differently, but the actual fact of the apple dropping from tree to earth did not change.) In any event, the dominance of the theological and ideological over bare facts does not wholly obscure the ethical issues in which we are interested; as was noted above, ideology and the ideals it espouses can be as informative for ethical ideas as reports of actual activities, though caution must of course be exerted to maintain the distinction between the ethical ideal and practical reality.

is therefore primarily a companion to the preceding section's ideological description of the Judahite kings, accounting for some of the practical outworking of that royal ideology.

6.2.2.2. Practice

There are too few incidences of detailed military activity to result in more than a scattershot impression of the habits of any particular king. A further distinction of the *Kings* and *Chronicles* texts as opposed to their (approximate) Assyrian counterparts is the near-inevitability of accounts in which neither Judah nor Israel were the aggressor. Because of the ethical implications of wars of aggression as opposed to wars of defence, this section proceeds first through events in which Judah is portrayed as the aggressor, then those in which Judah is the target of foreign attack. The same is then done for those accounts in which Israel is the primary actor.

6.2.2.2.1. Judah

6.2.2.2.1.1. Judah the aggressor

The first instance of Judahite aggression is an attack on Edom by Amaziah (2 Kg. 14.7 // 2 Chr. 25.11-16), in which Amaziah "smote ten thousand Edomites in the Valley of Salt and took Sela in battle". The only possible commentary is contained in the note that the place has been called "El supports" (יקתאל) ever since, though this really tells us little other than reiterating the idea of divine involvement in successful battles.[31]

31 As we have seen elsewhere, "the support of the deity is deemed necessary for victory; victory is indication of the god's favor and power as defeat is indication of his/her disfavor or impotence" (S. Niditch, *War in the Hebrew Bible: A Study in the Ethics of Violence* [Oxford: Oxford University Press, 1993], 125). It is the *Chronicles* account which most clearly indicates that the attack was initiated by Judah, though the *Kings* text gives the same impression (see J. Gray, *I & II Kings*, OTL [London: SCM, 1977], 605; G.H. Jones, *1 and 2 Kings*, NCB [Basingstoke: Marshall, Morgan & Scott, 1984], 2:509). Also in the *Chronicles* version, "the people of Judah captured another ten thousand alive, took them to the top of Sela, and threw them down from the top of Sela, so that all of them were dashed to pieces" (25.12). Aside from the issue of reliability (on which see e.g., M. Cogan and H. Tadmor, *II Kings*, AB 11 [Garden City, N.Y.: Doubleday, 1998], 155; J.M. Myers, *II Chronicles*, AB 13 [Garden City, N.Y.:

Commentators – as is common with other biblical passages in which large numbers of the enemy are supposed to have been killed or captured – tend to describe the number 10,000 as typologically indicative of a vast number, or attempt to minimise the death toll by arguing that 10,000 enumerates the enemy defeated rather than killed.[32] The verb is נכה *hi,* which can mean either to strike causing injury or to strike causing death. In either case, large numbers of enemy troops are said to have been involved. To suppose that all 10,000 were captured and none killed is implausible, and in any event the imprecision of the terminology indicates that the possibility that all 10,000 might be presumed killed was not sufficiently problematic as to warrant the use of more precise language. This, combined with the suspicion that 10,000 – dead or captured – is an implausibly high number in an engagement between two relatively minor nations, causes us first to note that there are no apparent qualms about exaggerating in this way, nor concern that the report be misunderstood as referring to more dead than really were killed; but second, to question the reason(s) that such numbers were deemed favourable. Though the reference to 10,000 smitten may seem mere hyperbole, the fact of hyperbole does little to diminish the citation's ethical implications. In that hyperbole is an expression of an idealised event in place of the more restrained actuality, the use of hyperbole in military rhetoric is indicative of the ethical ideal with regard to military behaviour (even if the text becomes, via the same hyperbole, less reliable for actual historical reconstruction).

Such vast numbers may have been intended to impress the audience with the king's military might. However, just as we are aware of an element of factual implausibility to the report, we must presume that the original target audience, knowing firsthand the size and military strength of Judah and of Edom, would have also recognised that 10,000 was probably not meant as a factual representation of reality. Given this, the number seems meant as a cipher for complete destruction: emphasising the totality of Amaziah's dominance over Edom.

That Amaziah's military exploits in Edom are not marked out for censure or as a means of sullying his reputation is indicated by the

Doubleday, 1965], 198-199), it is interesting that in this post-exilic version of events the agency is devolved from the king (*Kings* uses masculine singular verbs, referring to Amaziah) to the people. The capacity for such a shift is undoubtedly based on the theological developments demanded of a society in which there is no king to act as the earthly counterpart to the god in war.

32 Cogan and Tadmor, 155; Jones, *Kings*, 508; Gray, *Kings*, 605.

generally good portrait of Amaziah in *Kings*.[33] In addition, the report of the attack against Edom is also immediately preceded by explicit approval of killing his father's assassins but not killing their children (14.5-6), "according to what is written in the book of the law of Moses" (14.6). While neither this nor the overall assessment of Amaziah (which is based on his cultic record) is directly relevant to the Edom incident, it does suggest that there is no reason to suspect an effort to smear Amaziah's reputation by associating him with negative acts. Had the Edom incident been grossly inconsistent with his overall approval then the author could have readily omitted it.

Kings next recounts an encounter between Israel and Judah, which will be addressed below due to the special circumstances attending the confrontation of Yahweh's two nations.

The chronologically latest episode of offensive warfare occurs in the reign of Hezekiah. On the heels of cultic praise for the king is the report that Hezekiah "rebelled against the king of Assyria and would not serve him. He attacked the Philistines as far as Gaza and its territory, from watchtower to fortified city" (18.8). This is immediately preceded by the statement that "Yahweh was with him whenever he went out" – indicating deuteronomistic approval for his military actions at least.[34]

Though connected, there are two separate actions designated here. First, Hezekiah's rebellion most likely took the initial form of refusal of tribute. This we can recognise as the reversal of the acceptance of Assyrian hegemony and authority which the original payment of tribute had symbolised. Clearly consistent with the ideology of the later author, the act itself also reflected a reassertion of Judahite autonomy and the Judahite system of order. The rebellion is practically a proof text for the preceding statement of Yahweh's presence with Hezekiah, which, though an editorial association, is again consistent with the idea of royal-divine synergy which has been seen elsewhere.[35] Though less hackneyed than *Chronicles'* dogmatic correlation of military success with divine support, *Kings* also rests passages like this one on an underlying assumption that triumph on the battlefield is the consequence of the convergence of both the king's and the god's purposes.

33 Overall, Amaziah receives qualified praise, having done what was right in the sight of Yahweh and been buried in the city of David (14.3, 20). Note that the bearing of the following on our question presupposes a dual redaction of the Deuteronomistic History.

34 NRSV translates "wherever he went, he prospered", which obscures the use of יצא, the usual word for military excursions, and the less economically-slanted meaning of שׂכל *hi* as to achieve success.

35 R.D. Nelson, *First and Second Kings*, Interpretation (Louisville, Ky.: John Knox, 1987), 236. Cf. e.g. Dt. 20.1ff, 2 Sam. 8.14.

The second element is Hezekiah's attack on Philistia. This was by all appearances unprovoked, and seems to have been motivated by an attempt to expand Judah's authority in the region. M. Cogan and H. Tadmor draw a dependent connection between the reassertion of Judahite autonomy through the refusal of tribute and the expansion of Judahite authority in an imperialistic offensive manoeuvre and suggest that the attack on Philistia was part of the rebellion, perhaps coordinated with local anti-Assyrian elements.[36] This need not be the case, but it is certainly clear that both derive from the same resurgence of interest in Judah-centred order, both in its preservation and in its expansion. The attack's success, whether it was connected to the rebellion or not, supports the assertion that Yahweh was with Hezekiah whenever he went out.

Unfortunately, the details of the attacks themselves are problematically vague from the point of view of military practice and therefore military ethics; "from watchtower to fortified city" is hardly enough detail to make a confident assertion about the nature of the offensive manoeuvres involved. Two opposing suggestions on how best to interpret the phrase come to mind. First, the phrase may be intended to emphasise the thoroughness of the assault. Such an interpretation may be supported by the specification of Hezekiah's actions as extending "as far as Gaza and its borders".[37] Alternately, the naming of specifically military constructions is meant to emphasise that the offensive was directed strictly against military targets, and not against the general population of Philistia. Which is the correct interpretation of the phrase is impossible to tell; perhaps both are intended.

The other two reports of Judahite aggression occur only in *Chronicles*, which entails a greater level of uncertainty as to historical reliability, while at the same time entirely eliminating the relevance of the editorial layer of ethical judgment.

The first episode is at 2 Chr. 26.6-15. There is little suspicion of the text among commentators, despite the lack of a *Kings* parallel.[38] The straightforward character of the text lends it some of its authority; it simply recounts how Uzziah attacked the Philistines, breaking down

36 Cogan and Tadmor, 217; Jones, *Kings*, 563.

37 So e.g., T.R. Hobbs, who considers it an idiomatic expression emphasising extremes (*2 Kings*, WBC 13 [Waco, Tex.: Word Books, 1985], 232, 253).

38 The passage lacks the long expansions usually typical of the Chronicler's own compositions (H.G.M. Williamson, *1 and 2 Chronicles*, NCB [London: Marshall, Morgan & Scott, 1982], 334). R.B. Dillard observes that the incidents described would merely be further episodes in the ongoing conflict between Judah and traditional enemies (*2 Chronicles*, WBC 15 [Waco, Tex.: Word Books, 1987], 208).

the walls of Gath, Jabneh and Ashdod and how he was successful through divine aid against the Arabs and against the Meunites.[39] Uzziah's military efforts were evidently sufficiently successful to enable the extraction of tribute from the Ammonites, and his building projects seem to have extended into the defeated territories. The size of the army, in excess of three hundred thousand men, seems perhaps large, but if this includes all able-bodied men of a certain age, rather than professional soldiers – as the reference to the heads of the ancestral houses seems to suggest – then it seems slightly less so.

The passage does not itself reveal a great deal about tactics or about the treatment of the enemy, either on the field or after a successful campaign, but it does attest to an expansionist attitude on the part of the Judahite king. Though the ideology behind these actions is not made explicit, one may see how acts such as the breaking down of city walls and the receipt of tribute, though of course of practical purpose, simultaneously stood for the symbolic destruction of opposition to a Judahite sphere of influence.

The continuation of such policies on the part of Uzziah's son and successor, Jotham, is indicated in the note in 2 Chr. 27.5 that Jotham also received tribute from the Ammonites, this time on an annual basis for three years. The annualisation of the tribute indicates that the intent of Uzziah's offensive campaigns was the exertion of ongoing dominance on the part of Judah over its neighbours, rather than merely occasional forays aimed at material gain or at the prevention of expansion on the part of the opponent(s).

While it is of course possible that campaigns of aggression which occurred in the final decades of the Judahite kingdom were simply omitted from *Kings*, it is probably not a coincidence that accounts of Judahite aggression cease after the reign of Hezekiah; the one possible exception is the report that Josiah went up to meet the Egyptian pharaoh (2 Kg. 23.29).[40] After Sennacherib's siege of Jerusalem Judah consisted of little more than a rump state, centred on Jerusalem, and much of the surrounding territory was part of the Assyrian provincial system. The practical limitations of the army and its support system would have easily been enough to make a Judahite king think twice about challenging his very powerful neighbour. Judah thus entered a military holding pattern for almost the entire rest of its existence, satisfied with

39 A few manuscripts read Ammonites for Meunites in 26.7, but the Septuagint's assimilation of Ammonites to Meunites in 26.8 suggests that both variants are smoothing an original series of references to several opponents.

40 On the context of this act see Chapter 10.

simply maintaining the level of its ordered existence in the face of invading threat, and not attempting to expand it.

6.2.2.2.1.2. Judah under attack

This brings us to the episodes in which Judah is depicted defending itself against foreign attackers. Justification of violence after provocation is usually more readily forthcoming than justification for unprovoked violence; given the apparent tolerance of Judahites for offensive military violence, it would prove surprising should defensive acts be condemned.

Intellectually, there is unfortunately little which reveals how the experience of being under attack and sometimes defeated was incorporated into the cosmological system of warfare as a struggle against chaos. *Kings* and *Chronicles*, as we have already seen, usually include nothing more than plain, unembellished reports of military endeavours, with the focus of their interests elsewhere meaning that the intellectual underpinnings of these acts are not accounted for. In the case of offensive campaigns, this is not entirely unhelpful, in that – having sketched the intellectual side from the more cosmological texts of *Psalms* – we are able to locate the offensive acts against this background and to see how they fit within it. As, however, there is significantly less attention given in *Psalms* to the experience of being attacked or defeated, it is harder to locate the defensive activities in an intellectual context.

One may, however, engage in a small amount of speculation in this regard. First of all, defensive activities would have been initially perceived as engagement in the rebuttal of a threat to the Judahite system of order. Accordingly, acts undertaken in such a war may be perceived in a similar way to those undertaken in a war of aggression, namely, as acts engaged upon as a means of preserving (in aggression, expanding) the cosmic order as represented by the Judahite system. If successful, the synergy of the Judahite king with Yahweh in this preservation (or expansion) of cosmic order is affirmed.

If, however, the Judahites were defeated, the justification of the acts of the king on the basis of his synergy with the god seems to break down – since defeat indicates either the abandonment of the king by the god or the god's impotence. The most significant crisis to this effect was of course the exile, and it is difficult to tell the extent to which theodicies developed as a consequence of that event have coloured the biblical depictions of earlier defeats.

It is in fact almost certainly not mere coincidence that it is only in *Chronicles* that the outright defeat of Judah prior to the exile is ever reported: in neither of the two incidents in *Kings* which report Judah's defence of its territory against invaders is the actual defeat of the Judahite king reported. In the latter, both situations resolve via the intermediary stage of tribute-offering.

The first of these is early in the eighth century, in which Hazael of Aram is persuaded to abandon his thoughts of attacking Jerusalem through the prompt delivery of treasures from the temple and palace (2 Kg. 12.18-19).[41] The extent to which such a payment was considered an acknowledgment of Aramaean authority (and Aramaean order) by the Judahites is unfortunately far from clear; the text gives no further detail which might conclude one way or the other, though the absence of reference to perpetual payments of this kind may indicate that it was – or could be – seen as a one-off payment of an essentially material nature, without abiding political (and therefore intellectual) implications.[42] The key point is that the Aramaean king never so much as enters Judahite territory, according to the account in *Kings*, and he thus never truly challenges the Judahite system of order.

In *Chronicles'* version of the Aramaean incident, by contrast, the army of Aram "came up to Judah and Jerusalem, and destroyed all the officials of the people from among them" (2 Chr. 24.23-24). It is unclear whether the *Chronicles'* rendering is based on *Kings*, with typically chronistic elaborations, or is derived from an entirely different source.[43] That it is only after the exile – when a post-monarchic theological rationalisation of defeat in terms of divine punishment is fully articulated – that the complete defeat of a Judahite king is admitted is hardly coincidental. Especially if the extent of the defeat described by *Chronicles* is

---

41 The keen religious sensitivities of *Kings* might lead one to expect a condemnation of Jehoash's use of temple property for this purpose, but there is none. In other instances of this, including especially Ahaz in 2 Kg. 16, commentators will often assume that it is being repudiated by the *Kings* writer. Cogan and Tadmor, for example, argue that the use of שחד to describe Ahaz's payment to Tiglath-pileser is a criticism (Cogan and Tadmor, 188; also Hobbs, *Kings*, 214). Neither explains, however, why the involvement of temple property prompts such a negative reaction in Ahaz's case; they apparently assume that because Ahaz is generally condemned, he must be being condemned for this as well. However, Asa, Jehoash and Hezekiah, all judged "good" Judahite kings, also draw on temple properties for military purposes (1 Kg. 15.16-21; 2 Kg. 12.18-19; 2 Kg. 18.15-16).

42 Whether this is how the Aramaeans interpreted the payment, of course, is a different matter.

43 See S.S. Tuell, *First and Second Chronicles*, Interpretation (Louisville, Ky.: John Knox, 2001), 197; S. Japhet, *I & II Chronicles*, OTL (London: SCM, 1993), 851; Williamson, 325.

historically accurate, it indicates by way of contrast a strong pre-exilic aversion to conceding the king's defeat, presumably a consequence of the highly problematic nature of defeat for the cosmological framework in which the god and the king work together for cosmic order, and the king's military activities are legitimated as being the human enactment of a divine struggle.[44]

In the subsequent accounts of tribute payments – those of Ahaz and of Hezekiah – it is to this effect significant to note that in neither case is the ongoing nature of the tribute mentioned: both are again portrayed as one-off events. The episode with Hezekiah especially emphasises the temporary nature of the payment with the phrase "at that time". The intellectual implications of ongoing payment of tribute, symbolising the subordination of Judah to Assyria, are thereby avoided.[45] The differences in this respect between *Chronicles* and *Kings* are especially evident in the Ahaz episode (the so-called Syro-Ephraimite war): *Kings* stresses the ineffectiveness of the coalition's attempts to attack Judah – thus emphasising the legitimacy of Judahite resistance – while *Chronicles* focuses on its success.[46]

6.2.2.2.2. Israel

In a manner characteristic of the primarily southern orientation of *Kings* and the exclusively southern orientation of *Chronicles*, there is even less material on the warfare of Israel than the little provided for Judah. The perspective of these descriptions is also persistently Judahite, rather than being a direct reflection of Israelite thought on the acts in question. Therefore, though these are here treated separately from the Judahite activities, it is probable that they reflect more on Judahite morality of warfare than on Israelite, excepting of course the extent to which they are an accurate reflection of actual Israelite practices.

---

44 One notes the similar absence of accounts of defeat in the Assyrian inscriptions.

45 In the case of Ahaz, his message to Tiglath-pileser – "I am your servant and your son" – is in keeping with the language of a vassal to his overlord, and thereby may implicitly acknowledge the subordination of Judah attendant on the payment (see Cogan and Tadmor, 187-188). Similarly Hezekiah's statement to the Assyrian king – "I have sinned; turn back from me; whatever you set upon me I will bear" – may also implicitly acknowledge the Assyrian king's role as the determiner of correct orientation (note the use of the language of "sin", which is wholly in keeping with the language used of rebellious vassals by the Assyrians; contra Hobbs, *Kings*, 255). In both instances, however, the subordination is portrayed as fleeting.

46 See Dillard, 221.

6.2.2.2.2.1. Israel under attack

The instances of defensive Israelite actions are depicted differently from their Judahite counterparts. Menahem's tribute-offering to Tiglath-pileser is described as a means of maintaining his hold on power (2 Kg. 15.19-20), and the emphasis above on the singularity of such payments gives way to their implied perpetuation through the use of the participle. Given the similar payments described above, the description of tribute in such a negative way here indicates either a general anti-Israelite bias or a cynicism about Menahem in particular. The willingness to imply their ongoing nature also suggests that Israel was perceived as sufficiently outside the divine-human synergy as to not problematise that relationship through its subordination to a third party.

Even more strongly indicative of such an attitude to the status of Israel is the account of the oppression of Israel under Jehoahaz by the Aramaeans under Hazael (2 Kg. 13.3-7), in which the stereotyped language of "threshing" is used to indicate extensive destruction (see Chapter 7). It is also worth noting that, despite the obvious despair of Jehoahaz at the extent of Israel's devastation by the Aramaeans, there does not appear here to be any sense that the Aramaeans were acting outside of a morally tolerated framework of how war could or should be conducted.

The persistent victimisation of Israel by the Aramaeans is explicitly characterised as divine punishment – a characterisation which is taken to its most extreme manifestation in the explanation for Israel's final defeat at the hands of Assyria (2 Kg. 17). Unsurprisingly, the divine-human synergy, upon which military success is predicated, is broken by the human rejection of the god – and the failure of the king to succeed in battle is perceived as a sign that the king has in fact done so, knowingly or not.

6.2.2.2.2.2. Israel the aggressor

Given the impression of these episodes that Israel had been abandoned to its fate, it is initially surprising that there are, despite the problematic nature of Israel's relationship with Yahweh, instances in which Israel's kings are successful in their military endeavours.

According to 2 Kg. 14.25, 28, Jeroboam "restored the border of Israel from Lebo-Hamath as far as the sea of the Arabah...he recovered for Israel Damascus and Hamath, which had belonged to Judah". Ignoring for a moment the statement's location within a southern-orientated narrative, it is interesting to note that it asserts a restoration of the classic, "Solomonic" borders.[47] From Israel's point of view, such a campaign could have readily been conceived as pushing back the chaotic forces which had temporarily impinged upon Israelite order.

From the southern perspective of the extant narrative, however, the acknowledgment of Israelite military success is unusual. It may not be insignificant that here as well as at 2 Kg. 13.23 the survival of Israel seems to require an extenuating explanation: here the intervening text explains Jeroboam's success as the result of Yahweh's concern for Israel.[48] The territory itself is also said to have belonged to Judah, and so its recapture may have been perceived as a restoration of Judah's order, as much as Israel's.

The unusual historical relationship of Judah and Israel seems to have resulted in a peculiar conception of the latter's appropriate military fate. Insofar as Israel was seen as a constantly rebellious part of Judah, this seems to have allowed the dissociation of the Israelite king from Yahweh and the justification of Israel's military defeats. Yet at the same time Israel's successes may have been allowed, grudgingly, as somehow connected to the restoration of Israelite-Judahite order.

Before addressing the accordingly theologically difficult situations in which Israel and Judah faced each other in battle, there is one text which details specificities of Israelite warfare: "At that time Menahem sacked Tipsah, all who were in it and its territory from Tirzah on; because they did not open it to him, he sacked it. He ripped open all the pregnant women in it" (2 Kg. 15.14-16).[49]

It is difficult to ascertain the extent to which such extreme violence was typical of Israel or the rest of the ancient Near East at the time. The practice elsewhere is attributed once to the Aramaeans (2 Kg. 8.12), once to the Ammonites (Amos 1.13) and once to an unidentified enemy

47 Cogan and Tadmor, 162.

48 Cogan and Tadmor also contend that such concern is highly unusual for the deuteronomistic editor, and that the passage is therefore pre-deuteronomistic in origin (162-163). Second Kings 13.23 appeals to Yahweh's "covenant with Abraham, Isaac and Jacob, and would not destroy them; nor has he banished them from his presence until now"; the latter may likewise indicate the pre-deuteronomistic origins of the text, perhaps near to 721.

49 So the Masoretic text; several commentators read Tappuah for Tipsah (e.g., Gray, *Kings*, 623; Hobbs, *Kings*, 196; Jones, *Kings*, 522-523). Jones similarly argues that, rather than being connected to Shallum, Tappuah was the site of another rival uprising – maintaining the element of intertribal rivalry as a contributing factor to the violence (*Kings*, 523-524).

of Israel (Hos. 14.1); the one extra-biblical attribution is to Tiglath-pileser I circa 1100.[50] T.R. Hobbs claims that

> the brutality of Menehem's actions was, sadly enough, a very common feature of warfare in the ancient Near East. Such deeds were regarded as the right of the victor...[it is] stereotyped language of the description of the horrors of warfare in the ancient Near East.[51]

Given the almost complete lack of corroborating evidence for the practice outside the Hebrew Bible, however, it is difficult to tell whether this generalisation is accurate. Given the diversity of the perpetrators, it seems probable that it was a known element of ancient Near Eastern warfare, particularly in the Levant. The lack of frequent mention, however, may indicate that the parties involved nonetheless registered it as morally offensive.

As for its practice in Israel, it is possible that Cogan and Tadmor are correct in arguing that the report of ripping open the pregnant women is a critical comment of the editor, equating Menahem's evil with that of the Aramaeans (cf. 2 Kg. 8.12).[52] The lack of other mention of it in reference to the activities of either Israel or Judah, in addition to the condemnation in *Amos*, could equally plausibly point toward a rejection of the practice.

In light of the observations on the extreme nature of military actions undertaken in the late stages of the Assyrian empire (see Chapter 8), one further explanation presents itself. A number of commentators have argued that if the Septuagint's Tappuah is read in the place of the Masoretic text's Tipsah in 15.16, then the extremity of the act may have been the result of intertribal rivalry, in that Shallum, Menahem's rival for the throne, seems to have been from near there.[53] If this is an accurate reading, the extremity of Menahem's behaviour may have been provoked by similar circumstances to those observed with regard to the late Assyrian kings, namely a heightened threat to the king's legitimacy and a consequent need to assert it on the basis of military power.

---

50 Quoted in Barton, *Amos's Oracles*, 57.
51 Hobbs, *Kings*, 102.
52 Cogan and Tadmor, 171.
53 See Gray, *Kings*, 623; Hobbs, *Kings*, 196.

6.2.2.2.3. Israel and Judah face off

The nature of Israel and Judah as "divided kingdoms", both worshipping the same deity, provides an unusual theological and cosmological situation in those instances in which they meet each other in battle.[54]

As the only narrative accounts of these encounters come from the Judahite tradition of *Kings*, our information on the Israelite point of view is limited to non-existent. Admittedly the Judahite point of view is almost equally scarce, given that such encounters are reported infrequently and, like most accounts of military encounters, almost wholly without intellectual commentary. Thus in 2 Kg. 14 is a report of Amaziah's challenge to Jehoash, followed by Jehoash's capture of Amaziah and rout of his troops. The episode tells us that Amaziah thought he could defeat Jehoash; given the kingdoms' relative strengths, this may thereby indicate that Amaziah believed that his actions, and not those of Jehoash, were the ones mirroring Yahweh's cosmological struggles for order in the midst of chaos. While unfortunately the episode really does not give enough detail to allow certainty or much elaboration, a Judahite point of view in which the true divine-king synergy against chaos lay between Yahweh and the Judahite king coheres well with the overall *Kings* picture of an apostate northern kingdom whose religious practices eventually led Yahweh to abandon it, and whose royal house(s) were in a more or less constant chaotic state. This is doubtless not how the Israelite kings saw the situation, but as a Judahite depiction of their nearest and most important neighbour, it goes well with the Judahite royal ideology in which the king works with Yahweh to expand order and combat chaos. Israel, as a territory once part of "order" yet since disordered by rebellion, would have been a natural object of the Judahite king's military efforts toward order.

The unusual nature of the Judah-Israel relationship is affirmed by the fact that the only instance in which Judah's defeat at the hand of an attacking force is clearly acknowledged is Jehoash of Israel's assault on Amaziah, in which Amaziah himself is captured along with a number of hostages (2 Kg. 14.8-14 // 2 Chr. 25.17-24). This is the only recorded hostage-taking in the Hebrew Bible, and it is unclear whether they were taken as pledges for war indemnity or for some other purpose.[55] Whatever the reason, there seems to have been no significant concern, even from the Judahite side, as to the moral permissibility of hostage-taking.

---

54 Though see also Chapter 8 on the relationship between Assyria and Babylon and the shifts in the *Enūma eliš* which seem to derive from a similar problem (albeit handled differently due to the allowances of polytheism).

55 Gray, *Kings*, 611; Cogan and Tadmor, 157; Dillard, 202.

There being no description of the fate of the prisoners, either their fate was fairly benign, or a more gruesome fate was not considered objectionable.

According to the sequence of events in both *Kings* and *Chronicles*, Jehoash broke down the walls of Jerusalem and plundered the palace and the temple after he had captured Amaziah himself, thus extending the military offensive beyond the enemy leader and onto the general populace. This generalisation is not condemned. S. Japhet hypothesises that the destruction may have been for one of two reasons: either punitive damage, extending Amaziah's personal punishment to the whole of the city, or the result of continued resistance by the city's inhabitants despite the capture of its king.[56] It suggests a belief that the people of a city were in some way also responsible for acts on the part of their king (or other leaders), though the limitation of capture and hostage-taking to the king and his family indicates that the general population was not perceived to be guilty and demanding of punishment to the same extent as the leadership.

6.2.2.3. Conclusions

Ultimately, there is little in *Kings* or *Chronicles* to suggest that either Judahite or Israelite tactics in warfare were substantially different to those of the Assyrians. The underlying association of military success with divine-human alignment in the service of cosmic order – the basic premise of Assyrian warfare morality – seems to be supported by the narrative accounts, with the only peculiarities being related to the unusual nature of the relationship between Judah and Israel. The practical application of violent offensive warfare against Israel's and especially Judah's enemies was restricted by its relatively minor political and military standing in comparison to its other neighbours, but the narrative books give no reason to suspect that their kings would have acted in any substantially different way had they been in a similar situation to the kings of Assyria.

---

56 Japhet, 871.

7. Ethics of the non-élite

7.1. Amos

The most concentrated single source of information on ethics in the biblical prophetic literature, if not the entire Hebrew Bible, is the first chapter of the book of *Amos*.[1] His role as a prophetic figure immediately alerts us to the possibility that he may reflect a distinct ethical perspective from that which we have just described in Chapter 6; though prophets can be part of the élite social stratum, the Amos tradition sustains such a persistent attack on the Samarian monarchy that his place within its court is improbable. As we will see, his approach to warfare also confirms that he does not share in the royal military ideology of the ruling élites.

Unfortunately for our purposes, *Amos* makes no direct comment on Israel's own conduct in war; in the oracle against Israel Amos rounds on his audience to place sins of social justice on par with those committed by the nations in battle, rather than speaking of Israelite military offences. However, in the prophet's preceding oracles against the nations he speaks explicitly of acts of war committed by other nations, in a prophetic sequence whose logic appears to suppose that both the prophet and his audience consider such acts morally repugnant and worthy of condemnation and punishment.[2]

With the exception of a recent paper by N. Wazana, those oracles against the nations have not been discussed in the context of other ancient Near Eastern attitudes to warfare, nor in comparison to the atti-

1 For a thorough review of the literature on the origins and nature of the oracles against the nations, see S.M. Paul, *Amos*, Hermeneia (Minneapolis, Minn.: Fortress, 1990); cf. e.g., J.H. Hayes, "The usage of oracles against foreign nations in ancient Israel", *JBL* 87 (1968): 81-92. Current scholarship on *Amos* usually concludes that, besides the oracle against Israel, only the oracles against the Aramaeans, the Philistines, the Ammonites and the Moabites are authentic to an eighth century prophetic figure (e.g., J.L. Mays, *Amos*, OTL [London: SCM, 1969]; H.W. Wolff, *Joel and Amos*, Hermeneia, edited by S.D. McBride Jr., translated by W. Janzen, S.D. McBride Jr., and C.A. Muenchow [Philadelphia, Pa.: Fortress, 1977]; but contra Paul, *Amos*). The following will therefore concentrate on these oracles; for a provocative proposal as to the message conveyed by the remaining oracles, see R.B. Coote, *Amos Among the Prophets: Composition and Theology* (Philadelphia, Pa.: Fortress, 1981).

2 See Barton, *Amos's Oracles*.

tudes evidenced in other Hebrew Bible texts.[3] When such a comparison is undertaken, a number of differences between the intellectual and ethical approach to warfare which is evidenced elsewhere and that which is contained in the book of *Amos* are revealed.

7.1.1. Cosmology

As already described, the Assyrian, Israelite and Judahite royal ideology of warfare involves the correlation of the military activities of the human king with those of the divine king at creation. Amos' ethical thinking with regard to warfare differs from this framework. First and foremost, there is a lack of cosmological language in *Amos*. The only hint of it occurs in the doxologies, and these, if they do derive from the eighth century prophet, are lacking in allusions to a creative struggle against chaotic forces. In 9.3 there is a reference to a serpent who dwells in the sea, but there is no struggle and the creature is merely one of Yahweh's creatures to command; likewise 5.8 and 9.6 describe Yahweh as the one "who calls for the waters of the sea, and pours them out on the surface of the earth", but without any sense of struggle.[4]

In the absence of cosmological intellectual framework for thinking about warfare, it may naturally be supposed that Amos relies on some alternative understanding of the place of war in history and society.

7.1.2. Agency

As in the royal ideological framework discussed in the preceding chapters, there is a strong emphasis on divine agency in *Amos*. This is brought to the fore by a consistent use of first person verbs, with Yahweh as their subject. This emphasis on a divine agent, combined with the tendency in biblical texts for the object of the divine action to be Israel or Judah, has caused many to draw attention to the idea that military defeat is a means of divine punishment for sin.

It is not, however, only Israel and Judah which are the object of punishment through war, either in *Amos* or in the rest of the Hebrew Bible.[5] In Amos' oracles against the nations, divine punishment is di-

3 N. Wazana, "War crimes in Amos' oracles against the nations", European Association of Biblical Studies 2008 Annual Meeting, Lisbon (5 August 2008).

4 הקורא למי־הים וישפכם על־פני הארץ

5 As has already been noted, the Assyrian inscriptions emphasise the enemy's defeat in battle as the result of their sinful actions, defined with respect to their (intended)

rected against other nations before ultimately being directed at Israel. The sentiment is conveyed especially by the language of transgression (פשׁע) which is used in the recurring formula "for three transgressions of N and for four".[6] While broadly in keeping with the general ancient Near Eastern perception of military encounters reflecting the divine pleasure or displeasure with nations and armies, the particular manifestation of the concept in *Amos* is highly distinct, once examined closely.[7]

---

subordination to Assyria. The Assyrian mention of the phenomenon is, of course, in the context of the punishment of other nations for their sins, rather than the punishment of Assyria, whereas the Hebrew Bible much more frequently refers to it in the context of divine punishment of Israel and Judah. This latter orientation is certainly present in *Amos*, which culminates the sequence of oracles against the nations with a condemnation of Israel which continues into the rest of the book.

Before too much is made of this difference in emphasis, however, one must note the circumstantial differences of these countries. The mighty Assyrian army was not immune to defeat, but was triumphant far more frequently than not. As a result, defeat was a far less pressing issue in Assyria than it was in Israel or Judah, which were far smaller and far less powerful on the international political and military scene. Whereas Assyrian defeats were rare enough and geographically distant enough to enable royal annalists to gloss over them, and its prophets seem to have preferred to avoid discussion of the possibility altogether, the Israelite and Judahite populaces were less able to avoid the issue – though, as we have already had reason to note, the accounts of *Kings* appear to have done their best to downplay the ideologically problematic instances of defeat.

Literary efforts to obscure the problem aside, it is the case that the converse of divine good will in victory – which is so clearly evident in Assyrian materials – is divine ill will in defeat, and historical reality has meant that the articulation of military defeat as divine displeasure is significantly more prominent in Israelite and Judahite texts than in the records from Assyria. The ultimate fates of both nations sealed this emphasis permanently. The underlying premise is the same, but the emphasis has fallen differently according to each nation's particular international political circumstances.

6 על־שׁלשׁה פשׁעי ... ועל־ארבעה לא אשׁיבנו

7 There has been some dispute over the precise nature of the punishment anticipated by Amos in these pronouncements. The language in the oracles is reminiscent of both war and storm, and this is no doubt due in part to the amalgamation of characteristics of both war god and storm god into the one Yahweh. Ultimately phrases such as "shouting on the day of battle" (1.14) and "shouting and the sound of the trumpet" (2.3) and references to exile makes it more plausible that Amos had in mind some sort of military defeat. Given the relative absence of cosmological language in *Amos*, however, what is particularly striking about these "natural" disasters is that they are essentially limited to references to fire and earthquake: neither of which are associated with the cosmological battle against chaos at creation. The language of flood, thunder and lightning which appeared in clearly cosmological allusions are completely lacking in *Amos*.

Though no scholar has examined the oracles against the nations against the background of the cosmological ideology we have been describing, several have attempted to analyse the intellectual background which has enabled Amos' condemnation of the nations for their various military activities.

The most common explanation is that Amos' oracles against the nations presuppose a universally valid law of Yahweh. In H. McKeating's formulation: "God is concerned with the doings of all nations, and…all are responsible to the same moral law."[8] As Barton especially has pointed out, however, there are certain difficulties with this explanation. First and foremost, a universal moral law does not necessarily require derivation from Israel's god, Yahweh. Such an assumption is in fact logically problematic: if Amos's condemnations and Yahweh's attendant punishments are based on the belief that the nations were responsible to a universal law originating with Yahweh, this as yet gives no indication as to how the nations were to have been aware of this law, since the only law clearly identified as originating with Yahweh was revealed explicitly only to Israel. If Amos believed that his condemnation was grounded on the nations' responsibility to the law of Yahweh, he appears to have been condemning the ignorant.

This problem is the starting point of Barton's *Amos' Oracles Against the Nations*, which ultimately contends that the underlying moral assumption of Amos' oracles against the nations is some form of international customary law, not explicitly revealed by Yahweh but a sort of "natural" law to which all human beings are privy by virtue of their membership in the human race. Barton writes that

> the principles at stake in these oracles are essentially part of a conventional morality, which God is assumed to back up with fiery sanctions, rather than actual laws supposed to be issued by him for all the nations of the world to observe…Israel's neighbours are not denounced for sins which they could not have been expected to recognise as such (e.g. idolatry), but for offences against common humanity; not for disobedience to God, but for failing to follow the dictates of their own moral sense.[9]

As already noted, Yahweh is the designated agent of punishment for these offences; it is Yahweh who acts as defender of the moral order by destroying those nations whose actions contradict that order. Given the consistent depiction of Yahweh as promoter of justice and right-

8 H. McKeating, *The Books of Amos, Hosea and Micah*, CBC (Cambridge: Cambridge University Press, 1971), 14; cf. Wolff, *Joel*, 152; H.S. Gehman, "Natural law and the Old Testament", in *Biblical Studies in Memory of H.C. Alleman*, edited by J.M. Myers, O. Reimherr and H.N. Bream (Locust Valley, N.Y.: J.J. Augustin, 1960), 114.

9 Barton, *Amos's Oracles*, 43.

eousness, the emphasis on Yahweh as agent is a sign of the moral rectitude of the judgment and of the guilt of the offending nations.

That said, two points relating to the means of Yahweh's intervention on behalf of order are in need of further examination. First, it is worth noting that the punishment for immorally conducted warfare is to be destroyed by means of war. There is a hint here of a concept similar to the legal principle of *lex talionis,* to which we will return momentarily, but for now suffice it to note that this choice of punitive method, associated as it is to Yahweh himself, is a clear indication that there are no moral objections to the existence and pursuit of war in and of itself. Certainly it is impossible to agree with M.L. Barré that Amos supposes a universal sovereignty of Yahweh which forbids Yahweh's subject nations from engaging in war with each other.[10] The impossibility of Barré's argument is evident as soon as it is carried to its natural end, since it leads to the conclusion that warfare cannot be permitted in any circumstances, all nations being subject to Yahweh. Though N.K. Gottwald may have reasonably observed, albeit with that faintly exculpatory sentiment so common in biblical commentators' discussions of Israelite and Judahite warfare, that "so emphatically is the attack of the enemy asserted to be the work of Yahweh that the agent may fall from view and only the stark terror of Yahweh's judgment stands forth", the fact already repeatedly emphasised, that earthly interventions ultimately require a human agent to enact them, makes inevitable the conclusion that war is not fundamentally objectionable.[11] This, given the preceding chapters, is hardly a surprising conclusion. Where the issue takes on an interesting new twist in *Amos* is in the question of the identity of the human military agent.

In all of the instances thus far discussed, the human agent corresponding to the divine agent is the king of the nation of the god in question. That is, Yahweh's agent is the king of Israel or Judah, while Marduk's or Aššur's agent is the king of Assyria. In the royal cosmology, the mirroring of the divine military agent by the human king is a key aspect in legitimating the king's military acts, since the king can thereby be portrayed as working with his god against those forces which threaten the proper order of the created universe. Amos' oracles against the nations, however, do not make this normal parallel relationship between human king and national god explicit.

Of the four oracles under consideration, none specify the divine agent; in the fifth oracle, against Israel, an Israelite agent is impossible.

10 M.L. Barré, "The meaning of *l' 'šybnw* in Amos 1:3-2:6", *JBL* 105 (1986): 619.

11 N.K. Gottwald, *The Tribes of Yahweh: A Sociology of the Religion of Liberated Israel, 1250-1050 B.C.E.* (London: SCM, 1980), 97.

Nothing in the preceding four make the identification of Israel as Yahweh's agent impossible, though there are some difficulties with the idea. First, the threats of exile against both Aram and Ammon are of dubious plausibility when attributed to an Israelite agent. Large-scale deportation of the kind the oracles suggest was practiced at this time only by Assyria (who had only just begun employing them as part of imperial policy), and it is unlikely that the Israelite army would have succeeded in doing the same. More concretely, the destination of the Aramaean exiles in Kir is certainly not by any stretch of the imagination a location within Israelite territory; its location is uncertain, but it was probably in Mesopotamia.[12] This too then points toward an Assyrian or other foreign agent of Yahweh. If Amos conceived of an Israelite empire of proportions sufficient to exile multiple nations, including into Mesopotamia, he could have done better rhetorically than presuming it from the start and expecting his audience to unquestioningly catch on. Such an idea is also entirely at odds with the fate decreed for Israel in the final oracle and by the book as a whole. While an Israelite agent is not absolutely excluded by the oracles, it is seriously implausible.[13]

If, however, Amos has foregone the normal assumption that the human agent be the king of the nation where the divine agent is worshipped, this has a series of significant implications.

In and of itself, there is nothing in the structure of the royal ideology which inherently prevents the employment of the king of some other nation as the agent of the cosmic order, though it does significantly undermine the close relationship between national god and king which is important for acts of a more extreme kind. In such a scenario, Yahweh would have been perceived as having chosen to employ some king and army other than those of Israel or Judah in order to eradicate perpetrators of acts which contravene the created order. One might explain this decision as a function of the historical reality, with both Amos and his Israelite audience aware that the military strength of the Israelite army was insufficient for the task.

We could thus see a recognition of practical reality influencing both theology and ethics: Israelite military limitations provoke Yahweh's use of non-Israelite armies to police the created order, this in turn implies a much wider scope for Yahweh's influence than would have been otherwise the case, and the moral acceptability of engagement in warfare is implicitly extended to nations other than Israel and Judah.

12 Rodd, *Glimpses*, 583.

13 It is perhaps worth noting to this end that no commentator of whom I am aware makes any assertion or assumption that the agent is Israel.

Even as we recognise the possibility of a universalising tendency, however, we note that, sociologically, this would be a very unexpected shift. As discussed in Chapter 2, the sociological function of ideology is to define the subject culture as the norm, over and against other cultures, which are accordingly described as opposed to and threatening the natural – read moral – order, and in need of eradication. War enters the equation as the means by which eradication of the foreign threat takes place. The purpose of war is to protect the indigenous order (objectified and naturalised through attribution to divine creation), not the order of foreign neighbours and their god.

Such a universalising trend on both theological and ethical levels would also imply a high level of reliance on some form of natural ethics, given that Yahweh's agent, if not Israelite, cannot rely on revelation to know how to properly behave in war. As was already discussed, of course, Amos's oracles have already been used by Barton as evidence for natural ethics in the Hebrew Bible, and this then seems no particular surprise. The only modification of this which might seem advisable in light of the preceding is that the shift in agent away from the Israelite king more obviously requires that Israelite kings consider their own military activities, since they cannot simply refer to the necessity of preserving the created order in taking a no-holds-barred approach – legitimated by divine revelation – to the destruction of opposing forces.

A problem arises, however, when this evidence for a strong natural component in Amos' moral outlook is confronted with the practical inconsistencies between the indictments of the nations and the announcements of Yahweh's judgment. That is, we have Yahweh engaged in war as a means of judgment and, more importantly, engaging in it in ways which are notably similar to those acts for which the nations are condemned. Prior to addressing this issue, an examination of the acts of war attributed to the nations is in order.

7.1.3. Practice

Before addressing the specifics of each oracle, a few general remarks. Throughout the oracles there is a consistent concentration of interest in national leaders. This is particularly evident in the descriptions of punishment, but also occurs in the enumeration of the offence in the Moab oracle. Thus the phrase "the one who holds the sceptre" occurs in both the Damascus (1.5) and Philistia (1.8) oracles, and likewise the ruling élite of Ammon and Moab are targeted (1.15; 2.3; reading מלכם as "their king" in the Ammon oracle). Such an interest is consistent with the

Assyrian tendency to target leadership figures in their military campaigns, and consistent with the (admittedly sparse) evidence of *Psalms* and *Kings*.

While the emphasis on the national leadership is notable, it is only the Moab and Ammon oracles which direct punishment exclusively at leaders. The general population is also explicitly mentioned in the Aram and Philistia oracles: "the inhabitants of the Valley of Aven" and "the people of Aram" (1.5) and "the inhabitants of Ashdod" and "the remnant of the Philistines" (1.8). We could also argue that an attack on the general populations of Ammon and Moab is implicit in the references to the burning of the capital cities of Rabbah and of Kerioth. Gottwald notes that the oracles considered authentic to Amos lack any indication of discrimination in the punishment of Israel; such discrimination in the punishment of the nations would thus be more highly nuanced than that accorded Israel.[14] It seems most likely that the oracles are in keeping with the tendency observed elsewhere to concentrate punitive attention on the opposing leaders, but not excluding the general population as innocent. The impression that the oracles are more discriminatory than other parts of *Amos* perhaps suggests that they were more influenced by normal practices of international warfare; the more theologically dominated oracles against Israel speak deliberately of total destruction, even though this was a rare occurrence in ancient Near Eastern warfare.[15]

Moving on to the individual oracles, it should be noted that concerns about the dating of the various events will not be addressed here, since precise dating is of limited necessity for the purposes of this study. Though accurate dates might furnish information about non-Israelite practices in waging war at some given time, the information the oracles provide about Israel's moral response to such practices is limited to Amos' time regardless of the date of original events.[16]

14 Gottwald, *Tribes*, 114.

15 It may also be that the "total destruction" announced against Israel is just as ideological as the claims of such made in the Assyrian inscriptions and *Psalms*.

16 For a discussions of the possible historical referents see e.g., Paul, *Amos*, 43-74; H.M. Barstad, "Can prophetic texts be dated? Amos 1-2 as an example", in *Ahab Agonistes: The Rise and Fall of the Omri Dynasty*, edited by L.L. Grabbe, LHBOTS 421 (London: T&T Clark, 2007).

7.1.3.1. Aram

The most ambiguous of the actions attributed to the nations is that of Damascus, *pars pro toto* for Aram: threshing Gilead with threshing sledges of iron (1.3).[17] Though none of the other oracles speak metaphorically, the most plausible interpretation of the passage is to suppose that it is a metaphorical way of speaking of the (complete) destruction of the enemy.[18] The same terminology occurs in Tiglath-pileser III's descriptions of his victories over opposing nations as threshing them "as though with a threshing sledge" and in 2 Kg. 13.7, which states that "the king of Aram had destroyed them [Jehoahaz's army] and made them like the dust at threshing."[19]

The inclusion of this essentially general condemnation suggests that Amos and his audience expected a certain general restraint in war. If one looks for corroborating evidence for an Israelite ethic of restraint, however, one finds that nations are elsewhere not condemned for excess in the conduct of war. Generalised condemnation is in fact very rare, and normally related only to hubris on the part of foreign armies, and this only from the exile onwards.[20] Within *Amos*, we may also note that the oracles against the nations describe similarly expansive destruction in their indictments of the nations, and though the visible agent there is divine rather than human (on which see below), the idea that Aram is being condemned for its excess is incongruent with this, as well as with the thorough destruction Amos forecasts for Israel. If the issue is not a matter of general restraint, one might suppose there to be some more specific atrocity concealed behind the metaphor, but the nature of such is unfortunately now wholly obscure. In the ancient Near Eastern context Amos' condemnation of "threshing" – whether general or specific in intent – is unusual, given the attribution of it to Aram (here and 2 Kg. 13.7) and the use of the same phrase in the Assyrian annals. If general, it is exceptional to the Hebrew Bible as well.

7.1.3.2. Philistia

Similarly obscure is the act attributed to the Philistines: "they carried into exile entire communities, to hand them over to Edom" (or perhaps

17 על־דושם בחרצות הברזל את־הגלעד
18 See arguments for and against in Wolff, *Joel*, 154; Barton, *Amos's Oracles*, 19.
19 Tadmor, *Inscriptions*, 123, 131.
20 See C. Westermann, *Isaiah 40-66* (London: SCM Press, 1969), 191-192; K. Baltzer, *Deutero-Isaiah* (Minneapolis, Minn.: Fortress Press, 2001), 273-274.

"Aram"; 1.6).[21] It is unclear where the emphasis is meant to be in this oracle; most exegesis has been devoted to the element of "handing over" rather than that of exile, but it seems probable that the initial element of exile stands equally under censure. If so, it reiterates the correlations noted below with regards to divine agency. As for the reference to "handing over", the offence may refer to regular slave-trading activities, or specifically to the enslavement of prisoners of war.[22]

The problem with either proposal is that the enslavement of captives was common practice, and one in which Israel and Judah engaged, though perhaps with a certain ambiguity.[23] Condemnation of the Philistines for handing over their captives, presumably meaning their sale into slavery, may thus have not been as widely accepted as Amos' rhetorical logic presumes. Similarly, if equal censure lies on the initial aspect of exile, the preponderance of evidence for the practice indicates that Amos' audience may not have been as immediately acquiescent to his premises as expected.

7.1.3.3. Ammon

The act attributed to the Ammonites is probably the most offensive to modern sensibilities: "they have ripped open pregnant women in Gilead in order to enlarge their territory" (1.13).[24] Most commentators suppose that the moral offence is due to the murder of innocent civilians, particularly the double victim of pregnant woman and unborn foetus.[25] Again, Amos' rhetorical logic indicates that he believed that his audience would find it morally repulsive, and the attribution of the practice only to the negatively-assessed Menahem in 2 Kg. 15.16 seems to indicate that it was not generally practiced by Israelites or Judahites.

21 על־הגלותם גלות שלמה להסגיר לאדום

22 See discussions in McKeating, *Amos*, 16; Wolff, *Joel*, 157; Barton, *Amos's Oracles*, 20.

23 There is no doubt that the Israelites owned slaves, and one must imagine that a significant source of such slaves was war, whether their own or that of other nations which led to the capture of persons then sold into slavery to Israelites. Deuteronomy 20, from the Judahite perspective, allows the taking of female captives (presumably for slaves, since Dt. 21 then lays out the procedure which must be followed if a man wishes to make one of these women his wife instead). Second Chronicles 28 condemns the Israelites for taking Judahites captive, but no similar condemnation occurs at 2 Kg. 14.8-14 // 2 Chr. 25.17-24, in which Jehoash captures Amaziah and a number of others and takes them as hostages (see Chapter 6).

24 על־בקעם הרות הגלעד למען הרחיב גבולם

25 J. Limburg, *Hosea-Micah*, Interpretation (Atlanta, Ga.: John Knox, 1988), 89; Wolff, *Joel*, 161; Mays, *Amos*, 37.

It is also attributed to the Aramaeans at 2 Kg. 8.12, while a description of similar conduct by Tiglath-pileser I is referred to by some commentators as an ancient Near Eastern parallel for the Ammonites' actions, albeit more than 300 years prior to Amos.[26] On the basis of these two pieces of evidence, Barton cites it as an example of a unilaterally accepted norm of international conduct, which Israel rejected though at least the Assyrians and the Ammonites tolerated it. He writes that "it obviously serves as a paradigm of the worst destruction possible – but…it was apparently an accepted feature of ancient warfare, and not forbidden by any 'rules of war'".[27]

Two points, however, weigh against such a conclusion of such a unilateral ethical standard. First, as discussed in Chapter 9, there are two additional references to the killing of mothers with their children in Hos. 10.14 and 14.1. There the killing of women and children is clearly a cipher for the extreme horrors of war, but Yahweh also plans to wreak the equivalent on Israel, which seems to indicate acceptance of such an act as morally excusable, at least under certain circumstances. Second, it is noteworthy that the only Assyrian mention of a similar practice is from a much earlier period, not the imperial period which we have been examining, and that even there it is mentioned only once. This tends to suggest that the Assyrians did not consider direct attacks on women and children appropriate acts of war any more than the Israelites did – a supposition supported especially by the absence of mention or depiction of rape in Assyrian sources (see Chapter 8). This leaves only the two attributions of the act, to Ammon and to Aram, to reckon with, and the lack of evidence means that any determination as to the prevalence and moral acceptance of the act in either culture would be premature.

7.1.3.4. Moab

The final act of war mentioned in an indictment is that of Moab, who is said to have "burned to lime the bones of the king of Edom" (2.1).[28] The translation of this verse will be discussed again below, but here it should be noted that no biblical commentators seem to have observed the similarities between late Assyrian practice (see Chapter 8) and the accusations against Moab, despite regular attention to the Ammonite parallel regarding the killing of pregnant women. Yet similar desecra-

26 E.g., Paul, *Amos*, 68; also Barton, *Amos's Oracles*, 57.
27 Barton, *Amos's Oracles*, 57.
28 עַל־שָׂרְפוֹ עַצְמוֹת מֶלֶךְ־אֱדוֹם לַשִּׂיד

tion of the bones of enemy kings is attested in the reign of Assurbanipal, who brought the bones of the ancestors of the Elamites and the Gambulu to Assyria (depriving them of food-offerings and peace in the afterlife); the Gambulu captives were forced to crush the bones before the gate in Nineveh.[29] McKeating's assertion that "to pursue the dead, even to the point of violating the corpse, is a mark of peculiar hatred and peculiarly offensive to the common conscience of mankind" is problematised by these specific parallels as well as the attestations of more generalised desecration of enemy dead (see Chapters 5 and 8). Biblical commentators seem to have focussed exclusively on the nature of Moab's treatment of the Edomite king (which none seem able to agree on, but see below), while largely failing to observe the military, political and religious purposes of such treatment.[30] In this case there are no other biblical references which might indicate whether Amos reflects popular Israelite sentiment with regards this phenomenon. If he does, it could be a unilateral Israelite condemnation.

On the other hand, it may be significant that the Assyrian references occur in late texts, when the imperial ideology was more fully developed and historical circumstances more extreme; such treatment could therefore be seen as a type of act which required more explicit legitimation in cultures such as Assyria and Israel, rather than one permissible under the general rubrics of war. Amos' condemnation would be in keeping with this attitude. At the same time, it may be significant that it is Moab which is named as the perpetrator here, and that it is also only among the Moabites that reference to a *ḥērem* has been found outside the Hebrew Bible.[31] The occurrence of these two acts, both of unusual extremity, in Moab specifically may suggest that Moab had a higher level of tolerance for military violence, than either Israel or Assyria. The fact that the *ḥērem* reference occurs in a ninth century text and the *Amos* reference must pre-date Amos himself perhaps indicates that, for reasons unknown, the Moabite ideological process was further advanced than either Israel or Assyria at the same time.

7.1.3.5. Amos 4

Outside the oracles against the nations, the only verses in *Amos* which offer much insight into the conduct of war in Israel and Israel's

29 *ARAB*, §§810, 866.
30 See Wolff, *Joel*, 162-163; Mays, *Amos*, 39; Limburg, 89.
31 See further discussion of the Mesha Stele in Chapter 10.

thoughts on the subject are 4.1-3. The announcement of punishment on Israel's élite women is that "they shall take you away with hooks, even the last of you with fishhooks. Through breaches in the walls you shall leave, each one straight ahead..." (4.2-3). The text here is difficult, and it is hard to tell what is meant.[32] The image is reminiscent of the lines of women leaving the city and going into exile in Sennacherib's Lachish reliefs, though the use of fishhooks on women, as part of the civilian population, would be otherwise unattested, the closest analogy being the leashing (through the lips, tongue or jaw) of enemies in two Sargon reliefs and in an Assurbanipal inscription:

> I pierced his chin. Through his jaw I passed a lead rope, put a dog chain upon him and made him guard a kennel of the east gate of the inner (wall) of Nineveh.[33]

Similar treatment of enemy leaders is suggested by Isa. 37.29, in which Yahweh's words against Sennacherib are that "I will put my hook in your nose and my bit in your mouth". All of these, however, refer to leaders, not the general population, and women in particular are certainly civilians rather than possibly mistakable as part of the military contingent.

Even if only metaphorical language for subjugation and deportation, it is difficult to tell what kind of moral assessment Amos and his audience would have made of this kind of treatment. It is obvious that deportation was perceived as an undesirable fate; otherwise it could not have been employed as a warning of the dire future awaiting the Israelites. There does not, however, seem to be much explicit reflection here on whether it was an acceptable means of warfare for the enemy to employ.

7.1.3.6. Conclusions

On the basis primarily of the indictments of the oracles against the nations, Amos suggests the following with regard to his moral thought on war. First, he expects some general restraint in the conduct of war (Aram). This is unparalleled by any other Hebrew Bible text. Second, he objects to the exiling of the defeated, apparently in connection to their sale as slaves (Philistia). The objection to exile will be pursued below; the apparent objection to the enslavement of prisoners tacitly contra-

---

32 See discussions in Mays, *Amos*, 73, and McKeating, *Amos*, 32.

33 Borger, *Assurbanipals*, A ix 106-109; *ARAB*, §829 (*ap-lu-uš ina la-aḫ-ši-šú at-ta-di ṣer-re-tú ul-li* ur-gi$_7$ *ad-di-šú-ma ina* abul *ṣi-it* ^{dingir}utu-*ši šá* murub$_4$ uru nina^{ki}).

dicts the assumption common elsewhere in the Hebrew Bible that slavery existed and that warfare was a significant source of slaves. The only ambiguity on the subject elsewhere is in the specific case of Israelite-Judahite relations, and even then the concern is inconsistent. Third, he objects to the killing of women and children. This is almost certainly not a unilateral objection, though it may not have been adopted by all ancient Near Eastern armies, and perhaps not even by everyone in Israel. Finally, he objects to the desecration of the remains of an enemy king.

7.1.4. *Lex talionis*

As this summary highlights, there are a number of discrepancies between the moral assumptions of Amos and those of the ancient Near East in general, but, more importantly, between Amos and the rest of the evidence on Israel and Judah. The peculiarity of this situation becomes all the more remarkable when the similarities between Amos' indictments and the announcements of Yahweh's judgment are noticed. As we have already discussed, the oracles against the nations exhibit an overwhelming emphasis on divine agency, which effectively obscures the human agents of the divinely-ordained destruction. We have also already noted that the emphasis on Yahweh's agency is a sign of the moral rectitude of the judgment and of the guilt of the nations. This does not raise any particular moral difficulties as long as Yahweh and the human agent act according to the same moral standards to which other morally accountable agents (the nations) are held. Here, however, there arises a problem.

In brief summary: Aram is chastised for lack of restraint in war, though Yahweh intends to destroy even the last remnant of the Philistines.

In Yahweh's reaction to Aram the object of his wrath ("Aram"), also seems to refer to a wider target than the original offender, which was identified with the more limited term "Damascus" (though this may be mere poetic license).

The Edomites are apparently condemned for targeting their enemies' leaders, in the form of their ancestors' bones. Yahweh consistently targets the same élite.

The indictment of the Philistines is based on having exiled entire communities. Yahweh promises to exile the populace of Aram to Kir, and to send the leaders of the Ammonites likewise into exile.

It may not be accidental that the most grievous offences of the nations, including the disembowelling of pregnant women and the desecration of the enemy dead, are not attributed to Yahweh – and it may not be insignificant that it is with regard to these offences that Amos seems most in keeping with other Israelite, Judahite and Assyrian considerations on war practices. Nonetheless, we are left with a situation in which the types of offences for which the nations are themselves condemned are, in broad terms, the same actions as those by which they and their neighbours are punished. Bearing in mind that divine acts require human agents, this creates something of a moral paradox: nations employed as Yahweh's agent are apparently permitted to do what the nations they punish are not. For ethics "on the ground", this would have the effect of any nation being able to claim divine authority for any military act they chose to employ.

Perhaps the most obvious solution – and the one perhaps most appealing to those cynical as to the existence of war ethics in the first place – is to assume that Yahweh can do what he likes, with whom he likes. In other contexts this could be more or less plausible (albeit unsatisfying), but the entire rhetorical basis of these oracles is the ability of humans to recognise certain acts as universally immoral.

These observations thus throw into disarray all previous attempts to address these oracles' underlying moral framework, usually articulated in terms of either positive or natural law. There is some risk here of becoming bogged down in the debate over the existence and dominance of positive versus natural law in the Hebrew Bible, but in this instance the paradox is not whether an act is right or wrong because Yahweh declares it so or simply because it (somehow) objectively is wrong, but that the fact that Yahweh appears to assume that certain acts are wrong (or sufficiently so as to warrant the pursuit of punitive measures) but then commits these same acts via an unnamed earthly agent.[34]

In the case of positive law – law which originates in Yahweh's divine command – it would seem a natural corollary to presume that God himself would be at least inclined, if not bound, to follow the same dictates. Natural law is undercut by the fact that the agent of Yahweh must ultimately be human, and human agents are thereby required to be knowing perpetrators of the same offences which they themselves

34 For one explanation of a similar phenomenon with regard to the book of Isaiah, see A. Davies, *Double Standards in Isaiah: Re-evaluating Prophetic Ethics and Divine Justice*, BIS 46 (Leiden: Brill, 2000). His assessment of Yahweh's morality with regard to the foreign nations, however, is tied closely to these nations' attitudes to Yahweh, which cannot be the dominating factor in Amos.

can condemn and have condemned on the basis of a universal human moral standard. To divorce human and divine morality and suppose that acts impermissible for humans remain permissible for Yahweh requires that the historical fact of human agency be entirely obscured, and for this there is no biblical or ancient Near Eastern basis.

The positive law theory thus falls on its attribution to Yahweh of acts which Yahweh condemns, while the natural law theory is faced with the bizarre paradox of a human agent committing offences which he condemns, according to a universal human morality, and furthermore, committing these acts in order to punish those who have already committed them.

It is the last phrase – committing these acts in order to punish those who have already committed them – which offers the key to the potential solution to the moral quandary posed by Amos' oracles.

M. Arneth has made a detailed study of the literary relationships among the oracles against Aram, Philistia, Ammon and Moab and has observed that both the Aram-Philistia pair and the Ammon-Moab pair have a series of internal linkages in ideas and phrases, and that some of these are chiastic in nature.[35] A similar chiasm, it transpires, occurs also in the indictments and announcements of punishment (Illustration 1).

In the Aram-Philistia pair, the punishment of the first (Aram) corresponds to the consequence for the second (Philistia). Philistia exiles; Aram is exiled. The other half of the equation is slightly less obvious, but both action and consequence emphasise the totality of the destruction of the populace; Aram destroys completely, the Philistines are completely destroyed. The same emphasis on total destruction and death occurs in the Ammon-Moab oracles, with Ammon said to have completely destroyed (symbolised by the destruction of pregnant women, that is, not only the present generation but also future generations), while Moab suffers complete destruction.

The last leg of this arrangement should pair the action of Moab with the consequence for Ammon. As in the Aram oracle, the consequence for Ammon is exile. This produces the expectation that the action of Moab was also an act of exile, but instead Moab is accused of having "burned the bones of the king of Edom לשיד". There is no support in the versions for anything other than לשיד as the final word of this verse, but its meaning is unclear. Did the Moabite king burn the

35 M. Arneth, "Die Komposition der Völkersprüche in Amos 1,3-2,16", *ZABR* 10 (2004):250-253. For an alternate interpretation of the paired elements of the oracles, see J. Jeremias, *Der Prophet Amos*, ATD 24.2 (Göttingen: Vandenhoeck & Ruprecht, 1995), 12-13.

Edomite king's bones "to ash", "for lime (that is, whitewash)", or something else?[36]

Oracle against	*Action*	*(Final) consequence*
Aram (Damascus)	*A* they threshed Gilead with iron threshing-sledges	*B′* the people of Aram will go into exile to Kir
Philistia (Gaza)	*B* they exiled entire communities to hand them over to Edom	*A′* the remnant of the Philistines will perish
Ammon	*C* they cut open the pregnant women of Gilead in order to enlarge their borders	*?* their king will go into exile, he and his officials together
Moab	*?* he burned the bones of the king of Edom *laśśid*	*C′* Moab will die...I will cut off the ruler in its midst, and all its princes I will kill with him

Illustration 1

Here I would like to propose, with due caution, that in the term לשׂיד we have a reference to a location, rather than something to do with lime or ash: Moab "burned the bones of the king of Edom *at Haśśid*".[37] The phrase עמק השׂדים is used in Gen. 14 to refer to the area now covered by the Dead Sea, and Moab lies directly to the east.[38] If a Moabite city by the name of השׂיד is behind the phrase עמק השׂדים, Amos would then be referring to the exhumation of the royal dead of Edom and the deportation of their bones to Moab, where they were burned. As noted above, a similar phenomenon is attested in the annals of Assurbanipal.

This is, of course, dependent on the existence of an otherwise-unattested Moabite city by the name of *Haśśid*, and must therefore remain speculative. If such an incident is behind the accusation against Moab, however, it would then complete the series of actions paired

36 For these and other interpretations, see the commentaries.

37 It is also possible that there is a deliberate play on words here, and both meanings are in mind (with thanks to J. Stökl for suggesting this possibility).

38 For a discussion of the term עמק השׂדים, see W. Schatz, *Genesis 14: Eine Untersuchung* (Frankfurt: Peter Lang, 1972).

with opposing consequences, in which both the Aram-Philistia pair and the Ammon-Moab pair focus on the twin ideas of complete destruction and exile (which is itself a form of complete national destruction).

Presuming that this sequence is deliberate – in this regard it is worth noting the consistent positioning of the motif of exile so that it leads from the announcement of punishment in the first half of each pair to the indictment in the second half of the pair, thus drawing attention to the phenomenon – and also assuming that the chiastic positioning of actions and punishments is artistic rather than strict, we may suggest that the moral logic of Amos' oracles against the nations is based on a loose form of *lex talionis*.[39] In other words, the punishment which will be enacted for a given offence is commensurate with and contained within the offence itself, and the reason that Yahweh appears to be depicted inflicting the offences of the nations back upon them is rooted in a belief that each action must have its corresponding consequence and that Yahweh is the divine guarantor of this relationship. Like the *lex talionis*, the punishment inflicted, though like the crime, is not itself subject to punishment. In terms of motivating ethical behaviour, the *lex talionis* engenders the attitude that if we are unhappy to have our enemies else do the same, even unto ourselves, then we ought to not do it either.

It might also be suggested, in light of the other echoes of wisdom sometimes identified in Amos, that this might be related to the connection between act and consequence which is evident in that tradition. There as in Amos, Yahweh is the divine enforcer of the link between act and consequence. Rather than throwing the moral system into disarray by acting in apparent contradiction of it, Yahweh upholds the system by ensuring that each act is accorded its appropriate consequence.

In terms of his relationship to the cosmological framework discussed prior to this point, it is worth noting that Amos is not completely alien to cosmological assumptions. In fact, it is clear that he shares the royal ideology's concern with the existence and preservation of order. The key distinction lies in Amos' abandonment of the king as the central human proponent of that order.

In the absence of the king as the figure responsible for earthly justice and righteousness, the human agent devolves into a more generally identified one, which correlates to a greater explicit focus on the divine

39 Paul also noted elements of the talionic principle in Amos; with regard to the oracles against the nations, the burning of Moabite ramparts in turn for Moabite burning of the Edomite king and the destruction of Israel's fortresses as the consequence of the heaping up of treasure there (*Amos*, 5). Here this principle is traced in greater detail and according to a more structured pattern.

agent whose actions all the various human agents' actions mirror.[40] The emphasis has shifted accordingly, to a more localised concept of order in which each act has a specific and direct consequence.

That the two systems share at least a part of their underlying intellectual framework is indicated by the depiction of royal military actions as punishment which is the natural consequence of the given offence(s) of the punished.[41] The idea that a given act is against the natural (moral, social) order and must therefore be rectified via an appropriate counter-action lies beneath both the royal approach – in which the unnatural action is insubordinance to or existence outside of the natural authority of the king – and the kingless framework – in which the unnatural act seems to be the violation of some sort of right to existence (that is, to be neither completely destroyed in actuality nor to be effectively destroyed through exile) accorded all nations.[42] Violation of order as understood by the former entails a necessary restoration of order by the incorporation of the renegade into the indigenous cosmos. The latter achieves the restoration of order via the counterbalancing effects of an equal and opposite. In both cases the ability of the offender to repeat the offence is eradicated: in one case through the elimination of the opponent by incorporation, in the other through actual eradication. Ironically, then, the apparently higher standards of military behaviour in *Amos*, in which total destruction is condemned, simultaneously entail the perpetuation of such acts as a means of maintaining order. As in the case of the *lex talionis*, however, the reactionary act is not objectionable but rather condoned, even necessary.

7.1.5. Conclusions

Amos' shift in the identification of the implied human agent of the god suggested a corresponding distinction from the usual ideological framework of military ethics, which in turn highlighted both an apparent disregard for the moral sensibilities attested elsewhere as well as problematic similarities between the condemned acts of the nations and

40 In the context of war one can see how the exilic attitude to warfare was able to develop from such a decentralised ethical framework. A complete examination of the changes to the Judahites' ideas about ethical warfare is beyond the scope of this study, but is a worthwhile project to be undertaken in future.

41 See e.g, K. Koch, "Gibt es ein Vergeltungsdogma im Alten Testament?", *ZTK* 52 (1955): 1-42; G.E. Mendenhall, "The 'vengeance' of Yahweh", in *The Tenth Generation: The Origins of the Biblical Tradition* (London: Johns Hopkins University Press, 1973).

42 Though note that something similar, albeit with limitations, seems implicit within most manifestations of the royal approach also. See Saggs, "Right to live".

the punitive acts of Yahweh. Neither positive nor natural law satisfactorily addressed this situation. However, it was observed that these similarities were structured in ordered pairs, and that the idea of *lex talionis*, in which the consequence is connected to the offence in question, might provide the basis for Amos' moral framework. In *Amos* as in the more typical ancient Near Eastern ideological framework, there is a connection between ethics and the maintenance of order, but the route by which order is achieved and maintained is distinctive.

The final question to be answered is the reason that *Amos* exhibits such a distinct moral framework compared to the material in *Psalms* and *Kings*. The clearest reason is that in *Amos* the figure of the king has been abandoned as the conduit for divine-human synergy towards the maintenance of order. Such a kingless approach to war may derive from either Amos' origins outside the royal circles or from his deliberate abandonment of his roots there, perhaps as a result of disagreements about social issues, as might be suggested by the rest of the book. However, given that the abandonment of the king extends also to the abandonment of even the mildest allusions to a struggle for order at creation, it would seem most likely that Amos was never originally part of the social context associated with the royal framework. His approach to warfare thus reflects the thinking of a separate, non-élite group on the border between Judah and Israel. It is unfortunately beyond the scope of the evidence to determine whether such thinking was at that time adopted among similar circles in both nations.

Part III

Ethics and history

8. Developments in Assyrian ethics

At the end of Chapter 5 we saw the beginning of changes in the Assyrian use of the king's synergy with the god in the battle against chaos as a means of legitimating military encounters. These changes accelerate in the reigns of the next three kings – Sennacherib, Esarhaddon and Assurbanipal – driven by historical, political and personal factors.

8.1. Sennacherib (705-681)

The majority of information about Sennacherib's military practices comes from his palace reliefs, rather than inscriptions; the latter comprise in large part stereotyped expressions of conquest rather than detailed accounts. With a few notable exceptions (see below), the inscriptions are elusive about what Sennacherib and his subordinates elected to do with their defeated enemies.

8.1.1. Practice

Perhaps unsurprisingly given the stereotyped language, many of the same acts of warfare which were present in the first part of the imperial period, under Tiglath-pileser and Sargon, continue to be present in the reign of Sennacherib. Cities were besieged, destroyed, plundered and burned;[1] agricultural resources were demolished;[2] people and their possessions were taken as spoil and deported (though this policy now seems to have been also employed against non-rebellious peoples).[3] The family members of enemy leaders were also still deported, but it appears that this was now restricted to the families of rebels.[4] Those who orientated themselves toward Assyria by giving tribute were left

1 See D.D. Luckenbill, *The Annals of Sennacherib*, OIP 2 (Chicago, Ill.: University of Chicago Press, 1924).

2 Luckenbill, *Sennacherib*, 54:51, 59:29. The depiction of this in the reliefs occurs for the first time with Sennacherib.

3 Luckenbill, *Sennacherib*, 27:74, 28:19-21, 58:22, 59:30, 63:12.

4 Luckenbill, *Sennacherib*, 34:46, 35:65-68, 56:9-10, 71:36.

alone, while those who resisted Assyrian authority were attacked.[5] The only substantial change with regard to these general acts is the language in which they are depicted. Though still typically emphatic on the eradication of the enemy, the language is in some cases more vivid; thus, for example, the people of Hilakku were "slaughtered like wild animals."[6]

The reliefs are both consistently more vivid and more detailed. In them it is not unusual to see Assyrian soldiers threatening prisoners or in the act of harming or executing a prisoner.[7] In one scene captives are naked, some being beaten by Assyrian soldiers (apparently to death).[8] All of these incidents appear in the presence of other deportees, indicating that the deterrent effect of earlier periods was still in mind, albeit on a more general level and wider scale. There is no indication of what offence the persons involved had committed, and it is unclear that the reliefs' audience would have necessarily been able to discern a logical connection, from the images alone, between an offence and the action of the Assyrian soldier. This may however indicate an assumption among members of the reliefs' audience that the infliction of punishment could itself be taken as an assurance that an offence had been committed.

The heads of enemy dead are frequently shown held high in triumph, piled before scribal eunuchs and paraded in front of the deceased's countrymen, now prisoners (including children).[9] In one scene, a soldier has a head in one hand and with the other drags along a pris-

---

5 Luckenbill, *Sennacherib*, 30:60-64, 31:69-72, 69:22.

6 Luckenbill, *Sennacherib*, 77:24 (*nišê*^{pl} ^{l}*Ḫi-lak-ki a-ši-bu-ut ḫur-ša-ni zak-ru-ti ú-ṭib-bi-iḫ as-li-iš*). Note that the earlier version says that the people were brought to Nineveh (Luckenbill, *Sennacherib*, 62:85). The change in language is especially evident in the episodes relating to the Babylonians and Elamites (see below).

7 Threat: Layard, Pl. 68; Layard II, Pl. 35; infliction of physical harm (pulling of hair, striking): Layard II, Pls.37-38 (R.D. Barnett, E. Bleibtreu and G. Turner, *Sculptures from the South-West Palace of Sennacherib at Nineveh* [London: British Museum, 1998] II, Pls. 56, 83); execution: *ASBM*, Pl. XLII (*SSP* II, Pl. 174); Layard II, Pl. 35.

8 Layard II, Pl. 34.

9 E.g., *ASBM*, Pl. XLII (*SSP* II, Pl. 174); Layard II, Pls. 37-38 (*SSP* II, Pl. 83); *ASBM*, Pl. XLII; *SSP* II, Pl. 56; Layard, Pl. 29 (*SSP* II, Pls. 131-132); *SSP* II, Pls. 464-466; Layard II, Pl. 26; Layard II, Pls. 19, 35. One room in the Southwest Palace, Court XIX, is debated with regards to its use; some scholars suppose it to be the *bīt redûti* rebuilt by Assurbanipal. Others, including G. Turner, argue that the description of the rebuild was found elsewhere, thereby making it unlikely that the Court XIX is the place in question (*SSP* I, 29). For this study's purposes it seems to make little difference whether the reliefs in the room are assigned to Sennacherib or to Assurbanipal; they show little of interest other than providing yet further examples of the delivery of enemies' heads to scribes alongside other types of spoil (*SSP* II, Pl. 193).

oner by the beard.[10] In three reliefs heads are presented to the king, echoing the earlier reliefs' impression that heads were war trophies or proofs of success – though the frequency of the decapitated heads in general indicates that decapitation was under Sennacherib not limited to the bodies of leaders. The delivery of heads to scribes perhaps also indicates a practical, accounting purpose.[11] In all, these scenes suggest that there was no attempt to limit the psychological trauma of the recently conquered, and rather suggests that the Assyrians exhibited the violent treatment of prisoners and the indignities of enemy soldiers' dead bodies deliberately and with an intent to impress upon the defeated the consequences of resistance to Assyrian authority.

Of final note with regard to these types of scenes in Sennacherib's reliefs is a scene near the end of the Lachish series, in which a number of deportees are shown supplicating the king, while among them one is about to be executed by an Assyrian soldier.[12] The surrounding captives (the nearest of which may be female, but the relief is unfortunately obscured) appear to be supplicating for mercy, producing a scene which a viewer might readily interpret as an example of the Assyrians', and specifically the king's, lack of mercy toward conquered peoples.

The Sennacherib reliefs also break new ground in their depictions of Assyrian soldiers cutting down trees in enemy territory.[13] Other acts, though previously attested, become more frequent and more extreme under Sennacherib. Sargon had one enemy leader flayed and publicly exhibited, but under Sennacherib this seems to have become a more widespread occurrence: all the (rebellious) warriors of Hirimme were thus executed, as were the rebellious governors and nobles of Ekron.[14]

---

10 Layard II, Pls. 37-38 (*SSP* II, Pl. 83).

11 *ASBM*, Pl. XLII (*SSP* II, Pl. 174); *SSP* II, Pls. 464-466); Layard II, Pl. 29.

12 Layard II, Pl. 23.

13 Layard, Pls. 73, 76; Layard II, Pl. 40. On this as a means of escalating pressure designed to encourage the submission of the besieged, see Cole, "The destruction of orchards in Assyrian warfare". This perhaps contrasts with Dt. 20.19-20, in which deforestation in the course of war is expressly forbidden – though there the prohibition is limited to fruit trees, and non-fruit-bearing trees may be destroyed. The trees in the Assyrian reliefs appear to be palm trees, none of which appear to be bearing fruit, though it is unclear whether they are types which do at times bear fruit or how this would relate to *Deuteronomy*'s provisions. For a rather pointed study of the destruction of agricultural resources in the ancient Near East, see M.G. Hasel, *Military Practice and Polemic: Israel's Laws of Warfare in Near Eastern Perspective* (Berrien Springs, Mich.: Andrews University Press, 2005).

14 The Hirimme warriors are staked outside their own city, as are the élites of Ekron (Luckenbill, *Sennacherib*, 26:59-60, 32:10). Interestingly it appears to only be in the final version of Sennacherib's annals that the impalements are recorded; the earlier

The prefect Kirua is deported to Nineveh after instigating rebellion in Cilicia, and Sennacherib has him flayed upon arrival in Nineveh.[15] In the reliefs depicting the siege and conquest of Lachish there is one scene of impalement, and it is also in this series that the one flaying scene occurs – it is a double flaying, with two enemy victims.[16] The process has been depicted directly in front of two children.

On two further occasions executions are depicted as occurring directly in front of child deportees.[17] In one scene a child is held by the hair by a soldier, though the fact that this never occurs elsewhere may indicate a reluctance to depict violence inflicted on children.[18] Similar deference to women and children is indicated by an absence of scenes in which women are bound, as well as the absence of any depictions of rape in the reliefs or in the inscriptions.[19]

Despite the overall increase in violence under Sennacherib there is evidence for some distinction among opponents on the basis of the extent of their threat to Sennacherib's cosmic authority. After the defeat of Ekron Sennacherib "slew the governors and nobles who had rebelled, and hung their bodies on stakes around the city", while

> the citizens who sinned and treated (Assyria) lightly, I counted as spoil. The rest of them, who were not guilty (carriers) of sin and contempt, for whom there was no punishment,–I spoke their pardon.[20]

---

versions omit the incident and simply state that they were killed (see e.g., Luckenbill, *Sennacherib*, 57:18, 67:8, 77:14-15, 86:12).

15 Luckenbill, *Sennacherib*, 62:86. This incident occurs in a campaign conducted not by Sennacherib himself but by one of his generals, though Sennacherib's report of the incident claims responsibility by employing first person language nonetheless. The incident did not, however, make it into most versions of the annals.

16 Layard II, Pls. 21, 22.

17 *ASBM*, Pl. XLII (*SSP* II, Pl. 174); *ASBM*, Pl. XLII.

18 Layard II, Pls. 37-38 (*SSP* II, Pl. 83).

19 There is one scene from Assurbanipal which is disputed: an Arab tribe is attacked in its tents, and those attacked include a woman. This is usually identified as a rape scene, but Arab tribes are known to have sometimes had queens at their head, and it would be much more consistent with the rest of the evidence were the scene not a depiction of rape but of the deliberate targeting of leadership. A text tentatively assigned to Esarhaddon's reign appears to corroborate an Assyrian rejection of rape; it describes Assyrian disapproval of the war practices of the Puqudeans, declaring that "the men they slay, the women they violate" (ṣâbê^{meš} i-duk-ku-u sinnišâte^{meš} ú-šah-ma-ṣu-ú; the verb is *ḫamāṣu* [Š], "to [allow to] despoil"; Waterman I, §275:12; with thanks to Dalley for drawing this to my attention).

20 Luckenbill, *Sennacherib*, 32:7-14 (*a-na* ^{c}*Am-qar-ru-na aq-rib-ma* ^{am}*šakkanakê*^{pl} ^{am}*rubûte*^{pl} *ša ḫi-iṭ-ṭu ú-šab-šú a-duk-ma i-na di-ma-a-ti si-ḫir-ti ali a-lul pag-ri-šu-un mârê*^{pl} *ali e-piš an-ni ù qil-la-ti a-na šal-la-ti am-nu si-it-tu-te-šu-nu la ba-bil ḫi-iṭ-ṭi ù qul-lul-ti šá a-ra-an-šu-nu la ib-šú-ú uš-šur-šu-un aq-bi*). There is one fragmentary letter in Sennacherib's correspondence which also seems to advocate a merciful attitude, in this case toward

The lessening of the drive toward imperial expansion which had started with Sargon continued into the reign of Sennacherib: Sennacherib's campaigns, fewer in number, were aimed at maintaining the empire rather than expanding it. This may be one reason for the more extreme violence which is suggested by his reliefs and the more explicit passages of his inscriptions: previous campaigns lacked the specifically punitive element which became prominent as the Assyrians' opponents transitioned from resistant but originally independent to rebellious vassals and provinces. With Sennacherib, the Assyrian empire reaches a stage in which it has fewer encounters with new opponents and is instead embroiled primarily with opponents already part of or engaged with the empire, whose activities therefore take on the character of rebellion in the more traditional political sense.

8.1.2. Ideology

This shift in the nature of Assyrian warfare under Sennacherib leads one to expect that the emphasis on rebelliousness which first arose under Sargon would have become a regular element of the royal inscriptions. Surprisingly, this is not the case.

Sennacherib does employ language of sin and wickedness to describe the reasons for his campaigns, but this language is far from comprehensive; it appears to have instead been replaced by a much greater emphasis on the king's righteousness. While Sargon describes himself once as "I, Sargon, guardian of justice, who do not transgress against Aššur and Šamaš, the humble and unceasing worshiper of Nabû and Marduk",[21] such language is much more common in Sennacherib's inscriptions. Sennacherib bears "a righteous sceptre, which enlarges the

---

rebels in Borsippa (this may relate to Sennacherib's defeat of Babylon, in which case it constitutes further evidence as to the essentially normal nature of that siege). In it an unidentified correspondent adjures the king: "The king, my lord, should examine the cri[mes ... of a]ll [...s], have [compassio]n on those whose crimes are *lig[ht like breath]*, count (them) among [his servants], and [appoint them] to the ro[yal] service" (SAA 17 83:2′-7′; LUGAL *be-lí-a* ⸢*x*⸣ 1 *x*[*x x ma-la*] *i-ba-áš-šú-ú hi-*[*ṭu-šú-nu*] *lu-sa-an-niq* [*x x x x x*] *šá hi-ṭu-šú-nu pa-*[*a-hi re-e-ma*] *liš-kun-ma it-t*[*i* ARAD.MEŠ-*šú lim-ni*] *ù a-na* EN.NUN *šá* LUG[AL *lip-qid*]). The fragmentary nature of the letter is problematic. It is interesting, however, to note the rationale given by the Borsippeans, which appears to be based on the belief that no further rebellion is to be feared. This would be in keeping with the suggestion that serious punitive measures against rebellious individuals or territories were intended to relate to their potential future threat to the empire and, as importantly, to their present submissiveness.

21 *ARAB*, §156; Mayer, "Sargons", 84:156 (*a-na-ku* ^{m}LUGAL-GI.NA *na-ṣer kit-ti la e-ti-iq i-te-e* ^{d}*A-šur* ^{d}UTU *šaḫ-tu la mu-up-par-ku-ú pa-liḫ* ^{d}AK ^{d}AMAR.UTU)

border, an unsparing lance of the overthrow of enemies", given to him by Aššur.[22] His titulary declares that he is "guardian of the right, lover of justice...perfect hero, mighty man, first among all princes, the powerful one who consumes the insubmissive, who strikes the wicked with lightning".[23]

The titulary's specificity in stating that Sennacherib's campaigns against the insubmissive were undertaken by means of striking with lightning (*barāqu*) may not be insignificant: lightning (*birqu*) is one of Marduk's weapons in *Enūma eliš*. Though naturally more frequently associated with Adad, the storm god, the reference may reiterate the emphasis on the role of the king in the cosmic struggle against chaos, and implicitly depict the enemy thus defeated as the embodiment of chaos, the human form of Tiamat.[24] That it is the "insubmissive" who are subject to this weapon ties in with the idea of the chaotic enemy being those who do not subordinate themselves voluntarily to the Assyrian system of order.

8.1.3. Developing cosmology

It is in the campaigns associated with Babylon, however, that Sennacherib's clearest allusions to *Enūma eliš* occur. As we have already seen, this allusiveness was begun already in Sargon's accounts of his dealings with the Babylonians and with Marduk-apla-iddina: it was with regard to the latter that the first unmistakable equation of an enemy figure with chaos occurred, in his identification as the "likeness of a *gallû*-demon", one of the minions of Tiamat in *Enūma eliš*.[25]

8.1.3.1. Historical review

The dealings of the Assyrians with Babylonia are a matter of some complexity, and a brief summary of the situation under Sennacherib is worthwhile. Unlike his father, Sennacherib does not appear to have

---

22 Luckenbill, *Sennacherib*, 85:5 (*[w]ḫaṭṭu i-šar-tu mu-rap-pi-šat mi-iṣ-ri ši-bir-ru la pa-du-ú a-na šum-qut za-'i-ri*).

23 Luckenbill, *Sennacherib*, 23:4-5, 7-9; 48:2-3; 55:2-3; 66:1-2 (*na-ṣir kit-ti ra-'-im mi-ša-ri ... id-lu git-ma-lum zi-ka-ru qar-du a-ša-rid kal ma-al-ki rab-bu la-'-iṭ la ma-gi-ri mu-šab-ri-qu za-ma-a-ni*).

24 Note also that Adad is one of the many names ascribed to Marduk in climax of *Enūma eliš*, in which case the use of *birqu* may be a more direct allusion to Marduk than it first appears.

25 Fuchs, Prunk. 122 (*ḫi-ri-iṣ gallî*(gal$_5$.lá$^!$) *lem-ni*).

courted Babylonian favour, and within two years of his accession Sennacherib was faced with a series of rebellions, first by a native Babylonian and then by the same Marduk-apla-iddina who had so plagued Sargon. Sennacherib's first campaign was undertaken to restore Assyrian dominance in the region; Marduk-apla-iddina fled to the marshes and was replaced by an Assyrian puppet ruler, Bel-ibni. A second campaign was undertaken to pursue Marduk-apla-iddina, and during this Sennacherib's son Aššur-nadin-šumi was placed on the throne in Babylon. In response to an Assyrian foray against Elamite and Chaldean territory, however, Aššur-nadin-šumi was captured and exiled to Elam. Sennacherib's response failed to succeed in taking Babylon itself, and the territory continued to resist Assyrian authority. The military excursions of Sennacherib's reign culminated with the eighth campaign, in which the Assyrians faced a coalition of Chaldaeans, Babylonians, Aramaeans and Elamites at Halulê and then laid siege to Babylon, which finally fell fifteen months later.

8.1.3.2. Early inscriptions

The allusions to *Enūma eliš* with regard to the battle at Halulê have been most thoroughly examined by E. Weissert, and to this we will turn in a moment. Before doing so, however, the versions of Sennacherib's inscriptions deriving from after his first campaign require attention. In the earliest version, Marduk-apla-iddina is described as "that evil prop of a *gallû*-demon".[26] This is a slight change from the phrase employed by Sargon, but the sense is very much the same. It is only in this early version of the account of this campaign that the phrase occurs, and it is also only here that any detail is related as to the nature of the treatment meted out to those who fell into Sennacherib's hands. Marduk-apla-iddina himself escapes, but "the enemy warriors, strong and proud (*alt.*, powerful), who had not submitted to my yoke, I cut down with the sword and hung on stakes".[27]

By contrast, in the inscriptions deriving from the second campaign onwards, there is no mention of Marduk-apla-iddina in terms of the

26 Luckenbill, *Sennacherib*, 50:17 (*šú-ú im-di gal-li-e lim-ni*); E. Frahm reads *ḫi-ri-iṣ gal-le-e* ("image of a *gallû*-demon"; *Einleitung in die Sanherib-Inschriften*, AfOB 26 [Vienna: Institut für Orientalistik der Universität Wien, 1997], T1:17).

27 Luckenbill, *Sennacherib*, 55:62 (*ba-ḫu-la-te na-ki-ri šip-ṣu be-ru šá a*[*-na ni-*]*ri-a la ik-nu-šú i-na* ^{w}*kakki ú-šam-qit-ma a-lul ga-ši-šeš*); Frahm reads *mit-ru* ("powerful") for *be-ru* (T1:62). In a subsequent campaign, however, the impalement of enemies is sufficiently legitimated merely by reference to their rebelliousness (32:9-10).

gallû-demon – but also no details which such language might be seen as legitimating. The much more generic declaration of victory over Marduk-apla-iddina and his allies which appears in the Nebi Yunus inscription, for example, is accompanied by the statement that "in open battle like a flood I cast down Marduk-apla-iddina...", similarly reduced in its allusive intensity.[28]

Further generalised cosmic language with regard to the second campaign itself, the purpose of which was to chase Marduk-apla-iddina into Elam, may occur in the description of the destruction of Ellipi: "over the whole of his wide land I swept like a flood".[29]

Very little of interest occurs in the subsequent five campaigns, however, and only one passage with language suggestive of the creation epic: the fifth campaign includes the flight of the king of Ukku, to the north of Nineveh, and the subsequent destruction of his country so that it was "like a tell (left by) the deluge".[30] No particular reason is suggested for the language, but it is intriguing to note that it is this particular incident which in the later Nebi Yunus inscriptions is relocated to appear in the midst of the final series of confrontations with the Babylonians and their allies.[31]

8.1.3.3. The accounts of Halulê

Turning then to the battle at Halulê in 691 and the siege of Babylon in 690, Weissert identifies five literary allusions to *Enūma eliš* in Sennacherib's account, as contained in the final version of his annals. First and foremost, the citizens of Babylon are directly and immediately identified as *gallû*-demons. The campaign's incipit reads: "after Šuzubu had revolted, and the Babylonians, wicked *gallû*-demons, had closed the city-gates,–their hearts planning resistance...".[32] As Weissert notes, this is a more direct association than had occurred previously, being neither an analogy nor a secondary association. He cites the Sargon reference to Marduk-apla-iddina as the "likeness of a *gallû*-demon"; the description of him by Sennacherib in the first campaign as "that evil prop of a *gallû*-

28 Luckenbill, *Sennacherib*, 85:6-7 (*i-na ta-ḫa-az ṣêri* ^{md}*Marduk-apla-iddina*(*na*) *šar* ^{l}*Kar-*^{d}*dun-iá-àš ... a-bu-biš aš-pu-un*).

29 Luckenbill, *Sennacherib*, 28:15, 59:28 (*gim-ri mâti-šú rapašti*(*ti*) *kîma zî as-ḫu-up*). The term *zū* is now identified as *imbaru* or *anzû*; the former is more likely here (*CAD* Z, 150).

30 Luckenbill, *Sennacherib*, 72:47 (*ki-ma til a-bu-bi*).

31 Luckenbill, *Sennacherib*, 77:23, 86:16-17.

32 Luckenbill, *Sennacherib*, 41:17-19 (*arki* ^{m}*Šú-zu-bi is-si-ḫu-ma mârê*^{pl} *Bâbili*^{ki} *gallê*^{pl} *lem-nu-ti abullâni*^{pl} *ali ú-di-lu ik-pu-ud lib-ba-šu-nu a-na e-piš tukmāti*).

demon" is similarly oblique. It is also worth noting that the Halulê reference is a sweeping application of the imagery to the entirety of the Babylonian population, rather than to an individual leader. In light of what follows, this may be the first means by which Sennacherib acts to legitimate his destruction of Babylon.

Nonetheless, the king of Babylon also comes in for association with the cosmic chaos of *Enūma eliš*: Mušezib-Marduk (also known as Šuzubu) is said to be enthroned "inappropriately for him", a rare phrase which is used to describe Tiamat's enthronement of Qingu as her puppet ruler.[33] Weissert observes that

> through the adverbial phrase...the reader is expected to deduce the existence of a striking parallel between the Babylonians and Tiamat, between Mushezib-Marduk and Kingu, and finally, between the earthly royal throne of Babylon and the mythic office of divine sovereignty.[34]

The relationship between Qingu and Tiamat is of interest here. In *Enūma eliš* Qingu is initially said to be defeated and counted among the dead gods (the significance of which is unclear), then brought before Ea accused of having started the war: "they bound him and held him in front of Ea, imposed the penalty on him and cut off his blood".[35] The nature of this penalty is unfortunately unclear, as is whether or not he is killed outright. Mušezib-Marduk, perhaps surprisingly, is never said to have been killed but is deported to Nineveh, fettered and caged; he is then tied up "in the middle city-gate of Nineveh, like a bear."[36] A number of other leaders were previously reported to have been captured alive, but lack further comment as to their fate, making any corollary estimation of Šuzubu's ultimate fate difficult.[37] Under later kings he might be thought to have been killed, but indications for this under Sennacherib is lacking.

---

33 En.el. IV 82 (*a-na la si-ma-ti-šu*).

34 Weissert, 194.

35 En.el. VI 31-32 (*ik-mu-šu-ma maḫ-riš* ^{d}É.A *ú-kal-lu-šú an-nam i-me-du-šu-ma da-me-šú ip-tar-'u-u*).

36 Luckenbill, *Sennacherib*, 87:34-88:36 (^{m}*Šû-zu-bu šar Bâbili*^{ki} *i-na taḫâz ṣêri bal-ṭu-su ik-šú-da qâtâ*^{du}*-šu-un e-ri-in-nu bi-ri-tu id-du-šú-ma a-di maḫ-ri-ia ub-lu-niš-šú i-na abulli qabal ali šá Ninua*^{ki} *ar-ku-su da-bu-ú-eš*); a variant reads "with a bear" (*it-ti a-su*; Frahm, T19:II'6', T61:36). Note the rise in animal language to describe the enemy in Sennacherib's inscriptions. According to Liverani, in a developed imperial ideology in which foreigners are literally "strange" (*nak(i)ru*), "the doubt arises that they are sub-human beings, belonging rather to the animal world, and as a matter of fact frequently compared to animals" ("Ideology", 310); compare references to animals crawling on all fours like dogs (Sargon; *ARAB*, §148), kept alongside jackals, dogs and swine (Esarhaddon; *ARAB*, §529), and chained and kennelled (Assurbanipal; *ARAB*, §§819, 830).

37 Luckenbill, *Sennacherib*, 82:37-38.

The remaining three allusions noted by Weissert are references to the hastiness of Sennacherib's response, using *urruḫiš*; to combat headwear, using the rare *rāšu*; and use of the motif of a weapon which pierces the throat. To this we would add Sennacherib's description of himself as "like the onset of a raging storm", using language already recognisable as allusive to *Enūma eliš*.[38] Immediately after the use of *urruḫiš*, Sennacherib also declares that "like a huge flood fed by seasonal rains, I made their gullets and entrails run down upon the wide earth."[39]

By far the most detailed and most extreme military actions of Sennacherib's reign occur in this account, and it is surely not a coincidence that it is here that the clearest and most extensive allusions to the creation struggle also occur. At length:

> speedily I cut them down and established their defeat. I cut their throats like a sheep, I cut off their precious lives (as one cuts) a string. Like the onset of a raging storm, I made (the contents of) their gullets and entrails run down upon the wide earth. My prancing steeds, harnessed for my riding, plunged into the streams of their blood as (into) a river. The wheels of my war chariot, which brings low the wicked and the evil, were bespattered with blood and filth. With the bodies of their warriors I filled the plain, like grass. (Their) lips I cut off, and tore out their privates like the seeds of cucumbers of Siwan (June). Their hands I cut off.[40]

The language is stronger and the acts more extreme than any previously attested, particular with regard to the mutilation of the enemy dead: "(Their) lips I cut off, and tore out their privates like the seeds of cucumbers of Siwan (June). Their hands I cut off." The strength of the allusions to *Enūma eliš* act to clearly identify the enemy with chaos and Tiamat and to legitimate the enactment of such extreme treatments as part of the ongoing struggle against chaos.

The linguistic allusions to *Enūma eliš* identified by Weissert occur in the final version of Sennacherib's annals, which date between the battle of Halulê in 691 and the final fall of Babylon in 689, but are absent in

---

38 Luckenbill, *Sennacherib*, 45:77 (*kîma ti-ib me-ḫi-e šam-ri*).

39 Luckenbill, *Sennacherib*, 45:3-4 (*ki-ma mîli gap-ši šá ša-mu-tum si-ma-ni ù mun-ni-šu-nu ú-šar-da-a ṣe-er er-ṣe-ti*). Whether this is an allusion is also dependent on whether the analogy refers to Sennacherib himself or to the manner in which the entrails move.

40 Luckenbill, *Sennacherib*, 45:1-46:11 (*ur-ru-ḫiš ú-pal-lik-šu-nu-ti-ma aš-ku-na taḫ-ta-šu-un ki-ša-da-te-šu-nu ú-na-kis as-liš aq-ra-a-ti nap-ša-te-šu-nu ú-par-ri-' gu-'ú-iš ki-ma mîli gap-ši šá ša-mu-tum si-ma-ni ù-mun-ni-šu-nu ú-šar-da-a ṣe-er er-ṣe-ti ša-di-il-ti la-as-mu-ti mur-ni-is-qi ṣi-mit-ti ru-ku-bi-ia i-na da-me-šu-nu gap-šú-ti i-šal-lu-ú* [d]*nâri-iš šá* [w]*narkabat taḫâzi-ia sa-pi-na-at rag-gi ù ṣe-ni da-mu u pir-šu ri-it-mu-ku ma-gar-ru-uš pag-ri qu-ra-di-šu-nu ki-ma ur-qi-ti ú-mal-la-a ṣêri sa-ap-sa-pa-te ú-na-kis-ma bal-ta-šu-un a-bu-ut ki-ma bi-ni kiš-še-e si-ma-ni ú-na-kis qat-ti-šu-un*).

the version of events inscribed at the Bavian waterworks, which is to be dated after the fall of Babylon. Weissert has on this basis argued that the cosmic allusions reflect "the intense and zealous atmosphere prevailing close to, and during" the campaign's final stage, the siege of Babylon:

> the mythic presentation of the past events of Halule served in effect to create the right political climate in Assyria for the impending materialisation of Sennacherib's horrendous plans; and that the passionate rhetoric became superfluous once Babylon had been sacked, and the frustration and hatred felt toward her stubborn inhabitants had found their outlet in the final victory.[41]

While the ongoing reinforcement of the characterisation of Babylon and its associates with chaos for the purpose of legitimating the siege and extensive destruction of Babylon should not be overlooked, we contend that the cosmic language noted by Weissert serves not so much to whip up anti-Babylonian fervour in preparation for siege but to legitimate the unusually extreme actions taken against the Babylonians and their allies at Halulê itself. The absence of the more specific linguistic allusions in the Bavian inscription correlates to an absence of specific descriptions of the extreme fates meted out to the enemy soldiers. In the Bavian inscription the battle at Halulê is glossed over without detail, and the siege of Babylon described thus: "I advanced swiftly against Babylon, upon whose conquest I had determined, like the oncoming of a storm I broke loose, and I overwhelmed it like a hurricane".[42] Particularly fascinating is the description of the destruction itself:

> through the midst of that city I dug canals, I flooded its site (lit. ground) with water, and the very foundations thereof (lit. the structure of its foundation) I destroyed. I made its destruction more complete than that by a flood. That in days to come, the site of that city, and (its) temples and gods, might not be remembered, I completely blotted it out with (floods) of water and made it like a meadow.[43]

The classic allusions to the creation conflict reappear in a description of conquest which is essentially in keeping with previous military practices: once more the more general allusions to *Enūma eliš* suffice to le-

41 Weissert, 202.

42 Luckenbill, *Sennacherib*, 83:43-44 (*a-na Bâbili*[ki] *ša a-na ka-ša-di ú-ṣa-am-me-ru-šú ḫi-it-mu-ṭiš al-lik-ma ki-ma ti-ib me-ḫi-e a-ziq-ma ki-ma im-ba-ri as-ḫu-up-šú*).

43 Luckenbill, *Sennacherib*, 84:52-54 (*ina ki-rib ali šú-a-tu ⸢ḫi-ra⸣-a-ti aḫ-ri-e-ma ir-ṣi-is-su-nu i-na mê*[pl] *as-pu-un ši-kin uš-še-šu ú-ḫal-lik-ma eli šá a-bu-bu na-al-ban-ta-šu ú-ša-tir aš-šú aḫ-rat û-mi qaq-qar ali šú-a-tu ù bîtâti*[pl] *ilâni*[pl] *la muš-ši i-na ma-a-mi uš-ḫar-mit-su-ma ag-da-mar ú-šal-liš*).

gitimate a (apparently) normal military excursion.[44] This is a repetition of the phenomenon observed earlier in Sennacherib's accounts of the first campaign against Marduk-apla-iddina: the accounts written immediately after the campaign identify Marduk-apla-iddina with the *gallû*-demon, while those written subsequently merely record the defeat of his allies and make no explicit association with the forces of chaos. In the eighth campaign it is only in the exceptional case of Halulê, in which the treatment of the enemy goes well beyond normal practice, that more extensive legitimating allusions became necessary.[45]

44 The destruction of Babylon by Sennacherib was, of course, more dramatic than any before or after, and it may be for this reason that there are so many references to the storm and flood language of *Enūma eliš* (*kīma tīb meḫê, kīma imbari, eli ša abūbu*) interspersed with the description, but according to the report itself the destruction was essentially of the same variety known from previous sieges. The same expansive claims of destruction occur – e.g., "whether small or great, I left none; with their corpses I filled the city squares" – as were already seen in the reigns of Tiglath-pileser and Sargon (Luckenbill, *Sennacherib*, 83:45; *dannûte*^{pl}*-šu ṣeḫra ù rabâ(a) la e-zib-ma* ^{am}*pagrê*^{pl}*-šu-nu re-bit ali ú-mal-li*). It is particularly intriguing that it is the extreme treatments meted out to enemy people which require the most explicit allusions to legitimate them, and not the impersonal destruction of cities, for which the more generalised language suffices.

45 Rivaroli and Verderame have also suggested that Sennacherib's extreme violence is connected to an increasingly articulate ideological framework. They base their arguments on a general desire on the part of the inscriptions to demonstrate the king's superiority: whatever the specific fate of the king's enemies, the effect in every case is that the enemy king disappears, no longer able to threaten the order of the Assyrian king (302). The brutality of battle as well as the public humiliation of prisoners and bodies of the dead are intimately connected to the ideological necessity of demonstrating the king's superior power.

Their emphasis on the Assyrian king's superiority is one aspect of the order-against-chaos framework we have been describing, but Rivaroli and Verderame put too much emphasis on this superiority as the ultimate purpose of his violence. The object is rather the king's involvement in and contribution to the cosmic struggle against chaos; it is because of his identification with the forces of order that his enemies are identified with chaos, and it is because of this dichotomy that violence – aimed at eradicating the chaotic threat which they pose – is necessary. The king's superiority in battle is only the by-product of the necessary triumph of order over chaos; the enemy must disappear because he is anti-order, not simply to demonstrate the superiority of the Assyrian king. Also, by examining only Sennacherib's inscriptions Rivaroli and Verderame underestimate the extent to which Sennacherib's interactions with his opponents reach a previously unparalleled extreme, and, in connection to this, do not draw attention to the specific ideological means by which these acts are legitimated. Their general point, however – that a more articulate ideological framework undergirds higher levels of violence – is in fact reflected in Sennacherib's inscriptions: violence in battle reflects – and provokes – an increasingly articulate connection between the acts of the king and the acts of the gods at creation.

8.1.3.4. Enūma eliš

Of final note with regard to the development of the *Enūma eliš* allusions under Sennacherib is the apparent effort by his scribes to rewrite the epic, replacing the chief Babylonian deity, Marduk, with that of Assyria, Aššur. As W.G. Lambert has pointed out, these attempts were seriously hampered by the havoc wreaked on the divine genealogy, and they do not seem to have dominated in later recensions.[46] They do, however, reflect a recognition that the identification of Marduk as the divine warrior could be problematic in engagements with the Babylonians; while previously this seems to have been surmounted by identifying the human king and his counterpart, Marduk, as both acting for the benefit of Aššur, Sennacherib seems to have preferred to revise the mythology in order to eliminate the problematic Marduk and to identify Aššur himself as the divine warrior.[47]

The clearest application of the schema to Sennacherib's own battles occurs in a building inscription describing the new *bīt akîtu*, the house of the New Year festival, built by Sennacherib in Assur in place of the one in Babylon. The inscription describes temple gates which have been decorated with images of the altered version of *Enūma eliš*, culminating in an equation of Aššur and Sennacherib of unparalleled clarity:

> (this is) the image of Aššur as he advances to battle into the midst of Ti'āmat, the image of Sennacherib, king of Assyria...the weapon who conquers Ti'āmat and the creatures inside her, stationed in Aššur's chariot.[48]

---

46 Lambert, "Recension".

47 The acuteness of the issue may derive in part from the fact that *Enūma eliš*, with Marduk at its centre, is in large part about the origins and construction of the city of Babylon (see D.C.T. Sherriffs, "'A tale of two cities': Zion and Babylon", *TB* 39 [1988]: 19-57).

48 B. Pongratz-Leisten, *Ina Šulmi Īrub: Die kulttopographische und ideologische Programmatik der* akītu-*Prozession in Babylonien und Assyrien im I. Jahrtausend v.Chr.*, BF 16 (Mainz am Rhein: Philipp von Zabern, 1994), Nr.2: K 1356:26, 32-33 (*ṣa-lam* AN.ŠÁR *šá a-na* ŠÀ *Ti-amat ṣal-ti* DU-*ku ṣa-lam* [Id]30-PAP.MEŠ-SU MAN KUR *Aš+šur* ... [GIŠ].TUKUL *Ka-ši-du-*<*ti*> *ina* GIŠ.GIGIR AN.ŠÁR *šak-nu Ti-amat a-di nab-nit qer-bi-šú*); Luckenbill read [*ana*]-*ku ka-ši-du*, "I am one who conquers", but the sense is the same either way (*Sennacherib*, 142:1). Pongratz-Leisten prefers to distinguish the parallel descriptions of the "image of Aššur" and the "image of Sennacherib", contending that the latter is explicating the former as the "work" or "creation" of Sennacherib (209). She is right that this interpretation would be in keeping with the appearance of the phrase *ēpiš ṣalam Aššur* in Sennacherib's titulary, but as *ēpešu* is absent here and this interpretation denies both the syntactical structure of the passage and its coherence with the royal military ideology, the reading of the phrase as a straightforward parallel is preferable.

8.2. Esarhaddon (680-669)

There is a significant change in the language used to describe the battles of Esarhaddon which distinguishes him from all of his predecessors. While the heightened levels of violence which characterised the inscriptions of Sennacherib persist into that of his son – and, if anything, Esarhaddon appears to have been even more extreme – Esarhaddon very rarely uses cosmological language to legitimate these acts.

The perpetuation of high levels of extreme behaviour is of itself somewhat surprising, as that most scholars view him as having had a deeply ambiguous relationship with his father, particularly over the destruction of Babylon. Given what we have just seen with regard to Sennacherib, it may be that some of this ambiguity was related to the events at Halulê rather than to the destruction of Babylon proper. However, perhaps it is more likely, considering the continued employment by Esarhaddon of extreme acts akin to those perpetuated at Halulê, that the use of heightened cosmological language by Sennacherib to legitimate Halulê succeeded in increasing the moral tolerance of extreme levels of violence to the point that Esarhaddon did not feel the need to legitimate them individually, while the lesser levels of legitimation attached by Sennacherib to the destruction of Babylon failed to have a similar effect.[49]

8.2.1. Ideology

8.2.1.1. Cosmology

The cosmic language which does occur in Esarhaddon's inscriptions appears primarily in his titulary, though the nature of the allusions varies among the versions.[50] In the Zinçirli stele inscription he is "the king whose movement is like that of a flood, whose deeds like those of an enraged lion; before him is the storm, behind him the onslaught of

49 It may also be that Sennacherib's inscriptions deliberately played down the level of destruction wreaked upon Babylon (and that the legitimating language thereby associated with it was equally low), and that Esarhaddon's ambiguity towards his father is based on a more extensive destruction of reality.

50 Contributing to the peculiarities of Esarhaddon's reign is the non-chronological arrangement of his inscriptions; it may be in part due to this that the cosmic language of the titulary is considered sufficiently overarching as to act as legitimator for the entirety of an inscription's reports.

the beginning of his combat, a blazing flame".[51] In Prisms B and S Marduk's gift to Esarhaddon is explicitly designated as having made "the fear of my rule overwhelm the mountains of the four quarters like a mighty storm".[52] While there are a number of campaigns for which only fragmentary reports survive, and it is therefore possible that some of these included cosmological language, it is only in the campaign against Egypt that such language appears in reference to a specific encounter: against Egypt Esarhaddon advanced "like the onset of a raging storm"; in front of his troops he went "like a flood".[53] Maul writes with regard to this incident that it "ist folgerichtig, daß er seine realen Feinde in der Rolle der Mächte des Chaos, der Gegenspieler Ninurtas oder Marduks sehen mußte."[54] Overall and compared to his predecessors, however, Esarhaddon's lack of cosmological language is striking.

The lack of specific and repeated cosmological allusions does not correlate to a lack of extreme and explicitly described military actions. In general, the mercilessness of Esarhaddon is emphasised in his inscriptions as much as the justice of Sennacherib was emphasised in his.[55] He is called "king of kings, the unsparing, who controls the insubordinate, who is clothed in terror, who is fearless in battle, the perfect hero, who is unsparing in the fight."[56] He is "the unsparing weapon, which utterly destroys the enemy's land",[57] who wields the

51 R. Borger, *Die Inschriften Asarhaddons, Königs von Assyrien*, AfOB 9 (Graz: Ernst Weidner, 1956), 97:12-14; *ARAB*, §576 (*šarru šá tal-lak-ta-šú a-bu-bu-um-ma ep-še-ta-šú [lab]-bu na-ad-ru pa-nu-uš-šú zu(?)-um-ma ar-ke-e-šú ti-ib(?) qit-ru-ub ta-ḫa-zi-šú dan-nu nab-lu*). Note in particular the use of *abūbu*, which has occurred before; also *nablu*, which appears among Marduk's weaponry but has not appeared in the inscriptions prior to this.

52 Borger, *Asarhaddon*, 46:34-35; *ARAB*, §508 (^{d}*Marduk šar*$_{4}$ *ilâni*^{meš} *pu-luḫ-ti šarru-ti-ia ki-ma im-ba-ri kab-ti ú-šá-as-ḫi-pu šadê*^{meš}(*^{e}*) *kib-ra-a-ti*).

53 Borger, *Asarhaddon*, 65:11, 18; *ARAB*, §561, 563 (*kîma ez-zi ti-ib me-ḫi-i, a-bu-bu-niš*).

54 Maul, "König", 74.

55 Justice and righteousness are mentioned in a description of Esarhaddon as "king of Assyria, king of the four regions, who loves righteousness and whose anathema is dishonesty": language of righteousness as the means of achieving an ordered cosmos (Assyrian hegemony over the known world) (Borger, *Asarhaddon*, 54:25-26; *ARAB*, §518; *šàr mât Aš-šur*^{ki} *šàr kib-rat erbetti*^{ti} *šá kit-tu i-ram-mu-ma ṣa-lip-tú ik-kib-šú*). Compared to Sennacherib's annals, the idea of the king as emblem of righteousness is less prominent, while, like Sennacherib, Esarhaddon has largely abandoned Sargon's concern to identify enemies as universally rebellious. Such a decrease in the level of overt legitimation, despite an increase in the level of violence itself, suggests the absorption of ideology to the extent it need not be explicitly recalled.

56 Borger, *Asarhaddon*, 96:19-23; *ARAB*, §575 (*šàr šarrâni*$^{\text{m[e]š}}$ *la pa-du-u m-la-'-iṭ*⌉ *ek-ṣu-ti la-biš na-mur-[rati] la a-di-ru šá-áš-me qar-ra-du gít-*⌈*ma*]-[*lu*⌉ *la pa-du-u tu-qu-un-tu*).

57 Borger, *Asarhaddon*, 98:22; *ARAB*, §577 (^{giš}*kakku la pa-du-u mu-rib mât nu-kúr-ti*).

"unsparing javelin of Aššur".[58] Without apparent hesitation he declares that the gods empowered him "to rob, to plunder, to extend the border of Assyria."[59]

8.2.1.2. Divination and prophecy

In lieu of the use of cosmological allusions, Esarhaddon's military synergy with the gods – and thereby the legitimation of his wars – is established in a number of other ways, primarily divination and prophecy.[60] The synergy of the gods with their historical agent the king is clear from the texts; in the first collection of oracles to Esarhaddon, mostly from the goddess Ištar, it is the goddess who throws the king's enemies at his feet, and she who flays them.[61] "I will deliver up the enemy of the king to slaughter", she promises; "with an angry dagger in my hand I will finish off your enemies".[62] The oracles emphasise the universality of Esarhaddon's and the god's coming dominion. Ištar promises, "I will do away with the boundaries of the countries and give them to you"; Aššur announces "I slaughtered your enemies and filled the river with their blood".[63]

It is perhaps significant for our study that it is with Ištar that Esarhaddon appears to have had the closest relationship: though a war goddess, there is no indication that she was ever explicitly inserted into the role of Marduk in *Enūma eliš*, and it may be for this reason that the allusions to *Enūma eliš* are so much less prominent under Esarhaddon than under his predecessors.

The synergy of the gods with the king is also reiterated in the oracular texts through the range of acts attributed to the gods, which

---

58 Borger, *Asarhaddon*, 65:11; *ARAB*, §561 (*gišil-ta-ḫi Aššur la p*[*a-dû*]).

59 Borger, *Asarhaddon*, 98:34-35; *ARAB*, §579 (*a-na ḫa-ba-ti šá-la-li mi-ṣir mât Aš-šur*ki *ru-up-pu-ši*).

60 That divination for such purposes occurred prior to Esarhaddon is certain, but the collection and preservation of oracles and omens for legitimation purposes seems to have been a special phenomenon which began with Esarhaddon and continued into the reign of his successor, Assurbanipal.

61 SAA 9 1.1; Nissinen, Seow and Ritner no. 68.

62 SAA 9 1.2:31′-32′ (Nissinen, Seow and Ritner no. 69; *na-ak-ru ša* MAN KUR-*aš-šur* *⸢a!⸣-na ṭa-ba-ah-hi a-da-na*); SAA 9 1.6:7-10 (Nissinen, Seow and Ritner no. 73; *ha-an-ga-ru ak-ku ina* ŠU.2-*ia* LÚ.KÚR.MEŠ-*ka ú-qa-at-ta*).

63 SAA 9 2.3:15′-16′ (Nissinen, Seow and Ritner, no. 80; *ta-hu-ma-a-ni ša* KUR.KUR *ú-ga-am-mar a-da-nak-ka*); SAA 9 3.3:22-23 (Nissinen, Seow and Ritner no. 86; LÚ.KÚR.MEŠ-*ka uh-ta-ti-ip da-me-šú-nu* ÍD *um-tal-li*).

are of a kind with those reported of the kings.[64] The destruction of orchards[65] and the flaying of the enemy[66] are noted in both prophetic texts, where they are attributed to the gods, and in inscriptions, where they are attributed to the king. Destruction and burning appear, as does the description of a river running with enemy blood as a result of slaughter by Aššur.[67] The special punishment of rebels is noted, as is the violent punishment of conspirators: "I will cut the conspiring weasels and shrews to pieces before his feet."[68] There is also a reference to the practice of staking enemy conspirators.[69]

A parallel shift in the locus of military legitimation occurs in Esarhaddon's correspondence; there are two letters to Esarhaddon which make explicit appeal to the gods in relation to the king's military success. In one the writer reiterates the idea that it is the gods who are the active agents on the battlefield, bringing victory to the king whose role is passive:

> all the [gods of hea]ven are ready (for battle). [May they march] in the presence of the king, my lord, and [bring] the enemies of the king, my lord,

---

64 One of the curious aspects of the Esarhaddon prophetic texts in this regard is that a number of these incidents are not attested in the inscriptions of Esarhaddon himself, but are the types of treatments meted out by his predecessors. These references may suggest that, despite the absence of references to such actions in his inscriptions, Esarhaddon's military practices did include them. Alternately or additionally, these acts may have been taken by Esarhaddon to be representative of all the various extreme actions in which he engaged. Ultimately, regardless of the specifics, Esarhaddon receives a military *carte blanche* with the gods' instructions to "Go ahead, do not hold back! We go constantly by your side; we annihilate your enemies" (Borger, *Asarhaddon*, 43:61-62; Nissinen, Seow and Ritner no. 97; *a-lik la ka-la-(a-)ta i-da-a-ka ni-it-tal-lak-ma ni-na-a-ra ga-re-e*-ka*). Nissinen notes that the divine word may have been conveyed in this instance by haruspices rather than prophets, but that regardless of the method of mediation it fulfilled the same function (*References*, 34).

65 SAA 9 2.5; Nissinen, Seow and Ritner no. 82. Cf . Tadmor, *Inscriptions*, Ann. 23:11'-12', Summ. 7:24 (Tiglath-pileser); *ARAB*, §32, 39 (Sargon); Luckenbill, *Sennacherib*, 59:29 (Sennacherib).

66 SAA 9 1.1; Nissinen, Seow and Ritner no. 68; cf. *ARAB*, §10, 55, 56 (Sargon); Luckenbill, *Sennacherib*, 62:86 (Sennacherib); *ARAB*, §831 (Assurbanipal).

67 SAA 9 3.2; Nissinen, Seow and Ritner no. 85; SAA 9 3.3; Nissinen, Seow and Ritner no. 86; cf. the royal inscriptions of Tiglath-pileser (Tadmor, *Inscriptions*, Ann. 23:3', Summ. 7:48) and Sargon (*ARAB*, §154). The merit of the action is particularly obvious in this oracle, which follows "I slaughtered your enemies and filled the river with their blood" with the triumphant admonition "Let them see it and praise me, for I am Aššur, lord of the gods!" (SAA 9 3.3:22-25; Nissinen, Seow and Ritner no. 86; LÚ.KÚR.MEŠ-*ka uh-ta-ti-ip da-me-šú-nu* ÍD *um-tal-li le-mu-ru lu-na-i*[!]*-⌜du⌝-ni a-ki* ᵈ*aš-šur* EN DINGIR.MEŠ *a-na-ku-ni*).

68 SAA 9 1.7:3-7 (Nissinen, Seow and Ritner no. 74; *ka-kiš-a-ti pu-uš-ha-a-ti šá i-da-ba-bu-u-ni ina* IGI GÌR.2-*šú ú-bat-taq-šú-nu*).

69 SAA 9 3.5; Nissinen, Seow and Ritner no. 88; cf. Sennacherib and Assurbanipal.

> [quick]ly to submission before the feet of the king, m[y] lo[rd! May they let] the wishes of the king, [my] lord, [be fulfilled].[70]

The correspondence from the scholars is equally corroborative of this idea: they are to "constantly bless your kingship...may they defeat your enemies, slay your foes, dri[ve off your adversaries] and pick up their possessions".[71] The content of the gods' blessing is always military: "And [they will brin]g all the enemies [of] the king, my lord, [to submission] before the feet of the king, [my] lord."[72]

In these as well as the text which follows, the language describing the relationship between the king and the gods produces a sense that the gods are at the bidding of the king, rather than vice versa.

> The king of the gods, Marduk, turns graciously to the king my lord. Whatever the king my lord speaks, he will perform. Upon your throne you are seated, your enemies you shall take captive, your foes you shall conquer, and the land of your enemies you shall despoil. Bel has spoken, saying, "Like Marduk-šāpik-zēri, Esarhaddon king of Assyria is upon the throne and seated upon it, and the whole land is obedient to his instruction." The king my lord *knows*. Joyfully let the king do as he is able.[73]

While it seems unlikely that the kings would have seen themselves as overtly in control of the actions of the gods, it is interesting from a moral perspective that their synergy (and in this case it may not be insignificant that it is Marduk who is mentioned) is such that the direc-

70 SAA 16 132:5-8 (*ka-li-šú-nu* MURUB$_4$ *ra-a*[*k-su-t*]*e*.MEŠ *ina pa-na-at* LUGAL EN-*ia* [*lil-li-k*]*u* LÚ.KÚR.MEŠ-*te ša* LUGAL EN-*ia* [*ár-h*]*iš*$^{?}$ *ina* KI.TA GÌR.2.MEŠ *ša* LUGAL E[N]-*i*[*a lu-š*]*a*[*k*$^{!}$-*ni-šú*$^{!}$] *ṣu-um-mu-rat ša* LUGAL EN-[*ia lu-šak-š*]*i-d*[*u*]).

71 SAA 10 294:6-9 (*li*]*k*-[*t*]*ar*$^{!}$-*ra-bu* LUGAL-*ut-ka* ... L]Ú.KÚR.MEŠ-*ka lis-ki-pu li-šam-qí-tu a-a-bi-ka* [*ga-re-e-ka li-ṭa-a*]*r*$^{!}$-*ri-du lil-qu-tu bi-*⸢*iš*$^{!}$⸣-*šá*$^{!}$-*šú-un*). There are four such letters, three definitely from Esarhaddon's reign and one from either Esarhaddon or Assurbanipal. See also SAA 10 284, 316. More generally, another letter assures the king that his prayers are acceptable to the gods (SAA 10 351). It is very unfortunate that the final SAA volumes containing updated editions of the correspondence from the reigns of Esarhaddon and Assurbanipal are not yet published. Parts of the following have therefore had to be based on the old collections of R.H. Pfeiffer (*State Letters of Assyria: A Transliteration and Translation of 355 Official Assyrian Letters dating from the Sargonid Period (722-625 B.C.)*, AOS 6 [New Haven, Conn.: American Oriental Society, 1935]) and L. Waterman (*Royal Correspondence of the Assyrian Empire: Translated into English, with a Transliteration of the Text and a Commentary*, UMSHS 17-20 [Ann Arbor, Mich.: University of Michigan, 1930]).

72 SAA 16 126:17-18 (*ù ma-ri na-ga-ru-ti-ni* [*ša*] LUGAL *be-lí-ia i-na sa-pal* GÌR.2 *ša* LUGAL EN-[*ia ú-šak-nu*]-*šú*).

73 Waterman II, §1237:19-28 (šar ilâni^{me} ^{il}Marduk it-ti šarri be-lí-ia sa-lim mimma ma-la šarru be-lí-a i-qab-bu-ú ip-pu-uš ina ^{is}kussi-ka aš-ba-a-ta ^{amêl}nakre^{meš}-ka ta-kám-mu a-a-bi-ka ta-kaš-šad ù mât nakri-i-ka ta-šal-lal ^{il}Bêl iq-ta-bi um-ma a-ki-i ^{m} ^{il}Marduk-šâpik-zêri ^{m} ^{il}Ašur-aḫ-iddina^{na} šar ^{mât}⸢Ašur⸣ ina ^{is}kussi ù ina libbi a-ši-ib ù ⸢mâti⸣ gab-bi a-na qâtâ-šu ⸢a⸣(?)-man-ni šarri beli [i-di] ḫa-di-iš šarru a-ki-i ša i-li-['i-u] li-pu-uš).

tion of leadership may be obscured in this manner. The king again receives a *carte blanche* to do as he pleases on the battlefield.

Two further aspects of Esarhaddon's unusual methods of military legitimation are worth noting. First, in conjunction with the prophetic divinatory texts, there are a number of scholarly and epistolary texts which refer to other types of divinatory legitimation for warfare. One refers to the state of the moon as the reason why "the cities of the Mannean will be plundered, his people taken in captivity, and he himself will be encircled in his palace until he will be delivered into the hands of the king, my lord."[74] In another, the king is given *carte blanche* to pursue his opponent ("if there is an enemy of the king, my lord, in the West, the king, my lord, may do as he pleases") and the reassurance that he will succeed ("the king, my lord, will capture (him), and the king will defeat him. These are definite words").[75] This *carte blanche* is tied explicitly to the "just policy" of the king and presented as the gods' consequent reward.

8.2.1.3. Oaths

The final development in Esarhaddon's thinking on warfare is his persistent references to oath-breaking as a reason for punitive action against his enemies. Thus the attack, capture and deportation of the Mannean population and plunder of their assets are attributed to the fact that "they recognize neither the *oath* of a god nor a (human) agreement".[76] Similar sentiments appear in a letter from Esarhaddon's chief physician, Urad-Nanaya, in which he declares that "Aššur and the great gods bound and handed over to the king these criminals who plotted against the (king's) goodness and who, having concluded the

74 SAA 10 112:15-17 (*en-na* KUR.*man-na-a-a- ki-i pi-i an-nim-ma* URU.MEŠ-*šu iš-šal-la-lu* UN.MEŠ-*šú ih-hab-ba-tu ù šu-ú ina* É.gal-*šú ú-ta-sar a-di a-na* ŠU.2 LUGAL *be-li-a*). The assertion is analogous to a similar occurrence in the previous year (SAA 10 112).

75 SAA 10 168:13-r.1 (*ki-i* LÚ.EN-KÚR *šá* LUGAL EN-*iá ina* KUR-MAR.KI *i-ba-áš-šú-ú* LUGAL EN *ki-i šá i-le-'u-ú li-pu-uš* ŠU.2 LUGAL EN-*iá i-kaš-šad a-bi-ik-ta-šú* LUGAL *i-š[ak]-an dib-bi p[ar]-su-tum šú-nu*).

76 Waterman II, §1237:16 ([ma]-[am-ʾme-ti ša ili ù a-di-e ul i-du-ú). A subsequent letter from the same writer reports that "the army of the king, my lord, having attacked the Manneans, has captured forts, plundered towns and pillaged the open country" (SAA 10 112:8-11; *en-na e-mu-qa šá* LUGAL *be-lí-ia ina* UGU KUR.*man-na-a-a ki-i it-bu-ú bi-ra-na-a-ti iṣ-ṣa-bat* URU.ME *il-ta-lal hu-bu-ut* EDIN *ih-ta-bat*).

king's treaty together with his servants before Aššur and the great gods, broke the treaty."[77]

Esarhaddon's concern about his subjects reneging on loyalty oaths is equally clear in the letters surrounding the supposed conspiracy of Sasî.[78] In one the writer advises the king regarding the offenders, saying, "may the name and seed of Sasî, Bel-ahu-uṣur and their accomplices perish, and may Bel and Nabû establish the name and seed of the king, my lord, until far-off [days]!"[79] The advocated punishment is directly related to Sasî's violation of ("sin against") Sennacherib's Succession Treaty, to which vassals were required to swear upon Assurbanipal's and Šamaš-šuma-ukîn's investiture as crown princes, and which is mentioned specifically in both letters from this particular writer.[80] There also appears to have been a direct threat against Esarhaddon's life involved (presuming that Nabû-rehtu-uṣur is not being hyperbolic), thus justifying the interrogations aimed at identifying the conspirators and the execution of same.[81]

8.2.2. Practice

Esarhaddon's particular interest in oaths and oath-breaking appears to be tied to his own contested claim to the throne. Though invested by

77 SAA 10 316:20-r.3 (*an-nu-te* LÚ*.*par-ri-ṣu-te ša ina* UGU *ṭa-ab*$^{!!}$*-te id-bu-ub-u-ni a-de-e ša* LUGAL *ina pa-an aš-šur u* DINGIR.MEŠ GAL.MEŠ TA* LÚ*.ARAD.MEŠ-*šú iš-kun-u-ni ša ina* ŠÀ-*bi a-de-e ih-ṭu-u-ni aš-sur u* DINGIR.MEŠ GAL.MEŠ *uk-ta-si-iu-u ina* ŠU.2 LUGAL *be-lí-ia i-sa-ak-nu-šu-nu*). The "criminals" are almost certainly Sasî and his fellow conspirators (M. Nissinen, *References to Prophecy in Neo-Assyrian Sources*, SAAS 7 [Helsinki: Helsinki University Press, 1998], 128-129).

78 The nature of the conspiracy is unclear (see Baker 3/1, 1093-1094). Nissinen has argued that Sasî was himself an undercover royal agent infiltrating the conspiracy, on the basis of his apparent escape of the death penalty, on the basis of a legal document from around 664 (*The Prosopography of the Neo-Assyrian Empire* (P-Ṣ), volume 3/1 [Helsinki: Neo-Assyrian Text Corpus Project, 2002], 1093-1094; Nissinen, *References*, 145-150).

79 SAA 16 59:9′-10′ (MU NUMUN *šá* ^{m}*sa-si-i šá* ^{m}EN-PAB-PAB *šá* UN.MEŠ *šá is-si-šú-nu ú-du-*[*u-ni*] *li-ih-li-iq* MU NUMUN *šá* LUGAL EN-*ia* ^{d}EN ^{d}PA *a-na* ⸢*ṣa*$^{!}$*-at*⸣ [UD.ME *lu-ki*]*n-nu*).

80 Nissinen, *References*, 116-117; SAA 16 59, 60. The fact of Nabû-rehtu-uṣur's denunciation is itself probably also a product of the treaty, "where he personally urges his subjects to send denunciations to him...the dire fates of his father and grandfather clearly had made Esarhaddon strive to prevent history from repeating itself" (xxiv). For the text of the treaty, see SAA 2 6.

81 SAA 16 59, 60. "These exhortations make it clear that the writer believes the conspiracy of Sasî and his accomplices constitute a mortal danger to the king" (Nissinen, *References*, 127).

Sennacherib as crown prince, there was a dynastic struggle between Esarhaddon and his brothers upon the assassination of Sennacherib (by whom is disputed); after succeeding to the throne Esarhaddon imposed oaths of loyalty on a number of his subjects. The fortuitous portents and divinations discussed above appear to have been key in securing his accession to the throne, and his recourse to similar divinatory techniques to legitimate his subsequent endeavours is thus unsurprising.

Esarhaddon's particular attentiveness to his own legitimacy is likely also a key reason behind the change in military actions which occurs in his reign. To a certain extent Esarhaddon's practices repeat those of his predecessors, whose tactics tended to be limited to on-location practices like impalement; thus in an incident regarding the non-return of Assyrian fugitives by Šupria the body parts of the dead are abused, with "their skulls(?) they piled into pyramids. . . . . . they hung and surrounded their city with them."[82] Elsewhere it is said that Esarhaddon forbade the burial of the corpses of enemy warriors.[83] This left the corpses exposed to the public view, a vivid warning against resistance.

More significantly, however, Esarhaddon's reign sees a decisive change toward the return of captives to Nineveh for public display there. Thus the public exhibition of captured enemies and the body parts of the dead is reported in his description of a victory parade in Nineveh after a campaign to the west:

---

82 Borger, *Asarhaddon*, 104:9-11; *ARAB*, §600 ([...]-x-*šú-nu-ma gul-gul-li-šú-nu ir-ṣi-pu di-ma-ti-iš* [...*n*]*u*(?) *e-lu-lu-ma il-mu-u si-ḫi-ir-ti âli*-[*šu*]-*un*). Borger translates "…sie und ihre Schädel schichteten sie auf wie Türme. [Die Leichen ihrer Krieger?] hingen sie [an Stangen?] auf und umgaben damit ihre ganze Stadt." The treatment of the fugitives themselves: "the runaways, all who had deserted their masters and fled to Šupria – their fingers I cut off, their noses, eyes and ears I took away from them" (Borger, *Asarhaddon*, 106:23-24; *ARAB*, §606; *ḫal-q*[*u munnabtu ma-l*]*a bêlê*meš*-šú-nu ú-maš-šìr-u-ma ana mât Šub-ri-a in-nab-tú* x [xxx *qâtêšu*]-*nu ú-kar-rit ap-pu e-nu uz-nu e-kim-šú-nu-ti*). As with foreign rebels, it is probable that these acts were designed to make a public example of those who threatened the Assyrian order, but the fact that mutilations of this sort had not been reported in Assyria since the era of Assurnaṣirpal may suggest that that treason was considered a greater offence than the resistance of foreigners. One can see an analogy in the differentiation between previously independent entities, which constituted a sort of threat to Assyrian order by existing outside of it, and those which rebelled once subordinated, which threatened to disorder it from the inside. Esarhaddon explains his actions by explaining that "the gods had granted to me justice and righteousness, (to see) that oaths should be kept" (Borger, *Asarhaddon*, 106:32; *ARAB*, §607; [*aš*]- *šú a-de-e na-ṣa-rim-ma ki*(?)-*tú u mi-šá-ri iš-ruk-in-ni ilâni*meš *rabûti*meš). Note again the reference to justice and righteousness, the language of order, as well as the breaking of oaths, highlighting Esarhaddon's concerns with legitimacy (see below).

83 *ARAB*, §521.

> that the might of Aššur, my lord, might be manifested to (all) peoples, I hung them [the heads of Sanduarri and Abdi-milkutti] on the shoulders of their nobles and with singing and music (*lit.*, singers and musical instruments) I paraded through the public square of Nineveh.[84]

Prior to Abdi-milkutti's decapitation, he is depicted on two victory stele, one from Zinçirli and one from Tel Ahmar.[85] Both stele show Esarhaddon holding his enemies on leashes – the other enemy is Ushanahura, the son of Tarqa, king of Egypt and Nubia – though the location of the gesture is unclear.[86] The rebellious Uabu was brought in chains to Nineveh along with his soldiers, where they were tied to the city gate.[87] The king of Arzani was treated similarly: "beside the gate inside the city of Nineveh I kept him tied alongside *asi* (jackals?), dogs and swine."[88] A second account of the same campaign indicates that he was accompanied by other leaders of the area.[89]

The increased interest in bringing war captives home to Nineveh for execution suggests a concomitant shift in the understanding of the purpose of these acts. Saggs has argued that all such behaviour was aimed solely at the pursuit of psychological warfare, but this is problematised by the specification of Assyrians as the primary audience of these acts. While public exhibition of captives and their body parts in locations like the city gate entails the possibility, even probability, that foreigners might see them and be deterred from any thoughts of rebellion, the primary audience remains the Assyrians. Whereas previous Assyrian kings had concentrated the display of mutilations onsite, where the local populations would be able to see and be appropriately warned of the dangers of future rebellion, Esarhaddon's return of both the living and the dead to Nineveh for display indicates an altered target audience. This had certain practical implications: unlike in earlier reigns there is no reference to impalement during any of Esarhaddon's campaigns. Since the preceding kings' records indicated that impale-

84 Borger, *Asarhaddon*, 50:36-38; *ARAB*, §§214, 528 (*áš-šú da-na-an* (^{d})*Aš-šur bêli-ia nišê*^{meš} *kul-lu-mì-im-ma ina ki-šá-(a-)di* ^{lú}*rabûti*^{meš}*-šu-un a-lul-ma it-ti* ^{lú}*nâri ù* ^{giš}*sammî ina re-bet Ninua*^{ki} *e-te-et-ti-iq*).

85 Though Esarhaddon's palace at Nimrud was never finished, and therefore there are no reliefs from his reign, he is the only king for whom a stele has been preserved which depicts him victorious over his enemy. The lack of such stele for other kings is surprising, as they would have been opportune surfaces for imperial propaganda, but their absence may be merely the consequence of (non-)discovery.

86 Parrot, 35.

87 *ARAB*, §518.

88 Borger, *Asarhaddon*, 50:41-42; *ARAB*, §515 (*ú-ra-a ina ṭi-ḫi abul qabal âli šá* (^{uru})*Ni-na-a*(^{ki}) *it-ti a-si kalbi u šaḫî* (ŠAḪ) *ú-še-šib-šu-nu-ti ka-mì-iš*).

89 *ARAB*, §529.

ment was primarily directed at the leadership of a defeated state, this is hardly surprising in a dominant military-political climate in which these same individuals were instead transported to Nineveh for display there.

Almost certainly, the shift in purpose and the shift in practice reflect the increased instability of the internal political situation: Esarhaddon was not the eldest son and had faced significant opposition to his rule – hence the unprecedented interest in divination. The turn in attention inward, toward an Assyrian audience, suggests that the public exhibition and mutilation of foreign leaders was no longer a practice primarily intended to deter future rebellions in distant parts of the empire, but designed as living (or, frequently, dead) proof of the king's legitimacy: the fact of victory itself was a sign of the gods' approval of a king (and his acts), so Esarhaddon brought the evidence of their victories back to Assyria as evidence of his legitimacy. With the existence of the captives a sign of the king's legitimacy, the extremity of the treatments meted out to them becomes an exhibition of the king's power.

8.3. Assurbanipal (668-626)

Similarly extreme treatment of prisoners occurred in the reign of Esarhaddon's son, Assurbanipal, and is similarly associated with threats to his legitimacy. Assurbanipal's legitimation techniques include both those which arose under his father, such as divination and references to oath-breaking, as well as some reappearances of the more traditional cosmic allusions with which we are familiar from Esarhaddon's predecessors.

8.3.1. Ideology

8.3.1.1. Divination and prophecy

As to the former, Assurbanipal's records demonstrate a continued interest in legitimation through prophetic divination, though the support is expressed primarily in general terms, such as assertions that the god will "r]ise and slau[ghter] your enemy" and "will vanquish the

[e]nemy of Assurbanipal".[90] There are likewise a number of references in the king's letters to military success as the consequence of divine involvement. These references speak of both general as well as specific support:

> as to Upaqu, about whom the king my lord has written; (inasmuch as) Bel, Nabu, Ištar of Uruk and Nana hold sway from the rising of the sun to the setting thereof: may they utterly destroy him and deliver (him) into the hands of the king my lord; the kings of all countries may they bring into subjection before the weapon of the king my lord.[91]

Similarly, Bel-ibni writes to the king and attributes the troops' military success directly to the benevolence of the deities: "Since the gods of the king my lord lent their support to his servants, the (latter) slew seventeen of the enemy and wounded sixty or seventy among them; (the others) they routed".[92]

8.3.1.2. Oaths

This involvement of the gods in Assurbanipal's military affairs is frequently articulated as the involvement of the gods in the punishment of sin, but while similar language was observed already in the period of Sargon, in the reign of Assurbanipal the sin in question is persistently the breaking of treaties or oaths: thus assertions such as "Aššur and the great gods have bound those who sinned against the oath and given them into the hands of the king my lord."[93] This language recurs repeatedly in Assurbanipal's correspondence and may be attributed to Assurbanipal's concern with the loyalty of his subjects, as evidenced also by the imposition of extensive loyalty oaths at the time of his coronation as Crown Prince and the concern with establishing his legitimacy which these oaths reflected.[94] This is a concern which will resurface frequently in what follows.

---

90 SAA 9 9:26 (Nissinen, Seow and Ritner no. 94; *a-t]a-bi a-a-ab-ka a-ṭa-[ba-ah]*); SAA 9 11:4 (Nissinen, Seow and Ritner no. 96; [L]Ú.KÚR *a-kaš-šad šá* ^{m}*aš-šur*-DÙ-A[*x*).

91 Pfeiffer, §26:6-10 (^{m}*ú-pa-qu ša šarru bêli-a iš-pur-ra id-dan-nu-nu* ^{ilu}*bêl ù* ^{ilu}*nabû* ^{ilu}*ištar uruk*^{ki} *ù* ^{ilu}*na-na-a ul-tu ṣi-it* ^{ilu}*šamši*^{ši} *a-di e-reb* ^{ilu}*šamši*^{ši} *lu-qat-tu-ma a-na šarri bêli-ia lu-di-nu*), cf. §26:11-12.

92 Pfeiffer, §520:5-8 (*ne-mud ilâni*^{pl} *šá šarri bêli-iá it-ti* ^{amêlu}*ardâni*^{pl}*-šú ki-i iz-zi-zu ṣâbê*^{pl} *17 ina libbi*^{bi}*-šú-nu id-du-ku ù šuššu*^{šu} *70 ina libbi*^{bi}*-šú-nu un-da-ḫi-ṣu ina pa-ni-šú-nu it-ta-bal-ki-ti*).

93 Waterman I, §584:r.1-2 (a-di-e iḫ-ṭu-u-ni Ašur u ilâni^{meš} rabûte^{meš} uk-ta-si-ia-u ina qâtâ šarri be-lí-ia i-sa-ak-nu-šú-nu).

94 See e.g., Waterman I, §§301, 472, 584; Waterman II, §1380.

8.3.2. Developing cosmology

In addition to methods of legitimation continued from the reign of his father, Assurbanipal also returns to the more specific use of language of cosmic battle against chaos which characterised Esarhaddon's predecessors. This language did not, however, persist uniformly throughout Assurbanipal's reign. Rather, the type of language used of Assurbanipal's campaigns turns on the occasion of the war against his brother Šamaš-šuma-ukîn, who had been named Esarhaddon's successor in Babylon.[95] Almost all of the traditional types of allusions to cosmic conflict and references to Marduk (other than in exhaustive deity lists) appear in reports of events which occurred prior to this civil war.[96] During and afterwards cosmic language is absent and Marduk – whose appearances had already been sporadic – almost completely vanishes from the inscriptions.[97] The sole exception to this rule is discussed below.

8.3.2.1. Egypt

Prior to this watershed event, however, Assurbanipal undertook a number of other campaigns, about which we have varying degrees of detail. The first campaign was that to Egypt, and the reports of acts engaged upon on this campaign are essentially in keeping with the activities reported of his predecessor. The same generalised infliction of punishment for lack of subordination to Assyrian dominance, which began in the reign of Sennacherib and continued under Esarhaddon, is also attested in this campaign. Thus, in the case of the Egyptian allies of Taharqa,

---

95 Esarhaddon, despite boasting of having unified Assyria and Babylon under his one authority, redivided the two kingdoms between his sons, the older, Šamaš-šuma-ukîn, having Babylonia and the younger, Assurbanipal, Assyria. As Assurbanipal treated Šamaš-šuma-ukîn as a vassal, in 652 Šamaš-šum-ukîn rebelled, allied with the Elamites, Aramaeans and Chaldeans.

96 There is unfortunately some difficulty in determining the chronological sequence of Assurbanipal's military excursions due to the non-chronological arrangement of his historical inscriptions and the erratic inclusion of some episodes.

97 There is one reference to a "net" (*saparu*) in the description of the fall of Babylon, but it is explicitly described as the net of all the great gods, in what seems to be an attempt to diffuse its association with Marduk: "the net of the great gods, my lords, which cannot be eluded, brought them low" (R. Borger, *Beiträge zum Inschriftenwerk Assurbanipals* [Weisbaden: Harrassowitz, 1996], A iv 61-62; *ARAB,* §794 [*sa-par* dingir-meš gal-meš en-meš-*ia šá la na-par-šu-di is-ḫu-up-šú-nu-ti*]).

> the people of Sais, Pintiti, Si'nu and the rest of the cities, as many as had joined with them in plotting evil, they [the Assyrian troops] struck down with the sword, both great and small,–not a man among them escaped.[98]

That the motivation for Assurbanipal's treatment of the captured was, at least in part, the previously observed rationale of deterring future rebellions is indicated by the type of punitive measures employed: "their corpses they hung on stakes: they stripped off their skins and covered the city wall with them."[99] However, there is also a shift: those flayed cannot be the rebellious kings, as these are deported to Nineveh, which leaves only other leadership figures or members of the general population. Given the rationale for the deportation of enemy leaders to Nineveh, discussed above with regard to the practices of Esarhaddon and in further detail below, it seems that here Assurbanipal's practices have combined the old desire to deter future rebellion with his present concern to demonstrate his authority at home. That the latter has not yet reached its climax is suggested by the absence of any explicit indication that the kings were exploited in Nineveh as evidence of Assurbanipal's power.

8.3.2.2. Teumman and the Elamites

These were relatively ordinary campaigns, but there are two major military episodes which dominate the inscriptions and other material from Assurbanipal's reign.[100] The first of these is commonly referred to as Assurbanipal's war against the Elamites. The altercation commenced as a result of the invasion of Babylonia in 664 by the Elamite king Urtak, at the instigation of the leader of the Gambulu tribe, the governor of Nippur and one of Urtak's own officials. Despite the significant threat which an Elamite Babylonia would have posed to Assyrian dominance in the region, there appears to have been no immediate reaction on the part of Assurbanipal, perhaps because he was in Egypt on campaign at the time. Eventually Assyrian troops moved south, but the Elamites appear to have beaten a hasty retreat, and the incident reached a short-term resolution with the deaths of all of the major op-

---

98 Borger, *Assurbanipals*, A i 134-A ii 2; *ARAB*, §773 (un-meš ^{uru}*sa-a-a* ^{uru}*pi-in-d/ṭi-d/ṭi* ^{uru}*ṣi-i'-nu ù si-it-ti* uru-meš *ma-{la it-ti-šú-nu šak-nu} ik-pu-du* ḫul-*tú* tur *u* gal *ina* ^{giš}tukul-meš *ú-šam-qí-{tu e-du a-me-lu la} e-zi-bu ina* šá-*bi*).

99 Borger, *Assurbanipals*, A ii 3-4; *ARAB*, §§773, 844 (Adda-meš-*šú-nu iš-ḫu-ṭu ú-{ḫal-li}-pu* bàd uru).

100 For a detailed account of the following, see G. Frame, *Babylonia 689-627 B.C.: A Political History* (Istanbul: Nederlands Historisch-Archaeologisch Instituut, 1992).

position players within the course of the year (for none of which Assurbanipal claims credit). Eventually Assurbanipal's troops moved against the Gambulu, but this does not seem to have occurred until after the defeat of Teumman.

After the death of Urtak, one of the thrones of Elam had been taken by one Teumman (Elamite Tepti-Ḫumban-Inšušinak). Though apparently of the royal house, Teumman was not the heir apparent, and two of Urtak's sons fled to Assyria hoping to obtain Assurbanipal's assistance in overthrowing him. With Teumman demanding their extradition, Assurbanipal decided to use the sons to his own advantage: he moved against Teumman and put his rivals on the thrones of Elam as vassal kings. The key trigger for Assurbanipal's attack, however, was Teumman's apparent intent to attack Assyria, aiming at Nineveh in particular.[101] It is unclear whether Teumman's troops ever actually left Elam, but Assurbanipal pursued him as far as Susa and ultimately defeated him at the Ulai river, where he inflicted a bloody defeat.

Given that the sons – despite the almost certain imposition of loyalty oaths, either at this time or previously – were the descendants of one of Assurbanipal's own enemies, and that they then hardly submitted to Assurbanipal for a year before allying with his brother, Šamaš-šuma-ukîn, in rebellion, it seems clear that neither a humanitarian concern with their pleas for assistance nor a confidence in their loyalty were the motivating factor behind Assurbanipal's movement against Elam. Rather it was the direct threat posed by Teumman to Assurbanipal (real or perceived) which provoked Assurbanipal to formulate a response.

Though Teumman does not appear to have ever actually attacked Assyria, the ideological (as well as political, if theoretical) threat that he posed to the Assyrian heartland – the *māt Aššur* – was of a level not paralleled since Tiglath-pileser had begun the imperial project nearly a century earlier. By threatening the heartland itself, Teumman merited the most extreme identification with the forces of chaos: likening to a *gallû*-demon.[102]

It is in fact in the wars with the Elamites, and with Teumman in particular, that the majority of Assurbanipal's cosmic language appears. Thus in the Rassam prism Assurbanipal claims that "like the onset of a terrible hurricane I covered Elam in its entirety. I cut off the

---

101 This is according to one of Assurbanipal's own inscriptions; whether or not Teumman actually intended to invade Assyria, Assurbanipal evidently thought he did (see, e.g., SAA 3 31).

102 Borger, *Assurbanipals*, B iv 72-76 (bala-*e* lugal-*ti-šu iš-ki-pu be-lut* kur elam-ma[ki] *ú-šal-qu-u šá-nam-ma ar-ka* [I]*te-um-man tam-šil* gal$_5$-lá *ú-šib ina* [giš]gu-za [I]*ur-ta-ki*).

head of Teumman their king, the haughty one who plotted evil".[103] In (probably) the same campaign there is perhaps also a vague flood allusion in the description of the defeat of the Gambulu in the south: "I devastated, I destroyed, I laid waste by flooding it (*lit.* with water)".[104] An unusually generalised reference appears in a dedicatory inscription to the god Nergal, who is "lord of the storm": the inscription's report on Elam, similarly to those of the Rassam and B prisms, declares that "even more than before I laid it waste like a flood".[105]

Probably the most unusual allusion occurs in the Prism B report of the war, in which language familiar from *Enūma eliš* appears in reference to Ištar instead of Marduk. In his prayer to her, Assurbanipal pleas: "O hero of the gods, rip him open in the heat of battle like an encumbrance; let loose upon him a tempest, an evil wind".[106] The section culminates with a loose quotation from *Enūma eliš*, again with Ištar as agent rather than Marduk: "against Teumman king of Elam, against whom she was enraged, she turned her face".[107] While we have no evidence of a comprehensive literary attempt by Assurbanipal to revise *Enūma eliš* in favour of Ištar, it does seem that he was trying to merge the traditional cosmological legitimation of war with his and his father's special affinities for legitimation through divination and through Ištar in particular.[108]

The heightened rhetoric of cosmological opposition between chaos as represented by Teumman and order as represented by Assurbanipal correlated, unsurprisingly, to equally heightened extremity in Assurbanipal's campaign against Elam. Teumman's head was cut off and publicly displayed:

---

103 Borger, *Assurbanipals*, A iii 34-37; *ARAB*, §787 (*ki-ma ti-ib me-ḫe-e ez-zi ak-tu-um* kur elam-ma[ki] *a-na si-ḫir-ti-šá ak-kis* sag-du [I]*te-um-man* lugal-*šú-nu mul-tar-ḫu šá ik-pu-da* ḫul-*tu*).

104 Borger, *Assurbanipals*, A iii 69; *ARAB*, §788 (*ap-pul aq-qur ina* a-meš *uš-ḫar-miṭ*), cf. Borger, *Assurbanipals*, B vi 43; *ARAB*, §865.

105 Borger, *Assurbanipals*, 82:2; *ARAB*, §922 (*be-el a-bu-bi*); Borger, *Assurbanipals*, 84:56; *ARAB*, §926 (ugu *šá maḫ-ri a-bu-ba-niš as-pu-un*). The inscription is unfortunately quite fragmentary, making it impossible to determine whether further similar references were originally contained within it.

106 Borger, *Assurbanipals*, B v 44-46; *ARAB*, §859 (*at-ti qa-rit-ti* dingir-meš gim gun *ina qabal tam-ḫa-ri pu-uṭ-ṭi-ri-šú-ma di-kiš-šú me-ḫu-u* im *lem-nu*).

107 Borger, *Assurbanipals*, B v 75-76; *ARAB*, §862 (*e-li* [I]*te-um-man* lugal kur elam-ma[ki] *ša ug-gu-ga-at pa-nu-uš-šá taš-kun*), cf. En.el. IV 60.

108 Perhaps also related to this are the multiple references to a *bīt akītu* belonging to Ištar and the hints of cosmological language attributed to Ištar in an inscription found at her temple (*ra-ki-pat* ud-meš, *sa-par-šá šu-par-ru-ru a-a-bi šu-nu-*[*u*]*l-lu*) (*ARAB*, §§982-984; Borger, *Assurbanipals*, IIT 8-9).

> the head of Teumman, king of Elam, I hung on the neck of Dunanu. With the Elamite captives, the booty of Gambulu, which at the command of Aššur my hands had captured, with singers and music I entered Nineveh amidst rejoicing...The severed head of Teumman I displayed conspicuously in front of the gate inside Nineveh, that the severed head of Teumman, king of Elam, might show the people the might of Aššur and Ištar, my lords.[109]

The head is prominent in the reliefs, exhibited at a banquet attended by Assurbanipal and his queen and subjected to numerous other indignities, including being waved around from atop a chariot.[110] A similarly public humiliation is reflected in explicit description of Elamite captives as having their lips pierced and having been taken "to Assyria as a spectacle for the people of my land."[111] The Elamites' allies were similarly subject to extreme treatment:

> Mannu-ki-ahê, Dunanu's representative, and Nabû-usalli, the Gambulu's city overseer, who had spoken great disrespect against my gods: in Arbela I tore out their tongues and flayed them. Dunanu they laid upon a skinning-table in Nineveh and slaughtered him like a lamb. The other brothers of Dunanu and of Aplāia, I slew. I cut off their flesh and it was carried about for viewing by all lands.[112]

Even the Gambulu ancestors were deported; captives were forced to crush the bones publicly.[113] These same scenes also appear in the reliefs added by Assurbanipal to Sennacherib's palace at Kouyunjik.[114] Mirroring the reports found in the inscriptions, the onlookers are almost en-

---

109 Borger, *Assurbanipals*, B vi 50-56, 66-69; *ARAB*, §§865-866 (sag-du ^{I}*te-um-man* lugal kur elam-ma^{ki} *ina* gú ^{I}*du-na-nu a-lul it-ti- ki-šit-ti* kur elam-ma^{ki} *šal-la-at* kur *gam-bu-li ša ina qí-bit* an-šár *ik-šu-da* šu-min-*a-a it-ti* ^{lú}nar-meš *e-piš nin-gu-ti a-na* nina^{ki} *e-ru-ub ina* ḫúl-meš ... *ni-kis* sag-du ^{I}*te-um-man ina* gaba(*irat*) abul murub$_4$ uru *ša* nina^{ki} *ú-maḫ-ḫi-ra maḫ-ḫu-riš áš-šú da-na-an* an-šár *u* ^{dingir}XV en-meš-*ia* un-meš *kul-lu-me ni-kis* sag-du ^{I}*te-um-man* lugal kur elam-ma^{ki}).

110 Curtis and Reade, Nos. 20-22; R.D. Barnett, *Sculptures from the North Palace of Ashurbanipal at Nineveh (668-627 B.C.)* (London: British Museum, 1976), Pls. LXIII, LXIV, LXV.

111 Borger, *Assurbanipals*, A iv 135-137; *ARAB*, §800 (sag-du-meš-*šú-nu ak-kis* nundum$^{!}$-meš-*šú-nu ap-ru-u' a-na ta-mar-ti* un-meš kur-*ia al-qa-a a-na* kur an-šár^{ki}).

112 Borger, *Assurbanipals*, B vi 83-92; *ARAB*, §866 (*ša* ^{I}*man-nu-ki*-pap-meš ^{lú}min(*šanû*)-*u* ^{I}*du-na-nu ù* $^{I-dingir}$muati ^{lú}*šá* ugu(*muḫḫi*) uru(*āli*) kur *gam-bu-li ša* ugu dingir-meš-*ia iq-bu-u šil-la-tu* gal-*tú qé-reb* ^{uru}límmu-dingir eme-*šú-un áš-lu-up áš-ḫu-uṭ* kuš-*šú-un* ^{I}*du-na-nu qé-reb* nina^{ki} ugu ^{giš}*ma-ka-a-ṣi id-du-šú-ma iṭ-bu-ḫu-uš as-liš si-it-ti* šeš-meš-*šú ša* ^{I}*du-na-nu ù* ^{I}ibila(*apla*)-*a-a a-ni-ir* uzu-meš-*šú-nu ú-nak-kis ú-še-bil a-na ta-mar-ti ma-ti-an*). Aimu, brother and supporter of the enemy Abiate', was also taken to Assyria and flayed (*ARAB*, §831).

113 *ARAB*, §866. This scene is also depicted in the reliefs (Layard II, Pl. 45; Curtis and Reade, No. 21).

114 Layard II, Pl. 47.

tirely Assyrian soldiers: unlike similar scenes in earlier reigns, there are no other prisoners or deportees in the immediate vicinity.

As we already saw under Esarhaddon, the fact that the head of Teumman and the bodies of his supporters were brought home to Assyria for display to an Assyrian audience indicates that the old context of the more extreme military acts – to warn local populations of the consequences of resistance to Assyrian hegemony – has shifted to one in which the object is to reiterate to the native population the legitimacy of the king's rule. The direct threat which Teumman posed to Assurbanipal's authority makes this particularly likely.

As for the general population, Assurbanipal appears to have continued the general application of punitive measures begun under Sennacherib and continued under Esarhaddon. Thus "the people dwelling therein, who had not come forth and had not greeted my majesty, I slew. Their heads I cut off."[115] Various merisms emphasising totality are used to describe the Elamites carried off to Assyria, reiterating the completeness of the Elamites' submission to Assyrian authority.

That the use of cosmological allusions to legitimate the treatment of the enemy in warfare was already starting to show signs of weakening, however, is evident from the extent to which Assurbanipal also employs other legitimation tactics, including epigraphs inscribed on the palace reliefs depicting the campaign and references to divine imperatives conveyed through dreams and divination. One epigraph to the relief just mentioned explains that this treatment was the fulfilment of a prophecy:

> I, Assurbanipal, king of Assyria, put the head of Teumman king of Elam before the gate of the city centre in public. As from ancient times by prophecy was proclaimed "The heads of your enemies you will cut off, wine you will pour over them..." Šamaš and Adad have [fulfilled this] in my time: ... the heads of my enemies I have cut off, wine I have poured...[116]

The extremity of the treatment was also legitimated through direct appeal to divine authorisation: Teumman's head was cut off "at Aššur's

115 Borger, *Assurbanipals*, A iv 133-134; *ARAB*, §800 (un-meš *a-šib* šà-*bi-šú šá la ú-ṣu-ú-nim-ma la iš-'a-a-lu šu-lum* lugal-*ti-ia a-nir*). The gravity of these treatments is appreciated when it is also understood that the deprivation of burial and its attendant offerings denied the dead peace after death.

116 E.F. Weidner, "Assyrische Beschreibungen der Kriegs-Reliefs Aššurbânipalis", *AfO* 8 (1932-1933): 180-181 (a-na-ku ^{I} ^{d}aššur-bân-apli šar ^{mât}aš-šur^{ki} qaqqad ^{I}te-um-man [šar] ^{mât}elamti^{ki} ina tarṣi abul qabal âli muḫ-ḫu-riš u-[maḫ]-ḫir ša ul-tu ul-la ina ba-ru-ti qa-bu-u um-ma [qaqqad]ê^{meš} ^{amêl}nakirê^{meš}-ka ta-na-[kis] karânê^{meš} [elî-š]u-nu ta-naq-qi ša ..[................] e-nin-[na ^{d}šama]š u ^{d}adad ina *tarṣi*-ja ..[............] qaqqadê^{meš} [^{amêl}nakirê^{m}]^{eš}-ja ak-^{ki}kis karâna aq-qa [................]).

order".[117] Divinatory assurances also played a role in his treatment of the general Elamite opposition; having been encouraged by "good omens, dreams, speech omens and prophetic messages",

> with their bodies I [Assurbanipal] blocked up the Ulai river. With their corpses, as if with thorn and thistle, I filled the environs of Susa. On the command of Aššur I cut off the head of Teumman, the king of Elam, before his assembled troops.[118]

Further techniques include Assurbanipal's description of Teumman's military activities in language designed to identify Assyria, and Assurbanipal specifically, as innocents under attack; in describing his appeal to Ištar, he draws a connection between his worship of the goddess and the injustice of Teumman's assault, more or less explicitly articulating an idea of military defeat as divine punishment, and claiming that as he has not ignored the goddess then he is unfairly attacked.[119]

Given the relative scarcity of cosmic allusions – more extensive than under Esarhaddon but still less pervasive than among his predecessors – one gains the impression that such appeals to other indicators of divine favour were brought in to fill the shortfall between the legitimacy accorded by cosmic identification with the god at creation and reality.

The likely culprit behind the waning strength of cosmological allusions as a means of legitimation is the association of Marduk with Babylon, and of Babylon inevitably with Assurbanipal's brother, Šamaš-šuma-ukîn. We will examine the effects of this sibling relationship on Assyrian military practices in further detail momentarily, but with Marduk associated with Šamaš-šuma-ukîn, his usefulness as a means of identifying Assurbanipal's wars with Marduk's at creation seems to have been problematised. Already we have seen some evidence to suggest that Assurbanipal was attempting to shift the associations of Marduk over to the goddess Ištar. Corroborating this shift is the unprecedented report that Teumman and his family were brought before "Mullissu and the Lady of [Arbela]".[120] To claim that this reflects some sort of sacrificial notion behind Teumman's execution specifically

117 Borger, *Assurbanipals*, A v 7; *ARAB*, §801 (*ina na-áš-par-ti* an-šár).

118 Borger, *Assurbanipals*, B v 95-vi 3; *ARAB*, §863 (*ina* giškim-meš sig$_5$-meš máš-gi$_6$ inim-gar *ši-pir maḫ-ḫe-e* ... *ina* adda-meš-*šú-nu* íd *ú-la-a-a as-ki-ir šal-ma-a-ti-šú-nu ki-ma* ^{giš}dìḫ *u* ^{giš}kiši$_{16}$ *ú-ma-al-la-a ta-mir-ti* ^{uru}*šu-šá-an* sag-du ^{I}*te-um-man* lugal kur elam-ma^{ki} *ina qí-bit* an-šár *u* ^{dingir}amar-utu dingir-meš gal-meš en-meš-*ia* kud-*is ina* ukkin erim-ḫi-a-*šú*), cf. e.g., SAA 10 168.

119 SAA 3 31.

120 SAA 3 31:9 ([*ina* IGI ^{d}]NIN.LÍL *u* ^{d}GAŠAN-UR[U.*arbalìl*). The text is unfortunately very fragmentary.

or the execution of prisoners generally would surely be beyond the evidence, but it does emphasise Assurbanipal's shifting focus of military legitimation.

8.3.2.3. Šamaš-šuma-ukîn and the Babylonian rebellion

The second major event in the reign of Assurbanipal was the rebellion led by his older brother, Šamaš-šuma-ukîn, who had been designated by their father to be king over Babylonia as Assurbanipal was king over Assyria. The precise nature of the relationship Esarhaddon had intended between the two brothers and their respective kingdoms is unclear, but it is evident that in practice Assurbanipal was the dominant partner, with Šamaš-šuma-ukîn and Babylonia in the role of vassal king and kingdom respectively – albeit an arrangement preserving the traditional favoured status of Babylonia as a centre of learning and culture.

It is clear also that the status of Assurbanipal, the younger brother, as the ruler of Assyria was not the most natural of selections; that there were rumblings of dissent from the beginning of his reign is indicated by the oath of allegiance imposed on Šamaš-šuma-ukîn and others shortly after Assurbanipal's accession. Though the first decade and a half of Assurbanipal's reign record no trouble in Babylonia, then, Assurbanipal – like his father – seems to have been acutely aware of the dangers inherent to his situation. Perhaps it is for this reason that he appears to have maintained such a high level of personal involvement in Babylonian affairs, with officials nominally under Šamaš-šuma-ukîn reporting directly to Assurbanipal.[121]

Given the role of the creation mythology in legitimating royal military endeavours, and the traditional role of Marduk in the Mesopotamian cosmology (despite Sennacherib's apparent attempts to write Aššur into this role), the return of a (the) statue of Marduk to Babylon – it is unclear whether this statue was the same as the one removed by Sennacherib – in concert with the accession of Šamaš-šuma-ukîn would have exacerbated the difficulty attendant on Assurbanipal's situation, and it is probably not coincidental that at the same time that Assurbanipal was enquiring about the return of Marduk he was also enquiring as to whether the gods approved of the accession of Šamaš-šuma-ukîn to the Babylonian throne.[122]

121 See Frame, 107-114.
122 See Frame, 104.

Assurbanipal's concerns were in due course justified, when Šamaš-šuma-ukîn rebelled early in 652. Since Šamaš-šum-ukîn, the older brother, presented the first and foremost threat to Assurbanipal's legitimacy as king of Assyria, it is no surprise that it is the allies of his brother in Babylon which Assurbanipal subjects to his most extreme treatments:

> I did not give his [Nabû-bēl-šumati's] body to be buried. I made him more dead than he was before. I cut off his head and hung it on the neck of Nabû-qātī-ṣabat the *simmagir* of Šamaš-šuma-ukîn, the hostile brother, who had gone with him to rouse Elam to hostility.[123]

This particular sub-narrative of the Šamaš-šuma-ukîn revolt is one of the better-documented sequences of military events in the reign of Assurbanipal. Nabû-bel-šumati was a leader of the Chaldean tribe of Bit-Yakin, and probably governor of the Sealand before joining the revolt. He was also the grandson of Marduk-apla-iddina, who had given both Sennacherib and Esarhaddon so much trouble. Ultimately he betrayed his alliance with Assyria to become an ally of Šamaš-šuma-ukîn, joining the rebellion by 651 at the latest (if not having been one of its instigators). He was particularly involved in recruiting the Elamites to join the Šamaš-šuma-ukîn rebellion, and Nabû-bel-šumati took refuge there when Assurbanipal sent a new governor, Bel-ibni, to the Sealand. One of the letters which describes the Assyrians' efforts to hunt him down, after the main revolt had been quelled, reports that the approach of Assyrian troops "spread panic, like a pestilence", and provoked plans for the "every sort of destruction", apparently expected from the advancing Assyrian troops.[124] The army's attack on Elam fulfilled these expectations; speaking to his Bel-ibni and the Nippureans, Assurbanipal recalls the attack as follows:

> you know that, with the aid of the iron dagger of Ashur, my deity, you consumed that whole country with fire and when you withdrew, (that) country, being downtrodden, turned back its countenance to me.[125]

---

123 Borger, *Assurbanipals,* A vii 39-50; *ARAB,* §815 (adda-*šú a-a-din a-na qé-bé-ri* ugu *šá maḫ-ri mi-tu-us-su ut-tir-ma* sag-du-*su ak-kis ina* gú $^{\text{I-dingir}}$muati-šu-min-*ṣa-bat* $^{\text{lú-dingir}}$*sin-ma-gir* $^{\text{I-dingir}}$giš-nu$_{11}$-mu-gi-na šeš *nak-ri šá it-ti-šú a-na šum-ku-ri* kur elam-ma^{ki} *il-li-ku a-lul*). Elam, under a series of different kings, was again taking the anti-Assyrian part.

124 Pfeiffer, §32:9-11 (*la-pa-an* ^{amêlu}*e-mu-qu šá bêl šarrâni*^{pl} *bêli-ia ki-ma ṭi-e pu-luḫ-ti ul-te-ri-bu mimma šá ḫa-pi-e gab-bi-šú-nu i-dib-bu-bu*).

125 Pfeiffer, §35:5-9 (*at-tu-nu ti-da-a šá ina libbi paṭri parzilli šá* ^{ilu}*ašur ilâni*^{pl}*-e-a mâti ul-li-ti gab-bi šá i-šá-a-tu tu-šá-ki-la u mâti ki-i taḫ-ḫi-sa ta-at-tak-ba-as u pa-ni-šá ana muḫḫi*^{ki}*-iá tu-ut-tir-ra*).

The cause and effect relationship perceived by the Assyrian king between such treatment and a positive imperial outcome would have encouraged him to pursue such policies, and particularly when the royal military ideology correlated them with divine involvement.

Assurbanipal's attacks on Elam were, however, according to Assurbanipal entirely due to Nabû-bel-šumati's presence in their midst; had they given him up he would have left them alone. He reiterates the point twice: "(It is) on account of Nabû-bēl-šumati, Nabû-kātī-ṣabat, and Kiribtu that you have been treated like this" and "[I swe]ar by [Aššur and my gods] that it is because of [Nabû-bēl-šumati and the of]fenders who are with him that you have been treated like this."[126] Interestingly, however, immediate execution is not ordered for Nabû-bēl-šumati. Though anyone who brings him in or kills him will be rewarded with his (Nabû-bēl-šumati's) weight in gold, the instructions are to capture rather than kill him. Execution would almost certainly have been his ultimate fate, but it seems that Assurbanipal wanted the man alive first – perhaps to facilitate his employment as a public spectacle for those in Nineveh who doubted Assurbanipal's authority. As it turned out, Nabû-bel-šumati eventually committed suicide-by-proxy – but his body was nonetheless sent to and mutilated by Assurbanipal (above). Assurbanipal was thus deprived of the actual execution but not of the exhibition of power which was such a key part of his treatment of the enemy. Nabû-bēl-šumati's associates were killed, as expected.

By that point, however, Elam had sided too persistently against Assurbanipal and Assyria. When it finally succumbed, its successive kings Ummanaldaš, Tammarītu and Pa'e joined the many others subjected to public humiliation in Nineveh, being forced to draw Assurbanipal's royal coach as far as the gate of the city's temple.[127] Another ally of Šamaš-šuma-ukîn, Uaite' (the leader of one of the Arab tribes to the west), suffered still more for his allegiances:

> as I raised my hands, which Aššur and Mullissu had given me for the conquest of my foes, when my hands seized the *ḫutnû* of a *mašīru*-wagon, I pierced his chin. Through his jaw I passed a lead rope, put a dog chain

126 M.W. Waters, "A letter from Ashurbanipal to the elders of Elam (BM 132980)", *JCS* 54 (2002): 82 (*ina* UGU ^{md}PA.EN.MU.MEŠ ^{md}PA.ŠU^{II}-*ṣa-bat* ^{m}*ki-rib-tú ki-i ḫa-an-ni-i ep-šá-ku-nu* ... ⸢*an-ni-i*⸣ *ep-šá-a-*[*ni*] *ina* ⸢ŠÀ⸣ [*áš-šur* DINGIR.MEŠ-*iá at-t*]*a-ma šum-ma la ina* U[G]U ^{md}[PA.EN.MU.MEŠ *u* ^{LÚ}E]N-*ḫi-iṭ-ṭi šá is-si-šú k-i* ⸢*ḫa*⸣-[*an-n*]*i-e*$^{!}$ *ep-šá-ka-nu-ni*).

127 *ARAB*, §833.

> upon him and made him guard a kennel of the east gate of the inner (wall) of Nineveh.[128]

And yet: "that he might extol the glory of Aššur, Ištar and the great gods, my lords, I took pity on him and spared his life".[129] A similar fate befell Ammu-ladi, king of the Arab tribe of Qedar.[130]

As for the Babylonians themselves, it is hardly surprising that they too were subject to extreme punitive measures. The fate of Šamaš-šuma-ukîn himself is unclear. He seems to have died in a fire, which would explain why Assurbanipal's inscriptions never report mutilating his body. Despite the inscriptions' version of events, however, the response of Aššur to Assurbanipal's report on the revolt seems to indicate that Šamaš-šuma-ukîn was confined "in harsh imprisonment and bound... I [Aššur] placed lead ropes on his magnates and [lead] them to [*your*] presence."[131]

As for his troops –

> as for those men of slanderous mouth, who uttered slander against Aššur, my god, and plotted evil against me, the prince who fears him, I cut their mouths and brought them low.[132]

---

128 Borger, *Assurbanipals*, A ix 103-109; *ARAB*, §829 (*ina ni-iš* šu-min-*ia šá a-na ka-šad* ^{lú}kúr-meš-*ia am-da-ḫa-ru* an-šár *u* ^{dingir}nin-líl *ina* ^{giš}*ḫu-ut-né-e* ^{giš}*ma-še-ri ṣi-bit* šu-min-*ia* ^{uzu}me-zé-*šú ap-lu-uš ina la-aḫ-ši-šú at-ta-di ṣer-re-tú ul-li* ur-gi$_7$ *ad-di-šú-ma ina* abul *ṣi-it* ^{dingir}utu-*ši šá* murub$_4$ uru nina^{ki}).

129 Borger, *Assurbanipals*, A ix 112-114; *ARAB*, §829 (*a-na da-lál ta-nit-ti* an-šár ^{dingir}XV ù dingir-meš gal-meš en-meš-*ia re-e-mu ar-ši-šú-ma ú-bal-liṭ nap-šat-su*). This may have been the second time this ally, Uaite', had fallen into Assurbanipal's hands; previously, "to make known the majesty of Aššur and the great gods, my lords, I laid on him a heavy penalty. I put him into a kennel. With jackals(?) and dogs I tied him up and made him guard the gate, in Nineveh" (Borger, *Assurbanipals*, A viii 8-13; *ARAB*, §814; *a-na kul-lum ta-nit-ti* an-šár *ù* dingir-meš gal-meš en-meš-*ia an-nu kab-tu e-mid-su-ma* ^{giš}*ši-ga-ru áš-kun-šu-ma it-ti a-si* ur-gi$_7$ *ar-ku-us-šú-ma ù-šá-an-ṣir-šú* abul murub$_4$ uru nina^{ki}). Given the erratic chronology of the Assurbanipal inscriptions and the similarity of the accounts, however, these may merely be two versions of the same event.

130 This is "at the command of the great gods" (Borger, *Assurbanipals*, A viii 27; *ARAB*, §820; *ina qí-bit* dingir-meš gal-meš).

131 SAA 3 44:9-10 (*ina me-si-ri dan-ni e-si-ir-šú-ma ar-ku-us x*[*x x x*]*x* ⸢*x x*⸣[*x x*]⸢*x*⸣ *-ti* [L]Ú.GAL.MEŠ-*šú ṣir-re-e-ti áš-kun*$^{!}$*-ma a-na* IGI-[*ka ú-šar-di-šú-n*]*u-ti*). The highly fragmentary nature of the text makes its use as a reliable historical source problematic.

132 Borger, *Assurbanipals*, A iv 66-69; *ARAB*, §795 (^{lú}erim-meš *šá-a-tú-nu šil-la-tú pi-i-šú-nu šá ina* ugu an-šar dingir-*ia šil-la-tú iq-bu-u ù i-a-ti* nun *pa-liḫ-šú ik-pu-du-u-ni* ḫul-*tú pi-i-šú-nu áš-lu-uq* bad$_5$-bad$_5$-*šú-nu áš-kun*). In his treatment of the Babylonians Assurbanipal seems to have distinguished among "those men of slanderous mouth", whose mouths were cut, "the rest of the people", who were killed, and "the rest of the inhabitants of Babylon, Kutha and Sippar", but it is difficult to tell whether the

The report to Aššur recounts of the warriors that "the rest you [Assurbanipal] [handed over] to me [Aššur] alive and (later) slew with weapons in Nineveh, city of your lordship".[133] Again, the interest is in the use of the defeated to demonstrate the authority and legitimacy of Assurbanipal to his own subjects at home, rather than merely to deter any future rebellions by making an example of them on-site.

8.3.2.4. The final campaign

After the episodes against Elam and Šamaš-šuma-ukîn, Assurbanipal conducted one final major campaign to the west, which most scholars describe as an expedition aimed at punishing those who had supported the Šamaš-šuma-ukîn revolt. However, the campaign records mention alliances to Šamaš-šuma-ukîn specifically for some of these opponents and not for others, and the treatments meted out vary according to whether or not such an alliance is mentioned. Given the discrepancy between Assurbanipal's approach to the latter opponents in this campaign and his treatment of the supporters of Šamaš-šuma-ukîn in Mesopotamia (see above), it seems more likely that the campaign was also intended to deal with the rebellious vassals who had taken advantage of Assurbanipal's preoccupations in Mesopotamia, rather than only those who had actively supported Šamaš-šuma-ukîn.[134] Thus the

---

text is simply describing the same people multiple ways or if in fact some kind of distinction in culpability and consequent punishment was being made (Borger, *Assurbanipals*, A iv 70-75; *ARAB*, §795 [*si-it-ti* un-meš *bal-ṭu-sún ina* ^{dingir}alad ^{dingir}lamma *ša* $^{\text{I-dingir}}$*sin*-pap-meš-su ad ad dù-*ia* šà-*bi is-pu-nu e-nen-na a-na-ku ina ki-is-pi-šú* un-meš *šá-a-tu-nu ina* šà-*bi as-pu-un* uzu-meš-*šú-nu nu-uk-ku-su-u-ti ú-šá-kil* ur-gi$_{7}$-meš šaḫ-meš *zi-i-bi*; "the rest of the people, alive, by the *šēdu*-god and *lamassu*-goddess (?), between which they had cut down Sennacherib, the father of the father who begot me, at that time, I cut down those people there as a funerary offering. Their dismembered flesh I fed to the dogs, swine, wolves, and eagles, to the birds of heaven and the fish of the deep"]; Borger, *Assurbanipals*, A iv 92-95; *ARAB*, §797 [*si-it-ti* dumu-meš ká-dingir-ra^{ki} gú-du$_{8}$-a^{ki} zimbir^{ki} *ša ina šib-ṭi šag-gaš-ti ù né-eb-re-e-ti i-še-tu-u-ni re-e-mu ar-ši-šú-nu-ti ba-laṭ na-piš-ti-šú-nu aq-bi*; "on the rest of the inhabitants of Babylon, Kutha and Sippar, who had escaped the slaughter, carnage and famine, I took pity and ordered their lives to be spared"]). Particularly troublesome is that the clearly rebellious men have their tongues slit whereas at least part of a more general population is killed: punishments which would seem to be contrary to proportional expectations. In light of the statement in the *Letter to Aššur*, it seems most likely that the first group were taken to Nineveh and killed there.

133 SAA 3 44:24-25 ([*si -i*]*t-tu-ti bal-ṭú-su-un ina* ŠU.2-*ia t*[*am-nu*] *qí-rib* NINA.KI URU EN-*ú-ti-ka ina* GI[Š.TUK]UL.MEŠ *ta-nir-šú-nu-ti*).

134 See Frame, 133, 136, 208. The post-revolt campaigns, one to the west (discussed here) and one to Elam (see below), are distinguishable by the treatments meted out, which

people of Uššu, who had not paid tribute, and the people of Akku (Acre), who did not submit, were killed.[135] There is no mention of alliances with Šamaš-šuma-ukîn in reference to these enemies.[136] The corpses of the people of Acre were also hung on stakes around the city walls, in full view of its citizens and potential rebels.[137] Again, though expressed in violent language, the parts of this campaign which are not directed at Šamaš-šuma-ukîn's allies are in keeping with the mindset of the Egyptian campaign, being aimed at ensuring the subordination of vassal states with punitive treatments aimed primarily at local audiences.

Given the reversion to something more closely approximating "normal" warfare at this point, perhaps then it is not surprising that the one last gasp of the cosmic language of warfare appears in an inscription describing Assurbanipal's encounter with Tugdammê, king of the Umman-manda (Cimmeria, in Anatolia). In an unfortunately fragmentary context, Tugdammê is described as "Tugdammê, king of the Umman-manda, offspring of Tiamat, image of ...".[138] On the basis of what is clear, most fill in the obscured section as "image of a *gallû*-demon".[139] Even without it, the equation with Tiamat and chaos is clear.

What is perhaps more significant, however, is that it is in one and only one account of the battle that this language appears, and that is in a dedicatory text to Marduk from Esagila. In all the other texts which describe either this encounter – or indeed any other encounter from after the civil war with Šamaš-šuma-ukîn – there is no hint that the king's military endeavours were still conceived as part of a great cosmic struggle for order. Though the old language seems to have been inevitable in a text written for Marduk's own temple, it has otherwise entirely disappeared. The war with Šamaš-šuma-ukîn had destroyed the synergy between the Assyrian king and Marduk for good.

---

reflect the differing purposes of the campaigns: the former to punish general rebelliousness, the latter to punish the support for Šamaš-šuma-ukîn's rebellion and all it entailed (see below).

135 Borger, *Assurbanipals*, A ix 122-128; *ARAB*, §830.

136 Part of the campaign, against the Arab tribes in particular, is specifically aimed at those who had aided Šamaš-šuma-ukîn, and the treatments meted out are reflective.

137 Borger, *Assurbanipals*, A ix 122-128; *ARAB*, §830.

138 Borger, *Assurbanipals*, 202 (20 K 120B+ 20); *ARAB*, §1001 ([I]*tug-dam-mì-i* lugal erim-*man-da tab̩-nit ti-*géme(*amti*) *tam-šil* AN [...).

139 See M. Streck for the original rationale for this (*Assurbanipal und die letzten assyrischen Könige bis zum Untergange Nineveh's*, volume 2 [Leipzig: J.C. Hinrichs, 1916], 280).

9. Developments in Judahite and Israelite ethics I

For the most part, the Israelite and Judahite sources are too sparse and too uncertain of date and provenance to allow for the close historical contextualisation we have pursued with respect to the Assyrian material. In somewhat broader terms, however, we may be able to follow the course by which the *lex talionis* and cosmological approaches were merged. The process begins with Isaiah, is furthered by Nahum and finds its eventual culmination in works of the exilic period and beyond.

9.1. Isaiah

The majority of the oracles of Isaiah of Jerusalem are too vague to allow any conclusions about Isaiah's thinking on warfare to be drawn from them. There are, however, two oracles which suggest Isaiah as the initial intermediary between the strictly royal military ideology – to which he would have been exposed in his capacity as a royal advisor – and the concepts of *lex talionis* which makes its first Hebrew Bible appearance with Amos. Given the many other links between *Isaiah* and *Amos*, it is not surprising to note that Amos' younger compatriot has also made use of his distinct line of thought with regard to warfare.

The first of these which we will examine is the oracle against Aram and Israel in Isa. 17. Bearing in mind the difficulty of dating prophetic texts, the oracle would appear to antedate the incorporation of Aram into Assyria in 732 and of Israel in 721, probably relating to the alliance of these nations against Judah in the mid-730s and thus preceding Judah's own encounter with the Assyrian army at the turn of the century.[1]

The oracle is noteworthy for our purposes primarily in its use of cosmological language in the final passage, in which Isaiah speaks of

1 On issues of dating and origins see the commentaries. The strongest objection to the Isaianic association of 17.12-14 is its questionable coherence with the overall message of Isaiah, but on this see Wildberger (*Isaiah 13-27*, translated by T.H. Trapp [Minneapolis, Minn.: Fortress, 1997], 196). Wildberger insists that Israel and Aram cannot be the peoples in question, but is then faced with the difficulty of explaining the plural if the referent is Assyria alone (197).

the destruction of Judah's oppressors.[2] There the enemy is described in language associating it with watery chaos, making noise like the noise of the sea and a roar like the roar of oceans.[3] Against these chaotic forces comes a force for order which is described in terms of storm (סופה) and wind (רוח), and whose triumph is described as rebuke (גער).[4]

In the final verse of the oracle, however, there is an intriguing suggestion of the principle of *lex talionis*, albeit as yet faint and without expansion: "This is the fate of our despoilers and the lot of our plunderers" (17.14b).[5]

This principle is employed more extensively in Isa. 10.5-19, probably composed sometime after the siege of Sennacherib against Jerusalem in 701.[6] There Yahweh bemoans the problems which ensued from the attempted employment of a foreign king for divine punitive purposes, and declares that the misdeeds of the Assyrian king warrant his destruction.[7] The mirroring of act and consequence is not as explicit or

2 There is no indication as to the presumed human agent of this destruction; the divine antecedent of the masculine singular in 17.13 is אלהי ישעך in 17.10, if that passage is original to the oracle, but Yahweh's human counterpart remains anonymous. While cosmological language seems somewhat sparse in *Isaiah* as a whole, it is interesting to note that P. Cook's recent literary analysis of *Isaiah*'s oracles against the nations has identified this oracle as among the four original Isaianic oracles (*The Redactional Development of Isaiah 18-20*, University of Oxford D.Phil. thesis, 2009). According to this analysis, the cosmological language with which this oracle culminates may well be reflective of the intellectual framework behind all four.

3 הוי המון עמים רבים כהמות ימים יהמיון ושאון לאמים כשאון מים כבירים ישאון: לאמים כשאון מים רבים ישאון (17.12-13aα; the Masoretic text has some difficulties but the sense is clear). On the phrase מים רבים as referring to chaotic waters in Yahweh's battle against the sea, see H.G. May, "Some cosmic connotations of mayim rabbîm, 'many waters'", *JBL* 74 (1955): 10. Wildberger's observation that the descriptions of Yahweh as אלהי ישע and צור מעז are most reminiscent of passages related to the ideology of kingship is intriguing; if this language is purposeful, it may suggest that Israel's condemnation is tied to its abandonment of the identification of the king with Yahweh (though note the problems in identifying the addressee of 17.10-11; Wildberger, 180; cf. O. Kaiser, *Isaiah 13-39*, OTL, translated by R.A. Wilson [London: SCM, 1974], 81-82; J.D.W. Watts, *Isaiah 1-33*, WBC 24 [Waco, Tex.: Word, 1985], 240-241).

4 On all of this language as cosmological see below; a number of commentators have observed the cosmological aspects of these verses, though it is not always recognised that they need not be late eschatological-apocalyptic as a result (see e.g., Wildberger, 193-194; 199-201; O. Kaiser, 85-89; J. Jensen, *Isaiah 1-39* [Wilmington, Del.: Michael Glazier, 1984], 161-162; B.S. Childs, *Isaiah*, OTL [London: Westminster John Knox, 2001], 137-138).

5 זה חלק שוסינו וגורל לבזזינו:

6 On issues of dating and origins see the commentaries.

7 The links between the judgment language used of Israel in Isa. 10 and the language used of Assyria in Isa. 17 are noted by O. Kaiser, and corroborate the continuity of thought here (239).

thorough as it will be in *Nahum*, but the nation which sought to utterly destroy is in its turn utterly destroyed.

Isaiah's historical moment, coming as it did at the beginning of Judah's century-long encounter with Assyrian imperialism, was particularly conducive to his assumption of the *lex talionis* idea. In 701 Judah had had its initial first-hand experience of Assyrian military might, and in the wake of the destruction wreaked by the Assyrian army on Judah and the environs of Jerusalem the desire of Isaiah and his audience to see similar destruction wrought upon the perpetrators is understandable. Given Isaiah's familiarity with Amos, it is equally unsurprising that the theme of the *lex talionis*, as applied to warfare, was adopted by him to express this desire. At the end of the Assyrian century this concept, first introduced into élite Judahite military thinking by Isaiah, would be integrated extensively and explicitly with more traditional cosmological military ideology by Nahum, responding to the pressure of an intervening hundred years of subordination to foreign domination.

9.2. Nahum

The book of *Nahum* derives from the late seventh century, near the final collapse of the Assyrian empire, to whom it is formally addressed. It is not, unlike Assyrian prophetic texts, addressed to the Judahite king directly, though his presence is suggested in Nah. 2.[8] Like most poetic texts, it emphasises the role of the deity, in particular through the use of an opening acrostic describing the wrath of Yahweh against the enemy. The language used to describe Yahweh is a clear allusion to Yahweh's battle against chaos at creation, and sets the stage for the rest of the book's description of the military overthrow of Nineveh.

9.2.1. Cosmology

The allusions to a creation myth in the book of *Nahum* were first elucidated by A. Haldar in the early part of the twentieth century. Perhaps due to his somewhat inaccessible style, only the most general aspects of his conclusions have reappeared in the work of other biblical scholars,

8 A Judahite audience is of course also implied by the fact that the prophet speaks Hebrew, not Akkadian, in Judah, not Assyria, whatever the formal addressee, as C.A. Keller notes ("Die theologische Bewältigung der geschichtlichen Wirklichkeit in der Prophetie Nahums", *VT* 22 (1972): 404).

and the nature and significance of the mythological allusions which he adduced have not been considered further. This is unfortunate, since it is by appreciating not only *Nahum*'s allusions but also their significance for the book's outlook and intent that the book may be properly understood. Though flawed, Haldar's work is an important precursor to the following analysis.

Haldar undertook his *Studies in the Book of Nahum* for the explicit purpose of rebutting the arguments of P. Humbert and P. Haupt that *Nahum* is a liturgical text designed for use in ritual celebrations. According to Haldar, *Nahum* reflects an extensive familiarity with ritual texts, while not itself being intended for use in a ritual context. He purports to support this argument by establishing the close connections between *Nahum* and various mythological traditions known from the ancient Near East, making particularly frequent reference to the Tammuz tradition of a dying and rising god, *Enūma eliš* and numerous episodes of the Ba'al cycle from Ugarit. As this broad sweep suggests, however, Haldar's work is frequently little more than a compendious catalogue of possible allusions; one gains the impression that the author of *Nahum* could no more utter a sentence than allude in it to some great myth or another. The plausibility of some of the allusions listed by Haldar is not addressed, nor is the extent to which these are supposed to cohere (or not) toward a specific purpose.[9] Haldar supposes the book to have been composed for propagandistic purposes, but makes little attempt to explain how the allusions he adduces contribute to this aim. Rather than successfully arguing against the proposals for a liturgical background to the book, Haldar's allusions seem to support them.

A significant part of Haldar's failings in this respect are due to the assumptions of his time with regard to the nature of liturgy and ritual in the ancient Near East. While the myth and ritual school led to a number of significant insights into Judahite and other ancient Near

9 One particularly expansive example occurs in Haldar's discussion of 3.17, in which soldiers are likened to locusts on a cold day: "In this connection it may be mentioned that coldness is a feature in descriptions of chaos. In Ps. 68:15, for instance, we read that when Shaddai scatters the kings in the country, snow falls on Ṣalmon, and in Tammuz liturgies as well there are passages showing the same detail. Then it is said that when the sun arises they flee to an unknown place, exactly as in Is. 17.14 it is stated that the enemies, compared to water, disappear before the morning. This phrase is apparently here used as a stylistic formula, but perhaps this expression, too, reflects a ritual detail. ...The phrase saying that the enemy will disappear when the sun rises is such a pregnant one that I think we may assume that it derives from a concrete situation having its counterpart in the ritual..." (*Studies in the Book of Nahum* [Leipzig: Otto Harrassowitz, 1947], 143-144).

Eastern religious practices – some of which have been referred to elsewhere in this study – its emphasis on ritual and cult could also obscure the underlying historical significance of a given practice, and in this instance this has certainly been the case. Thus Haldar, though providing an invaluable starting point for the articulation of the mythological background of *Nahum*, failed to appreciate the extent to which the mythological allusions in the text were connected to and had their function in a particular historical context. Excepting a final vague suggestion as to the connection between the "cultic enemy" and the "historical enemy", Haldar's interests are exclusively ritual in character.

Turning to *Nahum*, we will attempt to examine the clearest and most convincing of its mythological motifs, bearing in mind the historical background as far as possible and drawing conclusions as to Nahum's understanding of warfare accordingly.

The cosmic language with which Yahweh is described has been most widely recognised in the opening psalm. First:

> His way is in whirlwind and storm,
> and the clouds are the dust of his feet.
> He rebukes the sea and makes it dry,
> and he dries up all the rivers;
> Bashan and Carmel wither,[10]
> and the bloom of Lebanon fades.
> The mountains quake before him,
> the world and all who live in it (1.3b-5).[11]

These verses include a number of significant allusions to a cosmological outlook based on a creative battle against chaos. First, the natural phenomena of storm and whirlwind (here סוּף and שְׂעָרָה) are also often used in the context of descriptions of Yahweh's creative actions.[12] More significantly, they occur as part of the divine repertoire of tools against chaos, against wickedness and against the nations. Thus סוּף is named as part of Yahweh's ordered creation (Job 37.9), and is employed by Yahweh as a means of destroying the wicked (Job 27.20) and as a force of order against chaos (Isa. 17.13) and the nations (Isa. 29.6); in the latter example it appears in conjunction with סערה. סער/שׂער occurs as a verb between ideas of creation and divine justice (Ps. 50.3) and is used to describe the destruction of the wicked (Job 15.30; 27.21). In nominal

10 To maintain the sequence of the acrostic this line should begin with ד. BHS suggests reading דללו; other alternatives include דאר (R.L. Smith, *Micah-Malachi*, WBC 32 [Waco, Tex.: Word, 1984], 74) or דאב (Christensen, "Acrostic", 21).

11 בסופה ובשׂערה דרכו וענן אבק רגליו׃ גוער בים ויבשׁהו וכל־הנהרות החריב אמלל בשׁן וכרמל ופרח לבנון אמלל׃ הרים רעשׁו ממנו והגבעות התמגגו ותשׂא הארץ מפניו ותבל וכל־ישׁבי בה׃

12 See Chapters 3 and 5 for the use of storm (*meḫû*) and related language in *Enūma eliš*.

forms it is a manifestation of Yahweh's punitive force against the wicked (Job 9.17; Am. 1.14; Jer. 23.19; 25.32; 30.23) and appears in the context of Yahweh's control over the sea (Ps. 107.29). The convergence of the sea, the wicked and the nations as the common opponents of Yahweh in the guise of the storm is not coincidental, but indicates the extent to which these three are perceived to be various manifestations of one chaotic enemy. The use of storm language to describe how Yahweh goes up against the sea affirms the location of this language in the ideological framework of a cosmic struggle against chaos.

That *Nahum* has in mind specifically the struggle against chaos which occurred at creation (and which continues in the historical present) is indicated by the language of the next verse. As we already know, sea (ים) and river (נהר) are the cosmological manifestations of chaos. The imagery could also be that of the exodus, but the particular combination of these is more strongly reminiscent of the parallelism between River and Sea, known from the Ugaritic tradition of the god's battle against chaos.[13] Here Yahweh exerts divine authority over chaos, corralling it into an ordered creation. גער "to rebuke, roar" is a motif word in Hebrew accounts of the cosmic struggle at creation, and a correlation between rebuke and the creation conflict is reiterated by the occurrence of the idea in other ancient Near Eastern accounts of the battle for order at creation, as catalogued by Haldar: Marduk rebukes Tiamat before killing her and likewise Ba'al rebukes Yam.[14]

Yahweh's control over chaos is probably reiterated by the reference to a flood in 1.8 (which most commentators identify as the Noachic flood), especially if the correct reading is to see Yahweh's actions against the enemies of that verse as occurring through the weapon of flood – a motif which we have seen used repeatedly in the Assyrian

13 C.A. Keller and R. Vuilleumier, *Michée, Nahoum, Habacuc, Sophonie*, CAT 116, (Paris: Delachaux & Niestlé, 1971), 112. W.C. Van Wyk argues for a deliberate fusing of traditions here, comparable to Isa. 51.10 ("Allusions to 'prehistory' and history in the book of Nahum", in *De Fructu Oris Sui: Essays in Honour of Adrianus van Selms*, edited by I.H. Eybers, F.C. Fensham, D.J. Labuschagne, W.C. Van Wyk and A.H. Van Zyl, POS 9 [Leiden: Brill, 1971], 223).

14 See A.A. Macintosh, "A consideration of Hebrew גער", *VT* 19 (1969): 474-475, 477-478; also Day, *Conflict*, 29n82; Haldar, 99. Keller, surprisingly, recognises these parallels yet rejects the presence of an allusion to the creation struggle, arguing that "l'idée de combat est en fait absente" (Keller and Vuilleumier, 112n4). Day considers 1.4 to be an allusion to Yahweh's "present power over that chaotic sea within the world of nature", not to a creation conflict, though he does identify the dual motif of drying up the waters and their defeat as derived from the driving off of the chaos waters from the earth at creation (*Conflict*, 60-61). The most straightforward resolution to this apparent tension is the recognition of the ongoing aspect of Yahweh's struggle against chaos, associated elsewhere as in *Nahum* with military conflict.

inscriptions in the allusions to the *abūbu* as part of Marduk's weaponry at creation.[15] Closer to home, it parallels references to other weather phenomena as Yahweh's weapons at creation (Chapter 6). J.M. O'Brien offers a literal rendering of the verse as "in a flood overflowing an end he will make, her place, and his enemies he will pursue darkness".[16] Though undertaking a literary and therefore final form reading, O'Brien implies that the hanging מקומה may have once stood in 1.9, where "he will make an end" is repeated, and J.D.W. Watts suggests that the מקומה might refer to "the creator's great enemy who represents chaos in the creation epic" (i.e., Tiamat, Yam or equivalent), and this would then reiterate the allusion to the idea of Yahweh battling the watery chaos.[17]

In 1.12 Haldar suggested following the Septuagint and Peshitta, re-dividing the consonantal text and reading the line as "I will cleave the great waters".[18] The idea of Yahweh cleaving the waters at creation appears also in Ps. 74.12-15 and survives even in the Gen. 1 account of creation, as well as being attested as part of the Mesopotamian account of creation, in which Marduk cleaves Tiamat in two after killing her, to make the upper and lower firmaments of creation. If the verse does refer to the great waters, it would emphasise the equation of the chaos waters with the enemies of the audience, which is identified in 2.1 as Judah.

Nahum thus begins its description of Yahweh's activity with terminology which has associations with Yahweh's combating of chaos at creation – historicised as battles against the nations and against the wicked – as well as showing clear affiliations to divine justice.[19] W.C. Van Wyk suggested that already in the introductory hymn *Nahum* makes the "transition from 'prehistory' to history", and while "transition" seems too strong, given the parallel repetition of the acts of crea-

---

15 E.g., R.L. Smith, *Micah-Malachi*, 75.

16 J.M. O'Brien, *Nahum*, Readings (London: Sheffield Academic Press, 2002), 50.

17 J.D.W. Watts, *The Books of Joel, Obadiah, Jonah, Nahum, Habakkuk and Zephaniah*, CBC (Cambridge: Cambridge University Press, 1975), 105.

18 Haldar, 114-115. See K.J. Cathcart for alternatives (*Nahum in the Light of Northwest Semitic*, BO 36 [Rome: Pontificio Istituto Biblico, 1973], 63).

19 Various scholars have associated *Nahum* with the annual festival celebrating Yahweh's kingship in Jerusalem since Humbert first made a case to this effect; this would connect it even more closely to the nexus of themes we have observed elsewhere in connection with royal military ideology; Haldar, though rejecting a liturgical setting for the book, associated it also to the king's engagement in ritual combat as part of the New Year festival, noting in particular the paralleling of historical and cosmological struggles (for a history of research see D.L. Christensen, "The acrostic of Nahum reconsidered", *ZAW* 87 (1975): 17-30; also e.g., Watts, *Joel*, 2-5; J. Gray, "The kingship of God in the prophets and psalms", *VT* 11 (1961): 5).

tion in history through military endeavour which we have seen elsewhere and which are reiterated in *Nahum* (see below), Van Wyk was right to note the easy movement between the primeval and historical planes.[20]

The overwhelming trend of scholarship, however, has been to see the cosmic language of the opening psalm as part of a universalising, eschatological interpretation of the historical references to Nineveh.[21] The entire book thus becomes "an eschatological prophecy of the end time", rather than a historically-situated prophetic text employing cosmological language and concepts to locate a historical event in the ongoing struggle of order against chaos. While this may be the way the book was later interpreted in an exilic and post-exilic canonical context, it underestimates the extent to which present encounters were conceived as battles against chaos. The idea that the characterisation of the enemy as chaos is only a late theme – the assumption from which these characterisations of the nature of the psalm and of *Nahum* as a whole derive – is wholly incorrect.

O'Brien – on the basis of a literary reading which observes the place of the superscription before the psalm – is one of the very few to come close to recognising that the introductory psalm is not designed to universalise the prophecies about Nineveh into a description of an eschatological *Endzeit* event, but to place the battle against Nineveh as part of the cosmic struggle against chaos:

> the mythological nature of the Divine Warrior poem suggests that Nineveh is not only a formidable military foe of Judah but also, more importantly, a suprahistorical enemy of Yahweh, one who threatens the cosmic order. ... When 1.1-10 is read sequentially, Nineveh does not become a general signifier for all forces that work against Yahweh; rather the historically specific Nineveh is demonized as the cosmic enemy of Yahweh.[22]

C.A. Keller also recognised that the use of cosmological language to portray the historical combat between Judah and Assyria was part of the divine struggle of order against chaos, though he tends to overstate the extent to which the historical element is obscured by its cosmologi-

---

20 Van Wyk, 230.

21 So e.g., B.S. Childs, who argues that the psalm turns the book into an eschatological prophecy of the End (*Introduction to the Old Testament as Scripture* [London: SCM, 1979], 444); L. Perlitt, who contends that it makes Nineveh into a paradigm of "aller gottfeindlichen Mächte" (*Die Propheten Nahum, Habakuk, Zephanja*, ATD 25.1 [Göttingen: Vandenhoeck & Ruprecht, 2004], 3-4); K. Seybold, *Nahum Habakuk Zephanja*, ZBK 24.2 (Zürich: Theologischer Verlag, 1991), 13; K. Seybold, *Profane Prophetie: Studien zum Buch Nahum*, SBS 135 (Stuttgart: Verlag Katholisches Bibelwerk, 1989), 82.

22 O'Brien, 52.

cal veneer: "das Drum und Dran der geschichtlichen Vorgänge ist uninteressant, wichtig ist allein die Tatsache, dass die Unordnung beseitigt und in suveräner Weise die Ordnung wiederhergestellt wird".[23] He supposes the description of the fall of Nineveh to be so general that were Nineveh not named it could not be identified, and that the point is not the particularities of the fall of Assyria but Assyria "als *Typus der gottlosen, herrschsüchtigen Metropole*", as that which is against Yahweh and Yahweh's order.[24] As will be evident from the discussion below, the details of the historical enemy are not as irrelevant as Keller seems to think, but he has at least correctly identified the general nature of the cosmological language in *Nahum*. The numerous allusions to the struggle against chaos at creation are not employed as a means of generalising the historical particularities of the fall of Nineveh into an eschatological description of the end, but are an essential aspect of the framework in which that city's fall are conceived.

That this is the case is apparent from the evidence for the same cosmological background in the rest of the book: though it is not generally recognised by commentators, the language of watery chaos which opens *Nahum* and contributes to this equation of Assyria with cosmic chaos also appears elsewhere in the book. Thus the description of the battle against Nineveh tells how "the river gates are opened...Nineveh is like a pool of waters..." (2.7, 9aα).[25] Keller himself argues that the river is the river *par excellence*: not just the Tigris and Khosr rivers which really flowed into Nineveh but the primordial river which had been contained by the act of creation itself.[26] Laying aside the practical dubiousness of flooding as a means of defeating Nineveh, Keller points out that Nineveh was not destroyed by flood but by fire (though this is not necessarily here nor there unless the oracle is a *vaticinium ex eventum*) and, more significantly, that the fact that it is נהרות, in the plural, makes the passage impossible to dissociate from other uses of נהרות, "où nous avons affaire aux *eaux souterraines* et cosmiques, aux eaux primor-

23 Keller, "Bewältigung", 418.

24 Keller, "Bewältigung", 410, 412 (italics in original). Likewise "Ninive und sein König sind Erscheinungsformen der gott- und ordnungsfeindlichen Macht; diese Macht aber nötigt die die [sic] ordnungschaffende und erhaltende Macht zum Eingreifen" (Keller, "Bewältigung", 415).

25 The Masoretic versification of Nah. 2 differs from that of the English and is followed here. The text of 2.9a is problematic; this translates the first half of the line according to the Masoretic text, wherein is a clear reference to מים. The possibility of an allusion to the "great cosmic waters" is noted by Watts (*Joel*, 113). Haldar takes the first part of the passage (2.7) as referring to "Tammuz-ideology" and the latter part (2.9) as a reference to chaos waters (128, 130).

26 Keller, "Bewältigung", 410-411; Keller and Vuilleumier, 123.

diales, au Grand Océan qui est identique au chaos... C'ést l'océan primordial lui-même qui déferle sur la ville...".[27] The lack of clarity on the exact nature of the allusion is indicated by the difference between this interpretation and that of J.J.M. Roberts:

> the well-watered city, whose mighty streams once inundated Israel and Judah (Isa. 8:7-8; 28:15, 17-19) like the unruly waters of chaos (Isa. 17:12-14), is here compared to a pool of water whose dam has broken, allowing its water to drain away.[28]

As is to be expected given the language which surrounds the creative struggle, it is difficult to tell whether the passage is meant to describe a flood as the weapon of the god (and king) against chaos or whether Nineveh is itself being identified as chaos. Given the associations noted by Keller, the latter should perhaps be preferred.

The identification of Nineveh as chaos by means of such an allusion would be in keeping with the description of Thebes (נא אמון) in terms of water.

> ...Thebes
> that sat by the Nile
> with water (מים) around her,
> her rampart a sea (ים),
> water (מים) her wall (3.8)

The extent to which this is a convincing geographical description of Thebes is debateable, but ultimately "all of the references to the sea and waters in v 8 seem to go beyond a factual description of the city's position". [29] Yet the nature of the excess is erratically described: despite an awareness of the cosmic battle imagery in *Nahum*, Keller dismisses it as mere poetic licence:

> la description que Nahoum fait de la ville doit être considérée comme l'image type d'une ville égyptienne (si ce n'est de l'Egypte tout court): elle est entourée d'eau, c'est-à-dire des bras du Nil et de l'océan – ce qui n'est pas vrai de Thèbes, mais Nahoum parle en prophète et en poète, non en géographe.[30]

Haldar somewhat overconfidently declares that the description refers to rivers which are "obviously...the rivers of the netherworld", and that Thebes is thereby associated with the waters of the netherworld, the

---

27 Keller and Vuilleumier, 124.

28 J.J.M. Roberts, *Nahum, Habakkuk, and Zephaniah*, OTL (Louisville, Ky.: Westminster John Knox, 1991), 66.

29 R.L. Smith, 88; see J.M.P. Smith for a discussion (J.M.P. Smith, W.H. Ward, and J.A. Bewer, *A Critical and Exegetical Commentary on Micah, Zephaniah, Nahum, Habakkuk, Obadiah and Joel*, ICC [Edinburgh: T&T Clark, 1948], 340-343); also Perlitt, 33.

30 Keller and Vuilleumier, 130.

waters of chaos.[31] More persuasive as to the significance of this description as an allusion to waters of chaos is the comparison made by P.R. Berger between this verse and one of the inscriptions of Esarhaddon.[32] Both scholars are right, however, in recognising that the description of Thebes in these terms is more likely to have been intended as a mythological allusion and part of the identification of Thebes as chaos than as a matter of factual description.

9.2.2. Agency

Though the book opens with a description of Yahweh's activity, Nineveh's destruction is described in human terms.[33] The agent (with regard to whom masculine singular nouns and suffixes are employed) is not identified, but his identity is implicitly royal, with the reference to "his officers" (אדיריו) suggesting that the unidentified leader is the king.[34]

The synergy of the king and Yahweh in the destruction wrought on Nineveh is evident from the framing of the description of the king's destruction with references to Yahweh's involvement (2.3, 14) as well as in the king's control over the waters (2.7; cf. Ps. 89.26).

The identity of this royal figure is of course a relevant question for our purposes, given the importance of the royal figure as mediator of the divine-human military synergy and the possibilities which such synergy allows in terms of military practice. Though commentators tend to assume that the invaders are the Babylonians and their allies, there is reason to believe that the Judahite king is implied as the royal agent in question: immediately preceding the description of the agent's acts is a direct address to Judah, culminating in the declaration in 2.13 that

> Yahweh is restoring the majesty of Jacob,
> as well as the majesty of Israel,
> though ravagers have ravaged them
> and ruined their branches.

---

31 Haldar, 139.

32 P.R. Berger, "Zum ugaritischen Wörterbuch, 1", *UF* 2 (1970): 346.

33 This is even clearer if 2.2 and 2.3 are reversed (see e.g., Keller and Vuilleumier, 114). Haldar and Roberts both presume that Yahweh is the agent, the latter on the basis of 2.14 and the use of פוץ in Num. 10.35 and Ps. 68.2 (Haldar, 123; Roberts, *Nahum*, 56, 64). As ever, however, there must be a human agent, and this is particularly inevitable in a text with such concrete descriptions of battle.

34 The head of the military was always the king, in principle if not always in practice. Commentators are divided over whether 2.6 refers to the invaders or the defenders (see e.g., R.L. Smith, 83; Smith, Ward and Bewer, 316-317).

How this national honour might be restored by a military demonstration of a king other than Judah's is obscure; though a foreign king is later employed to rescind the embarrassment of the exile, there it is the honour and reputation of Yahweh which is at stake, rather than the reputation of the nation as such.[35] In this situation, the defeat of Assyria by a third party would seem to do nothing to restore the majesty of Israel.[36]

The plausibility of such an attribution is not lessened by the relative strength of Judah in the late seventh century. An awareness of the waning power of Assyria had triggered a resurgence of nationalistic sentiments under Josiah. The report at 2 Kg. 23.29 that Josiah went up against the Egyptians indicates that the renewal of national pride extended also to confidence in military strength; if the Judahite army was considered a match for the Egyptians, the implication here that it would triumph over the Assyrians is not out of place. We have also already seen similar levels of confidence in the king's military strength in the royal psalms (Chapter 6).

9.2.3. Practice

If this is the case, we have an unusually lengthy depiction of the military manoeuvres of a Judahite king, albeit an impressionistic, poetic depiction rather than an annalistic one. True to poetic form, it is a depiction full of imagery and lacking in concrete detail. There is the reference to the river gates, already suggested to be a deliberate evocation of the theme of the cosmological battle at creation (2.7); exile (2.8), plunder (2.10) and hyperbolic claims about the number of enemy dead ("piles of dead, heaps of corpses, dead bodies without end"; 3.3b).[37] With Yahweh as the explicit agent, humiliating and making Assyria a "spectacle" are also mentioned (3.5-6), along with general references to destruction (2.11; 3.7). If the description of the fate of Thebes and the subsequent "you also" is meant to indicate that the same fate will befall Assyria, we

35 The fact that Deutero-Isaiah prepares his audience extensively before introducing Cyrus also suggests that the idea of a foreign king acting in the interests of Judah was an unprecedented idea as late as the end of the exile.

36 See e.g., Watts, *Joel*, 112; E.R. Achtemeier, *Nahum – Malachi*, Interpretation (Atlanta, Ga.: John Knox, 1986), 20. Achtemeier follows J.M.P. Smith in supposing that the reference to red shields in 2.4 is a reference to the Babylonians, on the basis of Ezek. 23.14 (Achtemeier, 20; Smith, Ward and Bewer, 313). Keller contends that the specificity is illusory, and that the invaders are deliberately "mysterious" and "unhistorical" (Keller and Vuilleumier, 416).

37 רב חלל וכבד פגר ואין קצה לגויה

may add an emphasis on punishment of leaders and a reiteration of the theme of exile; there is also a reference to the killing of children, perhaps meant as a sign of the totality of the destruction (3.10).

Excursus – The death of children in Israelite and Judahite warfare

There are a number of texts in the Hebrew Bible which mention the death of children or pregnant women in passing, but none in which the author's or audience's opinion on the tolerability of such targets is explicitly expressed.

As we already saw in Amos, it is listed as the accusation against the Ammonites as an indication of the complete destruction of an opponent, and it may not be insignificant that the form of complete destruction which is in turn wreaked upon Moab does not speak of such conduct. The Nahum reference is likewise once removed, with the original perpetrator being Assyria, and the description of Nineveh's defeat not explicitly mentioning the act.

The use of the fate as divine punishment may occur in Hos. 10.13-15.

You have ploughed wickedness,
you have reaped injustice,
you have eaten the fruit of lies.
Because you have trusted in your power and in the multitude of your warriors,
therefore the tumult of war shall rise against your people,
and all your fortresses shall be destroyed,
as Shalman destroyed Beth-arbel on the day of battle
when mothers were dashed in pieces with their children.
Thus it shall be done to you, O Bethel,
because of your great wickedness.
At dawn the king of Israel shall be utterly cut off.[38]

The original event which Yahweh's wrath will match is unidentifiable.[39] Gottwald supposes that the threat of atrocities against pregnant women, "if it is not merely a conventional phrase for war brutality, alludes to recompense for Menahem's similar atrocities against Tappuah" in 2 Kg. 15.16.[40] Gottwald's argument makes one wonder whether the principle of *lex talionis* is at work in Hosea as well, but Hosea's accusations against Israel are

38 חרשתם־רשע עולתה קצרתם אכלתם פרי־כחש כי־בטחת בדרכך ברב גבוריך: וקאם שאון בעמך וכל־מבצריך יושד כשד שלמן בית ארבאל ביום מלחמה אם על־בנים רטשה: ככה עשה לכם ב ית־אל מפני רעת רעתכם בשחר נדמה נדמה מלך ישראל:

39 Gottwald and Macintosh both suppose the most likely culprit was the Moabite Shalmanu (see Limburg, 135; Gottwald, *Tribes*, 128-129; Macintosh, *Hosea*, 429).

40 Gottwald, *Tribes*, 125.

so focussed on cultic activities that any extent to which the punishment might (also) be for military activities has been completely obscured.

The explicit agent of the punishment, whatever the reason for it, is Yahweh. Without obscuring the need for a historical agent as well, this attribution would apparently affirm the moral acceptability of the act. Further, though the statement is a simile rather than a direct expression of Yahweh's planned actions, it is clear that the reference is meant as a cipher for an extreme fate. Thus even if Yahweh is not threatening precisely the same fate for Israel, it may be expected to be something equivalently extreme. Moreover, in 14.1 the dashing to pieces of the children of Israel and the fate of its pregnant women are made explicit.

> Samaria shall bear her guilt,
> because she has rebelled against her God;
> they shall fall by the sword,
> their little ones shall be dashed in pieces,
> and their pregnant women ripped open.[41]

And as ever, the acts of Yahweh must also – by the nature of historical human agency – be acceptable in the human sphere. This is confirmed by the absence in Hosea of any sense of there being a need for the subsequent punishment of Yahweh's human agents.[42] In Hosea, at least, there seems to be no real objection to the practice.[43]

9.2.4. *Lex talionis*

What "you also" of 3.11 indicates even more strongly, however, is that in *Nahum* we have the melding of the classic royal tradition, in which military acts are described in terms of and legitimated as part of the cosmic battle against chaos and which we saw at work in *Psalms* and *Kings*, and a military ethic adopting as its motivating principle the *lex talionis* which we saw beneath the logic of *Amos*.[44] General observation of some sense of due recompense in *Nahum* has been made by a few scholars, but has not been pursued to its fullest extent.

---

41 תאשם שמרון כי מרתה באלהיה בחרב יפלו עלליהם ירטשו והריותיו יבקעו

42 When such a sense does occur it is in later texts and is almost always related to the agent's pride, rather than to the agent having over-stepped the bounds of moral tolerability in their violent treatment of Israel (e.g. Isa. 10; Zeph. 2.9-10; Hab. 1.11, 2.8).

43 Note that, unlike in *Amos*, the act engaged upon is not done as a means of counterbalancing an act perpetrated by the one now attacked: there is no indication that Israel will have such a fate inflicted upon it as a consequence of having killed women and children previously.

44 The reversal of judgment theme is taken up especially strongly in later prophecy (e.g., Jer. 51.44; Ezek. 33.2-10; Zech. 1.18-21 [2.1-4]).

K. Seybold, helpfully, suggests that the formula "are you better than" is a deliberate play "vom ethischen Zusammenhang zwischen Tun und Ergehen, Handlung und Geschick" common in prophetic and wisdom circles – in short, a question not only of superior political and military strength but also – and perhaps primarily – of ethical standing.[45] The question presupposes the common idea of military defeat as punishment, which we have seen throughout both Assyrian and biblical texts, but turns on Assyria – whose frequent victories were, under the purely royal framework, taken to imply divine approval – to suggest that it will soon experience the very treatment it has been meting out. The reason for the anticipated punishment is not explicit, though the extent to which Assyria's military exploits are emphasised suggests that they are the cause.

The appearance of the idea of Yahweh being involved in ensuring due recompense for extreme actions engaged upon during war is apparent from the start of the book: "A jealous and avenging God is Yahweh..." (1.2a).[46]

The depiction of acts followed by similar acts as consequences also appears in more practical terms. The Assyrians will be exiled (2.8), mirrored by the exile of the Egyptians in 3.10.[47] The plundering ordered in 2.10 is echoed in the description of Nineveh as "full of booty – no end to the plunder" (3.1).[48] More loosely, the emphasis on the extent of the Assyrian dead in 3.3 may be a response to the Assyrians' extension of destruction even to the children of Egypt (3.10).[49] There is certainly a play in the repetition of כבד in reference to Nineveh's treasure in 2.10 and to Nineveh's dead in 3.3.[50]

K.J. Cathcart interprets 3.18 as referring to the abandonment of corpses without burial, that is, the desecration of enemy dead, which was reported several times in the Assyrian material, in association with

45 Seybold, *Nahum*, 38. "Are you better than...?": התיטבי מן.

46 As is now widely accepted, the concept of נקם is badly conveyed by the English "vengeance", and is in its essence a term which conveys Yahweh's facilitation of the due consequences of wrong acts (see e.g., Koch, "Vergeltungsdogma").

47 Perlitt suggests that 3.10 is an exilic expansion on the basis that exile is a common exilic motif (Seybold likewise considers it a prose addition), but a programme of systematic deportations had been employed by the Assyrians for a century by the time of Nahum, including against the Egyptians, and the killing of children is also mentioned in pre-exilic texts (Perlitt, 34; Seybold, *Nahum*, 39).

48 *Lit.*, "prey does not cease".

49 It may be significant that this is not a direct reversal – suggesting that the execution of infants and children was not acceptable to a Judahite audience, even to enact the *lex talionis*.

50 So Achtemeier, 23.

varying degrees of bodily mutilation. Cathcart also suggests an association between the מפיץ, the "scatterer", in 2.2 and deportation, a practice similarly associated with the Assyrians.[51]

A less certain but nonetheless possible additional point of reversal may be suggested by J.M.P. Smith's interpretation of the one who came forth devising evil against Yahweh (1.11) and בליעל (2.1) as Sennacherib in 701.[52] If this interpretation is accurate, it would be an example of a much more direct form of reversal between two specific military parties (Judah and Assyria). As early as 1911 J.M.P. Smith hinted at this idea in his translation of 2.1 as "For not again will the destroyer pass through thee; he will be destroyed, cut off".[53] The extent to which this principle plays out in *Nahum*, however, was yet to be fully appreciated.

The allusion of 2.12-14 to Isa. 5.29-30 also strongly suggests that some form of *lex talionis* has been incorporated by Nahum into his conception of the king's role in war. In *Isaiah* Assyria (the "nation far away") is described in animal terms:

> Their roaring is like a lion,
> like young lions they roar;
> They growl and seize their prey,
> they carry it off, and no one can rescue (Isa. 5.29).[54]

In *Nahum* this same imagery is employed to show how Assyria has been undone:

> What became of the lions' den,
> the cave[55] of the young lions,
> where the lion goes,
> and the lion's cubs, with no one to disturb them?
> The lion has torn enough for his whelps
> and strangled prey for his lionesses;
> he has filled his caves with prey
> and his dens with torn flesh (2.12-14).[56]

---

51 K.J. Cathcart, "Treaty-curses and the book of Nahum", *CBQ* 34 (1973): 181, 182. Cathcart identifies a number of similarities between *Nahum* and curses which appear in ancient Near Eastern treaties – particularly those of Esarhaddon – which seems to further support the suggestion that *Nahum* has in mind a reversal of the punishments threatened or actually inflicted by Assyria.

52 Smith, Ward and Bewer, 310; followed by Perlitt, 13; and elaborated on the basis of the use of צרה in 1.9 and 2 Kg. 19.3 by Van Wyk, 226-227.

53 Smith, Ward and Bewer, 303.

54 שאגה לו כלביא ושאג ככפירים וינהם ויאחז טרף ויפליט ואין מציל

55 Following *BHS*; the Masoretic text has מרעה.

56 יה מעון אריות ומרעה הוא לכפרים אשר הלך אריה לביא שם גור אריה ואין מחריד: אריה טרף בדי גרותיו ומחנק ללבאתיו וימלא־טרף חריו ומענתיו טרפה:

The lion of Assyria is undone, and his undoing is attributed to his violent excess. The violence Assyria deployed against Judah (*Isaiah*) will now be turned against Assyria (*Nahum*). *Isaiah* is the book to which *Nahum* is the most closely related intertextually, and the use of this imagery by Nahum is unlikely to have been accidental.[57]

That the prophecy in *Nahum* is meant to signal Assyria's destruction in direct correlation to Assyria's actions is also further affirmed by 2.14: "I [Yahweh] will burn your [MT her] chariots in smoke, and the sword shall devour your young lions; I will cut off your prey from the earth, and the voice of your messengers shall be heard no more."[58]

Finally, the implication that Assyria's downfall is the direct result of its own military actions is evident in the last line of the book: "For who has ever escaped your endless cruelty?" (4.19).

9.2.5. Conclusions

What are we to make of this conflation of the royal ideology of warfare with a *lex talionis* system? Commentators often speak generally of oracles against Assyria as expressing a desire for revenge for the sufferings of Israel and Judah at the hands of the Assyrian armies. Such an explanation, though no doubt part of the reason for such oracles, underestimates the extent of the presence of the royal ideology of warfare in undergirding the king's role in redressing the military acts of other nations, and in particular the manner in which the royal ideology is employed to describe the acts of the enemy in the language of chaos (particularly by allusions to the chaos waters), and, by thus describing them, justifying the eradication of them.

This language is not, however, the purely dichotomous equation of the enemy with chaos, over against indigenous order, which we observed elsewhere. Rather, there seems to be an indication that the centre of "order" was located with the nation whose military might was

57 O'Brien, 50.

58 Note that Isa. 5.28 contains a reference to chariots, which may be being echoed here. This prose oracle may be a late addition, but it merely serves to confirm the impression of the preceding poetic verse. That the lion motif may also be an allusion to the chaos conflict was suggested by Haldar: Isa. 5.30 brings in clear chaos imagery in its description of the (Assyrian) lions – "they will roar over it on that day, like the roaring of the sea" – which Haldar extends through the equation of the *lābu* in Mesopotamian mythology with Tiamat (131-132). "The question about the lion's den [in *Nahum*] must then be taken as an allusion to its being destroyed, for when the water of chaos recedes, *i.e.* when Ti'āmat is slain, the *labbu* is also slain. Then, the state of chaos disappears, and consequently the lion's den is destroyed" (133).

dominant, and hence the language with which Assyria is described not only speaks of it as chaotic, but speaks of it as becoming chaotic as a result of losing its hegemonic authority. Thus turned, it becomes imperative that a new order be established, and this is the role of Judah.

It may also be significant that by the time of Nahum the Judahite and Israelite experience of the Assyrian conduct of warfare had given their leaders a taste of the possibilities of a military uninhibited by the practical constraints attendant upon a small nation-state. In keeping with the wave of nationalism which seems to have swept the upper classes in the late seventh century, *Nahum* expresses the hope that the power manifested by Assyrian military exploits might soon be manifested in those of Judah. In its reliance on *lex talionis Nahum* may reflect the aspirations of the Judahite monarchy, articulated in terms of the most significant locus of political power of the time. The proper centre of cosmic order is Judah; the "order" which has until now been centred on Assyria is about to be upturned and reoriented.

Finally, it is worth observing that *Nahum,* through its articulation of the royal military ideology in these terms, represents a key intermediary position between the classic royal ideology and that of the *lex talionis.* With the exile the Judahite king was ultimately removed from his role as the human counterpart to the divine military endeavour, and it was the *lex talionis* approach which proved victorious.

10. Developments in Judahite and Israelite ethics II

10.1. *Ḥērem*

Having pursued the ideological developments of Judahite warfare in Chapter 9, we now turn to one particular practice of war in which attentiveness to socio-historical factors may also prove useful. This is the most famed and most discussed of all biblical war practices: *ḥērem*.

10.1.1. Holy war

Most recent studies of warfare by biblical scholars have focussed on the subject of the so-called "holy war", a phrase used by G. von Rad in *Der Heilige Krieg im alten Israel* to describe what he saw as a uniquely Israelite sacralisation of the act of war.[1] Due to von Rad's identification of *ḥērem* as the final stage in the practice of "holy war", these two ideas have been frequently conflated by subsequent research. This was perhaps inevitable, and indeed not particularly problematic, as long as the term "holy war" was, following von Rad's original description, taken to include both the intellectual basis of the practice of war (the idea of divine involvement) and actual acts of war (especially the cultic rituals before, during and after a battle); according to von Rad's depiction of *ḥērem* as the religiously-motivated setting aside of the conquered (both animate and inanimate), it constituted one of the latter, practical aspects of war.[2]

Von Rad's theory of the cultic nature of war, however, was heavily modified by subsequent research and has to a large extent been abandoned as originally articulated. R. Smend cast serious doubt on von Rad's association of "holy war" with a tribal amphictyony, and then Gottwald pointed out that a tribal context was itself less likely than a

---

1 G. von Rad, *Der Heilige Krieg im alten Israel*, ATANT 20 (Zürich: Zwingli-Verlag, 1951), reprinted as *Holy War in Ancient Israel*, translated by M.J. Dawn (Grand Rapids, Mich.: Eerdmans, 1991).

2 Cf. F. Stolz, *Jahwes und Israels Kriege: Kriegstheorien und Kriegserfahrungen im Glauben des alten Israel*, ATANT 60 (Zürich: Theologischer Verlag, 1972).

statist context.[3] G.H. Jones identified the weaknesses of von Rad's argument for a fixed and required pattern for the cult rituals of war, though acknowledging that theological language reflected an idea of Yahweh's involvement in war.[4] Against von Rad's conception of the holy war as uniquely Israelite, M. Weippert demonstrated that the idea of divine-human synergy in warfare is a common ancient Near Eastern phenomenon, using Assyrian material as a case example.[5]

Since von Rad's idea of holy war as constituting a strictly defined series of cultic acts was abandoned, the term "holy war" has been used to refer more generally to the underlying concept of a military engagement in which the deity(ies) are thought to be involved, though, unfortunately, this usage tends to result also in the unconscious retention of the idea that cultic components are key to the phenomenon. With this revised version of "holy war", the importance of maintaining a clear distinction between holy war as intellectual background and *ḥērem* as specific battlefield act is evident, insofar as *ḥērem* is a possible component of a "holy war" but not a universal one.

Unfortunately, the recognition of this distinction has been erratic, as the innumerable theological discussions of the problematic nature of "holy war" for modernity indicate; P.D. Stern is one of the few if not the only scholar to emphasise the distinction.[6] As modern rhetoric of war makes clear, however, the "problem" of holy war is not the idea of the god(s)'s involvement on one side or another, but the extreme character of *ḥērem* in particular. S. Niditch is a good example of this; she complains that the perception of *ḥērem* as divine justice motivates and encourages war, "implying that wars of extermination are desirable in order to purify the body politic of one's own group, to eradicate evil in

3 R. Smend, *Jahwekrieg und Stämmebund: Erwägungen zur ältesten Geschichte Israels*, FRLANT 84 (Göttingen: Vandenhoeck & Ruprecht, 1963); Gottwald, *Tribes of Yahweh*.

4 G.H. Jones, "'Holy war' or 'Yahweh war'?", *VT* 25 (1975): 642-658.

5 M. Weippert, "'Heiliger Krieg' in Israel und Assyrien: Kritische Anmerkungen zu Gerhard von Rads Konzept des 'Heiligen Kriegs im alten Israel'", *ZAW* 84 (1982): 460-493. A few scholars continue to deny this, see e.g., Hasel. See also K.L. Younger, Jr., *Ancient Conquest Accounts: A Study in Ancient Near Eastern and Biblical History Writing*, JSOTSup 98 (Sheffield: JSOT, 1990) and Haglund, *Historical Motifs in the Psalms* for further discussions.

6 P.D. Stern, *The Biblical Ḥerem: A Window on Israel's Religious Experience*, BJS 211 (Atlanta, Ga.: Scholars, 1991); see below. Cf. P.D. Miller, *The Divine Warrior in Early Israel*, HSM 5 (Cambridge, Mass.: Harvard University Press, 1975); M.C. Lind, *Yahweh is a Warrior: The Theology of Warfare in Ancient Israel* (Scottdale, Penn.: Herald, 1980); P.C. Craigie, *The Problem of War in the Old Testament* (Grand Rapids, Mich.: Eerdmans, 1981); J. Cazeaux, *Le refus de la guerre sainte: Josué, Juges et Ruth*, LD 174 (Paris: Éditions du Cerf, 1998); N. Lohfink, "Der »heilige Krieg« und der »Bann« in der Bibel", *IKZ* 89 (1989): 104-112.

the world beyond one's group, and to actualize divine judgment".[7] This is not so much a complaint about *ḥērem,* however, as about ancient Near Eastern war in general, of which the practice of *ḥērem* is only one example. The identification of *ḥērem* as the source of the problem is simply because its extreme nature causes it to act as a lightning rod for criticism of biblical war.

The lack of scholarly distinction between holy war and *ḥērem* makes interaction with the secondary literature on the question of the historical location and development of *ḥērem* difficult. The situation is exacerbated by the fact that a number of these discussions are tied into attempts to emphasise that the *ḥērem* was either never implemented at all or was eradicated by the greater minds of later ages.[8] Thus A. de Pury traced "Yahweh war" to the deuteronomic and deuteronomistic sources of the strand(s) of the Hebrew Bible; both he and von Rad contended that the deuteronom(ist)ic interest in the practice of holy war (in von Rad's cultic incarnation) was part of a late, prophetic criticism of the monarchy, aimed at (re)emphasising the divine involvement in war (over and against human involvement, usually articulated prophetically as reliance on horses and chariots, etc.).[9] This argument stumbles, of course, on the fact that the ancient Near Eastern parallels for "holy war" theology are solidly based in royal ideology.[10]

---

7 Niditch, 68.

8 Stolz contended that holy war was a deuteronomistic fiction designed to emphasise the power of Yahweh (cf. de Pury and von Rad); Otto has argued that the entire phenomenon (both holy war and *ḥērem*) is, in its deuteronomic expression, part of an exilic "anti-Assyrian programme" for a New Israel, which programmatically pacifies war activities and counters Assyrian military practices (*Krieg und Frieden in der Hebräischen Bibel und im Alten Orient: Aspekt für eine Friedensordnung in der Moderne*, TF 18 [Berlin: Kohlhammer, 1999]). Stern makes a similar argument with a different motive: *Deuteronomy* is an attempt to end the actual practice of *ḥērem* by limiting its application to the native Canaanites and thereby making it irrelevant for *Deuteronomy*'s contemporaries. Ultimately, however, the point made most clearly by Gottwald cannot be overlooked: whatever the actual practical use or non-use of *ḥērem,* "the Deuteronomists believed: 1) that Canaanite civilians, including women and children, either *were* or *should have been* exterminated in the name of God, and 2) that one people had the religious right to dispossess another people, even though for various reasons the right had not been fully taken advantage of" ("'Holy war' in Deuteronomy: analysis and critique", *RE* 61 (1965): 307).

9 See S.-M. Kang, *Divine War in the Old Testament and in the Ancient Near East*, BZAW 177 (Berlin: Walter de Gruyter, 1989), 3-4.

10 This is implicit in Weippert's recourse to the Assyrian literature; that the phenomenon was no provincial or prophetic one in Israel or Judah either has been made explicit by this study, which has identified it most clearly in the royally-provenanced literature.

Since all the evidence indicates that an ideology of "holy war" in which human and divine worked together via military activity for the establishment of order and destruction of chaos – personified by the enemy – was a continuous part of Israelite and Judahite military activities up to the exile, it does us little good to dwell on such a general phenomenon. References to *ḥērem*, by contrast, are much more erratic.

10.1.2. *Ḥērem*

Scholars have, in the numerous studies of "holy war" and *ḥērem*, recognised that there are two main areas in which the *ḥērem* comes to centre stage: in the texts describing the pre-monarchical period of the "conquest" and in the texts associated with the deuteronom(ist)ic movement.[11] This connection between *ḥērem* and the deuteronom(ist)ic literature is not surprising, given that it is in the deuteronom(ist)ic literature (or literature deriving from it, in the case of *Chronicles*) that by far the majority of reports of Israel and Judah's war engagements are recorded. However, in the material comprising the deuteronom(ist)ic corpus, reports of *ḥērem* occur almost exclusively in the accounts of the Israelites' entry into the land. The practice is thus described most frequently in the early stages in the national and ethnic history, but in texts which are themselves largely the result of the work of a deuteronom(ist)ic editor working at a very late point in the same history.[12] In the interim there is almost no evidence that *ḥērem* (as such) was employed as a regular feature of either Israelite or Judahite warfare – in fact, it is almost entirely absent from both *Samuel* and *Kings*.[13]

---

11 The origins of Israel (and Judah) in the Levant is one of the least agreed-upon areas of Hebrew Bible scholarship. Without siding with any of the theories currently in vogue, we simply suggest that the description of the origins of Israel in war is not sociologically insignificant.

"Deuteronom(ist)ic" is used in what follows as a means of suspending linguistic judgment on the nature of *ḥērem* in *Deuteronomy* until the examination of Dt. 20 (below).

12 It is unfortunate that there are almost no reports of military activities for the last century of Judahite history, but this fact may not be itself insignificant (i.e., it is a further indicator of the level of the external threat to indigenous culture experienced during this period).

13 Stern notes Amalek (against whom is the only application of *ḥērem* after the conquest [1 Sam. 15]), as a special case; its opposition to Israel on the heels of the escape from the sea (the common ancient Near Eastern symbol of chaos) led to its perpetual personification as *Unwelt*, chaos, and its special vilification (169, 173). It is probably also not coincidental that 1 Sam. 15.18 is the only place in which the Amalekites are called sinners (חטאים).

The nature of this two-fold character of *ḥērem* in the Hebrew Bible has been variously interpreted, and this study is certainly not the first to note the prevalence of acts of *ḥērem* in deuteronom(ist)ic literature, nor the first to note its frequency in the narratives relating to the conquest.[14] What we are more precisely concerned with here, however, is the apparent disappearance of the practice of *ḥērem* for most of the middle part of the history of Israel and Judah. The significance of the dualistic nature of the phenomenon has not previously been recognised.

10.1.2.1. *Ḥērem* as battle against chaos

The practical aspects of *ḥērem* have been thoroughly examined by Stern and need not be re-examined in detail here. Most pertinent for our purposes is his description of *ḥērem* in terms of the cosmic struggle between order and chaos.[15] As expected, Stern identifies the enemy as the representation of chaos, who must be destroyed en route to the establishment of order.[16] He also extends the concept to the use of the term in the Mesha Inscription; the Moabite *ḥērem*, analogous to the Israelite *ḥērem*, is

> reasserting the rule of the god(s) and reflecting the victory of Kemosh and Mesha over the "monsters of chaos," i.e. YHWH and Israel. Moab was able

---

14 See the works already cited. Appearances of *ḥērem* are predominantly in deuteronomistic literature, but this is not an exclusive phenomenon, and though the emphasis on *ḥērem* in the Hebrew Bible seems to owe a good deal to the deuteronomistic interest in it, it does not seem to have been created *de novo* by the deuteronomists.

15 A decade and a half before Stern, Miller reached the opposite conclusion regarding the role of struggle against chaos in Israelite (and Judahite) warfare: though the gods of the ancient Near East fought to preserve order, Yahweh fought to save his people (*Divine Warrior*, 164-165). However, these objects are identical once identification of the enemy as chaos is recognised. Miller misjudges the distinctiveness of the Israelite emphasis on the historical battle against chaos, probably due to his concentration on Ugaritic texts; the Assyrian material makes clear that there too the gods fight on the historical plane, and it is in that material particularly that the struggle against chaos is most clearly perceived in historical terms (cf. also Albrektson).

16 Stern, 41. Somewhat surprisingly, Stern does not refer to Liverani's work on the Assyrian concept of the enemy as chaos; instead he refers to a similar Egyptian view of foreigners as chaotic forces. The depiction of the enemy as chaos elsewhere in the ancient Near East correlates with the general sociological phenomenon of ideology, described in Chapter 2. Otto reaches similar conclusions regarding the centrality of the struggle against chaos in *Krieg und Frieden in der Hebräischen Bibel und im Alten Orient*, though Otto's conclusions appear to draw on those of Liverani, and make no reference to Stern.

> to slaughter the Israelites without a qualm with the aid of this mythopoeic conception.[17]

Stern's study suggests that in the Hebrew Bible the term *ḥērem* is caught up in a matrix of terms having to do with the struggle for land and ordered existence.[18] This is most noticeable in the frequency of *ḥērem* language in the narratives relating the events of the conquest, especially in the conquest of Jericho – the only act of conquest in which the fullest and most expansive form of *ḥērem* is actually applied. Stern argues that the use of this most extreme form of *ḥērem* at Jericho is the result of the special place which Jericho holds in the overall struggle for a new, Israelite order: it is the initial act which begins the creative process. The echo of the seven day creation in the six/seven schema of Jericho's conquest is perhaps further indication of the creative character of this particular conquest.[19]

The contextualisation of *ḥērem* in the cosmic struggle of order against chaos is the key to its appearances in the conquest narratives and in the deuteronom(ist)ic literature. Stern, as described above, placed *ḥērem* into the historical context of the conquest, with its special interest in the struggle for ordered existence (focussed in particular on the possession of land). This, however, is only half of the story of *ḥērem*. Rather than the deuteronom(ist)ic emphasis on the practice reflecting a prophetic (or other fringe group's) attempt to reorientate national war practices toward Yahweh, it reflects a proportionate heightening of military response in a period in which the perceived threat to the Judahite socio-political order was equally heightened.

That is: *ḥērem* is an extreme expression of the struggle of order against chaos; it is sensible that it comes to the fore in periods in which the threat of chaos is felt particularly acutely. It is equally sensible that the threat of chaos, personified in the figure of the enemy (and its culture), would have been felt most strongly in the periods in which exposure to foreign cultures was highest. Though the histories of Israel and Judah are in many respects clouded and difficult to discern in detail, the peak periods of exposure to foreign cultures are most convincingly identified as during the period of the development of national identity (either through conquest or through a process of increased self-definition against other sub-groups in Canaan) and in the mid- to late seventh century, in which the commercial and political interactions among the small regional states of the Levant (including Judah) and between those states and the empires of the ancient Near East reached

---

17 Stern, 50, 83.
18 Stern, 49.
19 Stern, 143.

unprecedented heights.[20] Over the course of the eighth and seventh centuries, the extent of foreign – especially Assyrian – involvement in Levantine affairs progressively increased, and the *pax Assyriaca* facilitated, among other things, a sufficiently stable international environment to allow an unprecedented increase in international trade. [21] Between these two periods Israel and Judah – but especially Judah, being the smaller and less internationally prominent of the two – existed in a certain level of isolation.[22]

With the increase in foreign political incursions over the course of the seventh century, paralleled by rising numbers of foreigners in Judah as a result of trading activities, it is not surprising to find literary evidence reflecting an increased sense of the threat posed by foreigners to indigenous order. The advocated method for the eradication of this threat was, equally unsurprisingly, correspondingly extreme; it is thus that a renewed emphasis on *ḥērem*, the most extreme form of anti-chaos action, came to the fore in the deuteronom(ist)ic literature produced at this time.[23] Unfortunately the dearth of references to military activities in the final decades of the Judahite kingdom makes hypothesising about the practical enactment of *ḥērem* in the period of the deuteronom(ist)ic literature difficult, but we may say that *ḥērem* was again advocated as a battlefield technique, whether or not it was ever successfully enacted. We recall this exact same basic phenomenon – of unusual socio-historical factors influencing ethical tolerances – in Assyria, when the circumstances of Esarhaddon and Assurbanipal – namely,

20 See e.g., A. Faust and E. Weiss, "Judah, Philistia, and the Mediterranean world: reconstructing the economic system of the seventh century B.C.E.", *BASOR* 338 (2005): 71-92; N. Na'aman, "Ekron under the Assyrian and Egyptian empires", *BASOR* 332 (2003): 81-91.

21 See e.g., M. Cogan, *Imperialism and Religion: Assyria, Judah and Israel in the Eighth and Seventh Centuries B.C.E.* (Missoula, MT: Scholars Press, 1974); H. Spieckermann, *Juda unter Assur in der Sargonidenzeit* (Göttingen: Vandenhoeck & Ruprecht, 1982); Liverani, "Ideology".

22 N. Na'aman, "Population changes in Palestine following Assyrian deportations", in *Ancient Israel and its Neighbors: Interaction and Counteraction*, volume 1 of *Collected Essays* (Winona Lake, Ind.: Eisenbrauns, 2005); N. Na'aman, "The province system and settlement patterns in southern Syria and Palestine in the Neo-Assyrian period", in *Ancient Israel and its Neighbors: Interaction and Counteraction*, volume 1 of *Collected Essays* (Winona Lake, Ind.: Eisenbrauns, 2005).

23 It is surely not coincidental that the one extra-biblical attestation of *ḥērem*, in the Mesha Stele, is in a text in which the victors are reasserting their national identity in the face of a prolonged period of subordination to another national order (in this case, that of the Israelites). Stern, interestingly, contends that the Israelites acquired the practice of *ḥērem* from outside, and identifies the Moabites as a possible source, though how he believes the chronology of this cross-cultural adaptation to have worked is unclear (87).

a heightened threat to legitimacy as divinely-appointed ruler – resulted in correspondingly heightened levels of extreme behaviour in warfare.[24]

10.1.2.2. *Ḥērem* and the ancient Near East

The recognition of this underlying phenomenon provides an opportune moment to discuss Stern's assertion that *ḥērem* does not occur elsewhere in the ancient Near East, which he bases on M. Weippert's use of Assyrian "holy war" as the primary model for divine warfare in the ancient Near East. Assyria, Stern asserts, has holy war but not *ḥērem* (and "*ḥērem*" and "holy war" are therefore not interchangeable).[25] As far as it goes, there is nothing wrong with any individual part of Stern's argument; the problem appears with the image Stern creates when he puts all the parts together. The issue lies with Stern's assumption that *ḥērem* was a specifically cultic phenomenon, such that its supposedly sacral quality set it apart from any similar phenomena in surrounding cultures. He is certainly not alone in adopting this lingering inheritance of von Rad's classic description of holy war.[26]

Such a distinction, however, is over-emphasised. As already noted, the attempt to identify Israelite war as distinctly sacral due to a requirement of the performance of certain fixed cultic practices associated with it was proved false already by G.H. Jones. Indeed the association of cultic activities (particularly divination, both intuitive and technical) with warfare was wholly common in Assyria as well (see Chapters 5 and 8). More generally, that a separation between warfare and the gods was inconceivable in the context of the ancient Near East has been established beyond question.[27] The pursuit of war in and of itself, as well as the various treatments meted out to the defeated, is undertaken through a sense of divine-human synergy in the pursuit of an ordered cosmos. The triumph of the human agent is equally a triumph of the god(s); the demonstrations of power and authority enacted in the humiliation or execution of conquered enemies are demonstrations of the

---

24 See J.H. Tigay for an alternative explanation of the origin of *ḥērem* (*Deuteronomy*, JPS [Philadelphia, Pa.: Jewish Publication Society, 1996], 471-472).

25 Stern, 179. Stern's verdict on this point is especially surprising given that he appeals to a wide chronological and geographic range of activities to argue that there was a long pre-history to *ḥērem* in the ancient Near East prior to Israel's appropriation of the practice.

26 Cf. e.g., Kang.

27 See Chapters 3 and 4.

power and authority of the god(s) as much as the power of the human. Stern himself admits that the notion of "consecration" – the supposedly distinctive aspect of *ḥērem* – is implicit in all acts of killing: "by destroying those the gods hate, one makes the world a holier place".[28] In such a framework the persistence of scholars in trying to distinguish the Israelite and Judahite theology of warfare from the theology of warfare of the rest of the ancient Near East – Assyria, in the case studied here – can only be considered special pleading.

Thus, though Stern's assertion that Assyria has no *ḥērem* is accurate insofar as Akkadian has no equivalent root in its vocabulary, we must reiterate the observation made in the preceding discussions of the Assyrian material: the complete destruction of the enemy is frequently reported and, regardless of whether or not total destruction was actually achieved (or even attempted), makes clear the ideological importance of the eradication of the enemy.

In light of the language of order and chaos with which he describes *ḥērem* elsewhere, it is surprising that Stern does not come to a similar conclusion. The similarity between *ḥērem* and Assyrian assertions of total destruction is made particularly evident by this language; by boiling *ḥērem* down to a particular expression of the cosmic struggle against chaos it becomes eminently clear that the ideology underlying *ḥērem* is fundamentally identical to that which undergirds Assyrian military action, even though it uses different language. *Ḥērem* is clearly a military action in keeping with the common ancient Near Eastern conception of war as a struggle of order against chaos, even though it represents an extreme manifestation of that struggle (reasons for which were suggested above). The distinction made by Hebrew Bible scholars between *ḥērem* and the rest of Israelite (and ancient Near Eastern) military practice has been unfortunately facilitated by the use of a particular root to describe this most extreme form of the military eradication of chaos; it has obscured the extent to which this phenomenon is part of the broader ancient Near Eastern conception of war. *Ḥērem* is often the centre of attention in studies of war in the Hebrew Bible, but its importance has been fundamentally overstated.

What we are lacking elsewhere, therefore, is not so much the phenomenon of total destruction, but the articulation of the phenomenon as an imperative. To a certain extent, this is related to the issue of which Stern made so much, namely, the absence of a specific word in Akkadian (and most other languages) for total destruction. Why, in other

---

28 Stern, 72.

words, was this practice so significant in Israel and Judah as to warrant its designation with a particular item of vocabulary?

As already discussed, it is our contention that the deployment of *ḥērem* in the conquest (accounts) and subsequently in the late seventh century (though at both points probably more theoretically than actually) was a consequence of a perceived increase in the threat posed by outsiders to the indigenous order. There can be no doubt that the actual threat of foreign invasion was immeasurably higher in both Israel and Judah than it ever was in imperial Assyria. Such an extreme reaction to foreign threat never arose in Assyria simply because a correspondingly extreme threat never occurred in its historical experience. It is hardly surprising that a group for whom this threat and their reaction to it was so pronounced developed a particular word for the most extreme form of their reaction.[29]

Furthermore, in describing *ḥērem* as a creative act of order against chaos, it is significant to note that there is a very high level of inconsistency in the acts of war described by the term: it refers at various points to the execution of men, the execution of all human inhabitants, and the execution of all living creatures.[30] The supposedly paradigmatic narratives in Dt. 2-3, for example, conflict with the description of *ḥērem* in Dt. 20, and no amount of exegetical wriggling seems capable of eliminating this fact.[31] The erratic application of *ḥērem*, even in the early stages of

---

29 Given the close connection between the legitimation of acts of extreme violence and the divine, it also is not particularly surprising that the word employed for the most extreme act known to Israelite and Judahite warfare has religious overtones.

30 Gottwald explains its erratic application as the result of it having the nature of a vow, voluntarily invoked ("'Holy war' in Deuteronomy: analysis and critique").

31 There have been innumerable attempts to compensate for this basic inconsistency in the appearances of *ḥērem*. In the case of Dt. 2-3, Craigie considers Heshbon, at least, to be part of the territory ultimately identified as Israelite, though Christensen is doubtful. If Craigie is correct, Heshbon would not be eligible for the lighter treatment prescribed by 20.10-14 (in the traditional interpretation) (P.C. Craigie, *The Book of Deuteronomy*, NICOT [Grand Rapids, Mich.: Eerdmans, 1981], 118; D.L. Christensen, *Deuteronomy 1-11*, WBC 6a, [Dallas, Tex.: Word, 1991], 53). If Christensen is correct then *ḥērem* here goes beyond the men-only killing prescribed by 20.13-14. Bashan is in turn even less clearly identifiable as part of the territory meant to be Israel; the fact that the confrontation with its king is a consequence of the king's own initiative may suggest that it was not, and that the battle was by happenstance rather than design. The sequence of events in the two episodes is also distinct: Yahweh gives assurance of victory against Heshbon prior to the encounter with them, while the assurance of victory in the case of Bashan is prompted by the king's coming up against the Israelites. If Bashan was not part of the "promised" land, then, the treatment of Bashan in the same manner as Heshbon is further indication of the inconsistency with which *ḥērem* is applied. This inconsistency in the narrative application of *ḥērem*

national and ethnic identity formation, seems to provide evidence against it as a required (legislated or otherwise) component of Israelite or Judahite warfare. It makes much greater sense to consider *ḥērem* not an absolutely specific act, but rather to emphasise the *type* of act designated by the term: one which is aimed at the eradication of chaos, particularly in cases in which the perceived threat from chaos is especially high and the reaction against it consequently extreme.[32] Because of the high level of threat involved, *ḥērem* is correlated with acts of extreme violence against and destruction of the enemy.

10.1.3. Deuteronomy 20

The existence of an imperative to engage in acts of *ḥērem* in the Judahite and Israelite tradition raises the question of the nature of Dt. 20.10-18. We will treat the passage in two parts, commencing with Dt. 20.10-14:

> 10 When you drawn near to a town to fight against it, offer it terms of peace.
> 11 If it accepts your terms of peace and surrenders to you, then all the people in it shall serve you at forced labour.
> 12 If it does not submit to you peacefully, but makes war against you, then you shall besiege it;
> 13 and when Yahweh your God gives it into your hand, you shall put all its males to the sword.
> 14 You may, however, take as your booty the women, the children, livestock, and everything else in the town, all its spoil. You may enjoy the spoil of your enemies, which Yahweh your God has given you.[33]

We are first struck by the measured nature of these prescriptions. The instruction to offer terms of peace in the first instance indicates that military engagement is not sought for its own sake, but is a means to an end. The nature of that end is evident from Dt. 20.11a: subordination to Israelite authority, that is, acknowledgment of the correctness (inevitability, even) of the Israelite order. If the Israelite order is accepted vol-

---

is evident throughout Deuteronomistic History (of which these introductory chapters are an editorial part), whatever the theoretical imperatives of Dt. 20.

32 It is worth noting that, rather than mere existence being enough to classify these enemies as chaos in need of eradication, they must actively resist the Israelite expression of order. Sihon of Heshbon makes himself an obstacle to order by refusing passage through his territory; Og of Bashan comes up to fight against Israel of his own accord.

33 כי תקרב אל־עיר להלחם עליה וקראת אליה לשלום: והיה אם־שלום תענך ופתחה לך והיה כל־העם הנמצא־בה יהיו לך למס ועבדוך: ואם־לא תשלים עמך ועשתה עמך מלחמה וצרת עליה: ונתנה יהוה אלהיך בידך והכית את־כל־זכורה לפי־חרב: רק הנשים והטף והבהמה וכל אשר יהיה בעיר כל־שללה תבז לך ואכלת את־שלל איביך אשר נתן יהוה אלהיך לך:

untarily, there is no need for violence; the outworking of the enemy's subordination takes the form of forced labour. If, however, the opponent defies the extension of Israelite order by refusing to surrender, his consequent identification as anti-order, chaos, dictates that he must be eradicated. That this is not total is immediately clear from Dt. 20.14; again, the object is subordination, and acts of war are pursued only so far as necessary to achieve this end.

Though couched in legal phraseology, the instructions of Dt. 20.10-14 are very similar to the sequence of procedure adopted by the Assyrians: unsurprising, given that they share their underlying ideological logic. They both prefer that the enemy voluntarily submit to their system of order, and only pursue military means of enforcing it if the enemy defies subordination (and thus identifies itself with anti-order, or chaos). The treatment of the subordinated is proportionate to the degree to which they were identifiable with chaos: those who voluntarily submit are employed in the construction of the indigenous order (forced labour; deportation and employment in building projects or other commercial endeavours), while those who resist are eradicated more thoroughly.

There is, as has already been noted, some distinction between Assyrian practice and that expressed in *Deuteronomy* with regard to the treatment meted out to the combatants who have at first resisted. In *Deuteronomy*, the aggressors are explicitly instructed to execute all males. Extrapolating from the Assyrian sources, the Assyrians usually preferred to specify execution only with respect to the figurehead(s) of the defeated polity, though that this was a tendency rather than a strict rule is indicated by, on the one hand, the fact that the leaders of resistant populations were not killed in every case, and, on the other, the relatively frequent occurrence of sweeping statements to the effect that large numbers of the general male population were killed.

The reasoning behind this distinction is inevitably unclear, and the extent to which it was a real distinction is obscured by the fact that on the Assyrian side we have reports of actual engagements while on the Israelite and Judahite side we have a purely theoretical formulation, supplemented by only a handful of explicit military accounts. If, however, the distinction was actual and not merely theoretical, it is possible that it had something to do with the types of opponents normally encountered, namely large states versus small tribal groups. If the object is to prevent future resistance, the means employed to achieve this end would be modified according to the type of opponent encountered. The more developed a society, the more specialised are its inhabitants: in the case of a centralised state the military comprises only a portion of the overall population, and the execution of all males is superfluous. In a smaller, less industrialised society, military responsibilities fall broadly on all able-bodied males, and military incapacitation thus entails a much broader target of execution. In general, Mesopotamia was dominated by the former, while the Levant was mostly inhabited by the latter.

Deuteronomy 20.10-14, in any case, essentially prescribes military practices of exactly the sort we would expect. In Dt. 20.15-18, however, the prescriptions take a much more extreme form. First, Dt. 20.15 limits the preceding verses:

> 15 Thus you shall treat all the towns that are very far from you, which are not towns of the nations here.[34]

This leaves to be dealt with those opponents located in the territory claimed for the Israelites; for these Dt. 20.16-18 prescribes complete destruction:

> 16 But as for the towns of these peoples that Yahweh your God is giving you as an inheritance, you must not let anything that breathes remain alive.
> 17 You shall annihilate (חרם *hi*) them – the Hittites and the Amorites, the Canaanites and the Perizzites, the Hivites and the Jebusites – just as Yahweh your God has commanded,
> 18 so that they may not teach you to do all the abhorrent things that they do for their gods, and you thus sin against Yahweh your God.[35]

These verses have been identified by a number of scholars as a deuteronomistic addition to the instructions of Dt. 20.10-14.[36] They jar with preceding instructions to moderation, but coincide with the deuteronomistic interest in *ḥērem*, aiming for the most extreme level of eradication possible. The reason for the eradication is clear in Dt. 20.18: the cultural practices of the enemy are explicitly identified as a threat to the indigenous cultural order.[37] Again, the dual relevance of this prescrip-

---

34 כן תעשה לכל־הערים הרחקת ממך מאד אשר לא־מערי הגוים־האלה הנה׃

35 רק מ ערי העמים האלה אשר יהוה אלהיך נתן לך נחלה לא תחיה כל־נשמה׃ כי־החרם תחרימם החתי והאמרי הכנעני והפרזי החוי והיבוסי כאשר צוך יהוה אלהיך׃ למען אשר לא־ילמדו אתכם לעשות ככל תועבתם אשר עשו לאלהיהם וחטאתם ליהוה אלהיכם׃

36 E.g. J.G. McConville, *Deuteronomy*, AOTC 5 (Leicester: Inter-Varsity, 2002), 153; and Mayes, who considers all of 20.10-20 to be a deuteronomistic reformulation, though in such case the awkward limitation in 20.15 is difficult to explain (*Deuteronomy*, NCB [London: Marshall, Morgan & Scott, 1981], 293-296); see also Brueggemann, who considers Dt. 20.16-18 a deuteronomic addition (*Deuteronomy*, AOTC [Nashville, Tenn.: Abingdon, 2001], 210-211); and Tigay, 471. Deuteronomy 20.16-18 is very similar to 7.1-4, also recognised to be heavily deuteronomistic. The reversion in 20.19-20 to general conduct of war also indicates that 20.15-18 is an interpolation.

37 The address in Dt. 20.18 is plural, which Mayes takes as suggesting that it is an additional elaboration of the initial deuteronomistic radicalisation; Mayes divides

tion is evident: the description of the threat and the necessary response to it use terminology appropriate to the period of conquest (the Hittites, Amorites, etc.), but is clearly also a concern of the deuteronomistic writer who inserted the passage. The implausibility of Stern's argument that the deuteronomistic interest in *ḥērem* is a late attempt to ensure that it is not employed by the deuteronomist's contemporaries is made eminently clear by such an insertion: the more moderate instructions on warfare in Dt. 20.10-14 are radicalised by this insertion, not modified by them; a text in which total destruction is clearly excluded is extended to discuss the circumstances under which it may be enacted. The articulation of the instructions with reference to the Canaanites and other pre-Israelite populations is not an attempt to limit the practice to them alone, but an attempt to remain in keeping with the ostensible Mosaic setting of *Deuteronomy*.

Finally, a few brief comments on the absence of a king in Dt. 20.10-18, since we have observed elsewhere the king's special role in facilitating the legitimacy of warfare, by acting as the human half of the divine-human agency against chaos. There are a number of possible reasons for the king's absence. On the one hand, we may have a second instance akin to *Amos*, in which the absence of a king reflects the author's social location outside the monarchy, and thus outside the specifically royal divine-human synergy which occurs there. The origins of *Deuteronomy*, unfortunately, are terribly obscured. Alternately, the absence of a king in *Deuteronomy* may simply be the consequence of its purported Mosaic setting, and his absence in other texts of warfare similarly explicable. To a certain extent, this is surely true; no compiler could have plausibly inserted a king where it was known that there had not been one.

This emphasises, of course, that a king was not the only route by which the divine legitimation of warfare could be channelled; the accounts of pre-monarchic warfare certainly indicate this. We must remember that the sociological phenomenon in which war is a struggle against the chaotic enemy is a generalised expression of what happens when two alternative social orders meet; that this interaction was articulated in Israel, Judah and Assyria through the specific means of the

---

the theme of the destruction of the inhabitants of the land from the theme of avoidance of worship of other gods, and argues that they were conflated only later. However, he does this also in 7.1-4, again in the context of the application of *ḥērem*, and there the shifting between singular and plural is far too erratic to warrant taking it as an indicator of an additional editor. Note also that the Syriac of 20.18 employs the singular in the first half of the verse, rather than the levelled plurals of the Masoretic text.

king's identification with the god who battled chaos at creation is the result of these societies' monarchic structure. Such a close identification between king and god could be utilised to legitimate more specific and more violent treatment of the chaotic opponent, but the generally legitimating construct was readily able to legitimate lesser levels of violence.

This explains the ability of a pre-monarchic group to justify war in general. We, however, are interested in the pursuit of *ḥērem* in particular, given that elsewhere the justification of extreme military violence has been especially connected to the special role of the king as mediator of the deity's historical activity.

Ḥērem, as noted, dominates especially strongly in the account of the conquest, particularly in the narrative passages in Josh. 1-11. There is, of course, no king in these narratives. However, it can hardly be coincidental that these texts ascribe to Joshua a number of the characteristics normally associated with the king. The similarities between Joshua and Josiah in particular were enumerated by R.D. Nelson as part of his arguments for a double redaction of the Deuteronomistic History.[38] In *Deuteronomy*, it seems, the deuteronomistic radicalisation of warfare by the advocating of *ḥērem* could not be directly legitimated by reference to a royal figure, due to the Mosaic framework of the text. In *Joshua*, however, this legitimation was possible to achieve indirectly, through the association of *ḥērem* with Joshua in particular and the association of Joshua in turn with royal characteristics. The purpose of such royal associations, of course, is legitimation. For the deuteronomists working in the monarchic period, in which military legitimation is routed specifically through the figure of the king, the desired legitimation was most naturally expressed by employing royal associations.[39]

---

38 "Much of our present picture of Joshua is nothing but a retrojection of the figure of Josiah into the classical past" (*The Double Redaction of the Deuteronomistic History*, JSOTSup 18 [Sheffield: JSOT, 1981], 125); in detail, see R.D. Nelson, "Josiah in the book of Joshua", *JBL* 100 (1981): 531-540. Somewhat surprisingly, Nelson contends that the deuteronomist is tempering the violent traditions of Joshua to parallel Josiah's recovery of northern territories left open by Assyrian withdrawal – rather than, for example, the more nationalist and militaristic Josiah suggested by his confrontation with Neco ("Josiah", 537).

39 The underlying key to the king's legitimacy in undertaking military activities, however, is his intimacy with the deity, which could of course be expressed in other ways (compare, for example, Esarhaddon and Assurbanipal's reliance on prophecy). The use of *ḥērem* by Moses against Heshbon and Bashan in Dt. 2-3 is one example: in each case there is also an explicit quotation of Yahweh to express this intimacy.

10.1.4. Conclusions

Ḥērem is an extreme form of the military response to the chaotic threat of the enemy, but is not outside the range of what is observable in other Judahite and Assyrian texts, even if the latter did not develop a special language with which to refer to it. That such language did develop in Israel and Judah is most likely a function of these nations' higher exposure to foreign incursions over the course of their history. The frequency of references to *ḥērem* in accounts of the conquest and in deuteronomistic texts affirm its association with periods in which the perceived threat from outsiders peaked.

11. Conclusions

As the preceding demonstrates, successful comparison of ethical thinking in the ancient Near East entails an awareness of the social provenance of informants – including their ideological background – as well as an attention to changing historical circumstances.

We began by discussing the sociological phenomenon of ideology, and the conflation of society, nature and morality which it facilitates. Ethical thinking, we argued, could only be properly understood when its incorporation into the ideological system was appreciated: the identification of moral order with cosmic order meant that the submission of the chaotic other was not merely morally tolerable but morally imperative. We then turned accordingly to examine the peculiar manifestations of this phenomenon in Assyria and in Judah and Israel, where the confrontation between the indigenous order and its opposite, chaos, was conceived in terms of a divine battle with the watery forces of chaos at creation. In both cases this battle was intimately connected with the god's kingship. This association of cosmological creation motifs and both human and divine kingship provided strong evidence in favour of the proposal that the Judahite and Israelite royal ideology of warfare was founded on a similar cosmological basis to that which is evident in more detail in the Assyrian material.

The cosmological nexus of war, kingship and order proved central in the legitimation of military activities under the Assyrian kings Tiglath-pileser and Sargon, who use language alluding to *Enūma eliš* to evoke their role as the human counterpart of the god in the cosmic battle against chaos. The level of violence employed under these two kings is relatively moderate, and the most violent acts against enemy personnel are confined to leadership figures. Such acts always occur at the location of conquest, reflecting a purposeful use of targeted violence as a means of deterring future resistance to the Assyrian system. We also observed the use of religious-political language of sin and rebellion to describe the offences of the enemy, and noted that the offence was always a matter of resistance to Assyrian hegemony. The primary object of warfare was not the elimination of the enemy as such, but the elimination of it as opposed to Assyria. If an opponent could be relieved of its identification with chaos via a non-violent transfer of affiliation to

Assyria, this was sufficient to satisfy the ideological necessity that Assyria be the only system of order in existence.

Though the sources for Judah and Israel are less robust, we were nonetheless able to identify a similar use of cosmological allusions in *Psalms* to emphasise the synergy of Yahweh and the human king on the battlefield, and though the lack of a Hebrew rendering of the battle at creation made the identification of specific linguistic allusions to it inevitably tentative, we were able to suggest some such allusions. We saw that the language used of enemies frequently conflated political opposition with moral degenerateness, reiterating the conflation of social, natural and moral order, and noted the association of this ideology with an imperial programme designed to expand the cosmic order universally, in spite of the relatively minor political strength of both Israel and Judah in the ancient Near East.

We turned to the narrative texts of *Kings* and *Chronicles* in an attempt to flesh out the practical implications of this royal military ideology in Judah and Israel. Though these texts' interests elsewhere minimised the amount of technical detail about warfare which they relate, they were nonetheless able to confirm in a practical way certain elements of the ideological framework gleaned from *Psalms*, particularly with regard to a recurring imperialist attitude on the part of the Judahite king. Though the ideology behind the actions described is never made explicit, we saw how aggressive military actions stood for the symbolic destruction of opposition to a Judahite cosmic system. The texts unfortunately preserved no explicit explanation of how the experience of relatively little political power was incorporated into the cosmological system of warfare as a struggle against chaos, but we were able to argue that it was not mere coincidence that the outright defeat of Judah is only ever reported in *Chronicles*. The narrative accounts thus support the association of military success with divine-human alignment in the service of cosmic order. The practical application of violent offensive warfare was restricted by Judah and Israel's relatively minor political and military standing in comparison to other neighbours, but the narrative books give no reason to suspect that their kings would have acted in any substantially different way had they been in a similar situation to the kings of Assyria.

Having examined those texts pertaining to the ideology of warfare adopted by Israel and Judah's royal élite, we turned to the perspective of Amos, whose persistent polemic against the royal house and the upper classes suggested that he was not part of the social stratum reflected by the texts thus far considered. His oracles against the nations revealed a significant shift away from the ideological framework which we had observed thus far, with the new framework characterised especially by the dissociation of the implied human actor from the Judahite or Israelite king. This in turn highlighted key differences between the moral sensibilities attested in the oracles and those attested in *Psalms, Kings* and *Chronicles,* as well as problematic similarities between the condemned acts of the nations and the punitive acts of Yahweh. It was ultimately suggested that the concept of *lex talionis,* in which a consequence is connected to the offence in question, might provide the basis for Amos' moral framework. Though both Amos and the royal military ideology evinced a connection between ethics and the maintenance of order, the route by which order was achieved and maintained was distinctive in each.

The nature of the Assyrian sources meant that there was no equivalent non-élite material to consider, and accordingly we turned our attention to the implications of the second of our methodological concerns: namely, the impact of historical circumstances on ethical thinking.

The evidence in this regard was much more extensive in the Assyrian material, and we were accordingly able to trace a series of changes in the acts of warfare engaged upon by Sennacherib, Esarhaddon and Assurbanipal. These practical changes correlated to a series of changes in the use of cosmological language in the kings' records.

With Sennacherib, the Assyrian empire reached a stage in which opposition to its authority constituted rebellion in the more traditional political sense. The punitive character of the treatment of his opponents increased accordingly, but we noted that cosmological language varied according to the level of explicitness with which these punishments were described. The most extreme violence occurred in his conflicts with the Babylonians and their allies, and it was in descriptions of these encounters that the most pronounced cosmological allusions appeared, designed to cast Sennacherib as the counterpart of the god in the battle against chaos and to legitimate the extremity of his violence accordingly. The prominence of these conflicts with Babylonia under Sennacherib also led to attempts to rewrite *Enūma eliš* with Aššur as its protagonist, in an effort to circumvent the problematic nature of the identification of the Babylonian god Marduk as the divine warrior.

While the heightened levels of violence which characterised the reign of Sennacherib persisted under Esarhaddon, Esarhaddon's military synergy with the gods and the legitimation of his wars was primarily established not through cosmological allusions but through appeals to divination and prophecy, due perhaps in part to a recognition of the ongoing difficulties of the identification of Marduk as the king's cosmic counterpart. Both Esarhaddon and Assurbanipal also demonstrate a significant change in the treatment of defeated enemy personnel, namely, the return of captured leaders to Assyria for public exhibition and execution. It was argued that this change in practice was the consequence of these kings' heightened concern to demonstrate their authority and legitimacy as rulers, exacerbated in the case of Assurbanipal by both a direct attack on Assyria by the Elamites and by a civil war instigated by his brother in Babylon. The latter instance in particular appears to have been the final blow to the use of cosmological allusions in the legitimation of royal military endeavours.

The importance of historical factors in ethical thought about warfare in Assyria provoked the consideration of historical factors in the thought of Judah. The first suggestion of development surfaced in the traditions of Isaiah of Jerusalem, in which cosmological language was joined by hints of the language of *lex talionis*. This combination was taken further in the book of *Nahum*, which contained clear elements of the royal military ideology previously described, retaining the identification of the god's human counterpart with the Judahite king but also incorporating elements of the *lex talionis* concept observed in *Amos*. A number of explanations of this phenomenon were suggested, including a desire for revenge, re-orientation of the idea of cosmic order in relation to political power, and nationalistic aspirations couched in terms of the most significant political power of the time. Finally, we examined *ḥērem* as a particular manifestation of the struggle of order against chaos, and more specifically as a practice whose promotion was historically motivated by perceived increases in the threat to order, especially in the late seventh century.

In conclusion: we have argued that underlying similarities of cosmological and ideological outlook in the societies of Assyria, Judah and Israel have generated significant similarities in their ethical outlooks. In all three societies the mythological traditions surrounding creation reflect a strong connection between war, kingship and the establishment of order. Connections between the traditions' divine actors and the historical actions of the human king had the effect of making the king's military activities part of a cosmic struggle against chaos. Military violence was thereby cast not only as morally tolerable but as morally imperative.

Deviations from this point of view reflected two phenomena: the preservation of variable social perspectives and the impact of historical changes on ethical thinking. The relative frequency of the former in the Hebrew Bible as compared to the Assyrian libraries meant that earlier scholars emphasised the distinctiveness of ancient Israelite ethical ideas while failing to recognise that this distinctiveness was an illusion produced by the circumstances of preservation.

Finally, we have also drawn attention to a significant, yet underestimated, aspect of the study of ethical beliefs, namely the function of ethics in society. In order to understand violence on the battlefield and against defeated persons, it was not sufficient merely to catalogue the violence; rather we have put Assyrian, Judahite and Israelite warfare into their historical contexts, in order to understand how historical events affected the types of acts which could be legitimated and how the limits of acceptable behaviour shifted over time in response to historical factors. An appreciation of the importance of historical context for the origins and development of ethical thinking has facilitated a nuance of analysis which could not otherwise have been attained.

Abbreviations

AB	Anchor Bible
ABRL	Anchor Bible Reference Library
AfO	*Archiv für Orientforschung*
AfOB	Archiv für Orientforschung Beiheft
AJSL	*American Journal of Semitic Languages and Literatures*
ALASP	Abhandlungen zur Literatur Alt-Syrien-Palästinas und Mesopotamiens
AM	Arts of Mankind
AOAT	Alter Orient und Altes Testament
AOS	American Oriental Series
AOTC	Abingdon Old Testament Commentaries
Apollos	Apollos Old Testament Commentary
APR	R.D. Barnett. *Assyrian Palace Reliefs in the British Museum*. London: British Museum, 1970.
ARAB	D.D. Luckenbill. *Ancient Records of Assyria and Babylonia*. Chicago, Ill.: University of Chicago Press, 1926-1927.
ASBM	S. Smith. *Assyrian Sculptures in the British Museum from Shalmaneser III to Sennacherib*. London: British Museum, 1938.
ATANT	Abhandlungen zur Theologie des Alten und Neuen Testaments
ATD	Alte Testament Deutsch
ATM	Altes Testament und Moderne
BASOR	*Bulletin of the American Schools of Oriental Research*
BBVO	Berliner Beiträge zum Vorderen Orient
BETL	Bibliotheca Ephemeridum Theologicarum Lovaniensium
BF	Baghdader Forschungen
BHS	*Biblia Hebraica Stuttgartensia*
BI	*Biblical Interpretation*
BHT	Beiträge zur historischen Theologie
BIS	Biblical Interpretation Series
BJS	Brown Judaic Studies
BKAT	Biblischer Kommentar: Altes Testament
BM	*Baghdader Mitteilungen*

BerO	Berit Olam
BO	Biblica et Orientalia
BS	Biblical Seminar
BW	Bible World
BWANT	Beiträge zur Wissenschaft vom Alten und Neuen Testament
BZAW	Beihefte zur Zeitschrift für die alttestamentliche Wissenschaft
CAD	Gelb, I.J., et al. *The Assyrian Dictionary*. Chicago, Ill.: University of Chicago, 1956-.
CAT	Commentaire de l'Ancien Testament
CBC	Cambridge Bible Commentary
CBOT	Coniectanea Biblica Old Testament Series
CBQ	*Catholic Biblical Quarterly*
CBQMS	Catholic Biblical Quarterly Monograph Series
CHANE	Culture and History of the Ancient Near East
COP	Cambridge Oriental Publications
COS	Context of Scripture
CSHJ	Chicago Studies in the History of Judaism
EH	Essential Histories
EHS	Europäische Hochschulschriften
En.el.	P. Talon. *Enūma Eliš: The Standard Babylonian Creation Myth*. State Archives of Assyria Cuneiform Texts 4. Helsinki: Neo-Assyrian Text Corpus Project, 2005.
ET	*Expository Times*
FCB(SS)	Feminist Companion to the Bible (Second Series)
FRLANT	Forschungen zur Religion und Literatur des Alten und Neuen Testaments
GBS	Guides to Biblical Scholarship
GE	Geschichte der Ethik
HANEM	History of the Ancient Near East Monographs
HBM	Hebrew Bible Monographs
HER	Handbooks of Ethics and Religion
HSAO	Heidelberger Studien zum alten Orient
HSM	Harvard Semitic Monographs
IBT	Interpreting Biblical Texts
ICC	International Critical Commentary
ICT	Issues in Contemporary Theology
IKZ	*Internationale katholische Zeitschrift*
ILP	International Library of Psychology, Philosophy, and Scientific Method
IMJ	*Israel Museum Journal*
JAOS	*Journal of the American Oriental Society*

JBL	*Journal of Biblical Literature*
JCS	*Journal of Cuneiform Studies*
JJS	*Journal of Jewish Studies*
JNES	*Journal of Near Eastern Studies*
JNSL	*Journal of Northwest Semitic Languages*
JPS	JPS Torah Commentary
JSOT	*Journal for the Study of the Old Testament*
JSOTSup	Journal for the Study of the Old Testament Supplement Series
JTS	*Journal of Theological Studies*
KAT	Kommentar zum Alten Testament
LAI	Library of Ancient Israel
LAPO	Littératures anciennes du Proche-Orient
Layard	A.H. Layard. *The Monuments of Nineveh*. London: John Murray, 1853.
Layard II	A.H. Layard. *A Second Series of the Monuments of Nineveh*. London: John Murray, 1853.
LD	Lectio Divina
LDHS	Lectio Divina: Hors Série
LHBOTS	Library of Hebrew Bible/Old Testament Studies
LPR	Library of Philosophy and Religion
MDOG	*Mitteilungen der Deutschen Orient-Gesellschaft zu Berlin*
MLBS	Mercer Library of Biblical Studies
MVG	*Mitteilungen der Vorderasiatisch-ägyptischen Gesellschaft*
NCB	New Century Bible
NDA	New Directions in Archaeology
NICOT	New International Commentary on the Old Testament
NSBT	New Studies in Biblical Theology
OAC	Orientis Antiqui Collectio
OBO	Orbis Biblicus et Orientalis
OC	Orientalia et Classica
OBS	Oxford Bible Series
OIP	Oriental Institute Publications
OLA	Orientalia Lovaniensia Analecta
OPBF	Occasional Publications of the Babylonian Fund
Or	*Orientalia* (New Series)
OS	Oudtestamentische Studiën
OTL	Old Testament Library
OTM	Old Testament Monographs
OTS	Old Testament Studies
PID	Philosophical Ideas in Debate
POS	Pretoria Oriental Series

QGS	Quaderni di geografia storica
RE	*Review and Expositor*
RO	*Rocznik Orientalistyczny*
RSG	Regent's Study Guides
SAA	State Archives of Assyria
SAACT	State Archives of Assyria Cuneiform Texts
SAAS	State Archives of Assyria Studies
SBS	Stuttgarter Bibelstudien
SBLDS	Society of Biblical Literature Dissertation Series
SBLMS	Society of Biblical Literature Monograph Series
SBLSS	Society of Biblical Literature Symposium Series
SBTS	Sources for Biblical and Theological Study
SBT	Studies in Biblical Theology
SBT(SS)	Studies in Biblical Theology (Second Series)
SC	Scripture in Context
SEANE	Studies in Egyptology and the Ancient Near East
SFEG	Schriften der Finnischen Exegetischen Gesellschaft
SH	Scripta Hierosolymitana
SHR	Studies in the History of Religions
SNP	R.D. Barnett. *Sculptures from the North Palace of Ashurbanipal at Nineveh (668-627 B.C.)*. London: British Museum, 1976.
SOTSMS	Society for Old Testament Study Monograph Series
SS	Semeia Studies
SSP	R.D. Barnett, E. Bleibtreu and G. Turner. *Sculptures from the South-West Palace of Sennacherib at Nineveh*. 2 vols. London: British Museum, 1998.
TB	Theologische Bücherei
TF	Theologie und Frieden
TW	Theologische Wissenschaft
TynB	*Tyndale Bulletin*
UCPRE	University of Chicago Publications in Religious Education
UF	*Ugarit-Forschungen*
UMSHS	University of Michigan Studies Humanistic Series
UNHAIL	Uitgaven van het Nederlands Historisch-Archaeologisch Instituut te Leiden
VF	*Verkündigung und Forschung*
VT	*Vetus Testamentum*
VTSup	Supplements to Vetus Testamentum
WA	*World Archaeology*
WAL	World of Art Library
WAS	Wiener alttestamentliche Studien
WAW	Writings from the Ancient World

WBC	Word Biblical Commentary
WMANT	Wissenschaftliche Monographien zum Alten und Neuen Testament
ZABR	*Zeitschrift für altorientalische und biblische Rechtsgeschichte*
ZAW	*Zeitschrift für die alttestamentliche Wissenschaft*
ZBK	Zürcher Bibelkommentare
ZDMG	*Zeitschrift der deutschen mörgenländischen Gesellschaft*
ZTK	*Zeitschrift für Theologie und Kirche*

Multi-volume works are abbreviated as author followed by volume number, e.g., Eichrodt II.

Bibliography

Achtemeier, E.R. *Nahum – Malachi*. Interpretation. Atlanta, Ga.: John Knox, 1986.

Ackerman, S. *Warrior, Dancer, Seductress, Queen: Women in Judges and Biblical Israel*. London: Doubleday, 1998.

Adam, K.-P. *Der Königliche Held: Die Entsprechung von kämpfendem Gott und kämpfendem König in Psalm 18*. WMANT 91. Neukirchen-Vluyn: Neukirchner Verlag, 2001.

Albrektson, B. *History and the Gods: An Essay on the Idea of Historical Events as Divine Manifestation in the Ancient Near East and in Israel*. CBOT 1. Lund: CWK Gleerup, 1967.

Allen, L.C. *Psalms 101-150*. WBC 21. Waco, Tex.: Word, 1983.

Alter, R. *The Art of Biblical Narrative*. London: George Allen & Unwin, 1981.

Anderson, A.A. *2 Samuel*. WBC 11. Dallas, Tex.: Word, 1989.

Andersen, F.I., and D.N. Freedman. *Hosea: A New Translation with Introduction and Commentary*. AB 24. Garden City, N.Y.: Doubleday, 1980.

Anderson, C.B. "Biblical laws: challenging principles of Old Testament ethics". Pages 37-49 in *Character Ethics and the Old Testament: Moral Dimensions of Scripture*. Edited by M.D. Carroll R. and J.E. Lapsley. London: Westminster John Knox, 2007.

Arneth, M. "Die Komposition der Völkersprüche in Amos 1,3-2,16". *ZABR* 10 (2004): 249-263.

Arnold, B.T. *Babylonian Letters from the Kuyunjik Collection: Seventh Century Uruk in Light of New Epistolary Evidence*. PhD dissertation, Hebrew Union College – Jewish Institute of Religion, 1985.

Azarpay, G. "Proportions in ancient Near Eastern art". Pages 2507-2520 in vol. 4 of *Civilizations of the Ancient Near East*. Edited by J.M. Sasson. 4 vols. Peabody, Mass.: Hendrickson, 2000.

Bach, R. "»..., Der Bogen zerbricht, Spieße zerschlägt und Wagen mit Feuer verbrennt«". Pages 13-26 in *Probleme biblischer Theologie: Gerhard von Rad zum 70. Geburtstag*. Edited by H.W. Wolff. München: Chr. Kaiser, 1971.

Bahrani, Z. *Rituals of War: The Body and Violence in Mesopotamia*. New York, N.Y.: Zone Books, 2008.

Baker, H.D. *The Prosopography of the Neo-Assyrian Empire* (Ḫ-K). Vol. 2/1. Helsinki: Neo-Assyrian Text Corpus Project, 2000.

---. *The Prosopography of the Neo-Assyrian Empire* (L-N). Vol. 2/2. Helsinki: Neo-Assyrian Text Corpus Project, 2001.

---. *The Prosopography of the Neo-Assyrian Empire* (P-Ṣ). Vol. 3/1. Helsinki: Neo-Assyrian Text Corpus Project, 2002.
Baltzer, K. *Deutero-Isaiah*. Interpretation. Translated by M. Kohl. Minneapolis, Minn.: Fortress, 2001.
Barnett, R.D. *Assyrian Palace Reliefs in the British Museum*. London: British Museum, 1970.
---. *Sculptures from the North Palace of Ashurbanipal at Nineveh (668-627 B.C.)*. London: British Museum, 1976.
Barnett, R.D., E. Bleibtreu, and G. Turner. *Sculptures from the South-West Palace of Sennacherib at Nineveh*. 2 vols. London: British Museum, 1998.
Barnett, R.D., and M. Falkner. *The Sculptures of Aššur-naṣir-apli II (883-859 B.C.) Tiglath-pileser III (745-727 B.C.) Esarhaddon (681-669 B.C.) from the Central and South-West Palaces at Nimrud*. London: British Museum, 1962.
Barr, J. *History and Ideology in the Old Testament: Biblical Studies at the end of a Millennium*. Oxford: Oxford University Press, 2000.
---. "Natural theology and the future of biblical theology". Pages 199-221 in *Biblical Faith and Natural Theology: The Gifford Lectures for 1991 Delivered in the University of Edinburgh*. Oxford: Clarendon, 1993.
Barré, M.L. "The meaning of *l' 'šybnw* in Amos 1:3-2:6". *JBL* 105 (1986): 611-631.
Barstad, H.M. "Can prophetic texts be dated? Amos 1-2 as an example". Pages 21-40 in *Ahab Agonistes: The Rise and Fall of the Omri Dynasty*. Edited by L.L. Grabbe. LHBOTS 421. London: T&T Clark, 2007.
---. *The Myth of the Empty Land*. Stockholm: Scandinavian University Press, 1996.
Barton, J. *Amos's Oracles Against the Nations: A Study of Amos 1.3-2.5*. SOTSMS 6. Cambridge: Cambridge University Press, 1980.
---. "Approaches to ethics in the Old Testament". Pages 114-131 in *Beginning Old Testament Study*. Edited by J. Rogerson. London: SPCK, 1998.
---. *Ethics and the Old Testament*. London: SCM, 1998.
---. "Imitation of God in the Old Testament". Pages 35-46 in *The God of Israel*. Edited by R.P. Gordon. COP 64. Cambridge: Cambridge University Press, 2007.
---. "Natural law and poetic justice in the Old Testament". *JTS* 30 (1979): 1-14.
---. "Reading for life: the use of the Bible in ethics and the work of Martha C. Nussbaum". Pages 66-76 in *The Bible in Ethics: The Second Sheffield Colloquium*. Edited by M.D. Carroll R., M. Davies and J.W. Rogerson. JSOTSup 207. Sheffield: Sheffield Academic Press, 1995.
---. *Understanding Old Testament Ethics: Approaches and Explorations*. Louisville, Ky.: Westminster John Knox, 2003.
Beal, R.H. "Hittite military organization". Pages 545-554 in vol. 1 of *Civilizations of the Ancient Near East*. Edited by J. Sasson. 4 vols. Peabody, Mass.: Hendrickson, 2000.
Bellinger Jr., W.H. *Psalmody and Prophecy*. JSOTSup 27. Sheffield: JSOT, 1984.
Bentzen, A. *King and Messiah*. Translated by A. Bentzen. London: Lutterworth, 1955.
Berger, P.L. *The Sacred Canopy: Elements of a Sociological Theory of Religion*. Garden City, N.Y.: Doubleday, 1969. Reprinted as *The Social Reality of Religion*. Norwich: Penguin, 1973.
Berger, P.R. "Zum ugaritischen Wörterbuch, 1". *UF* 2 (1970): 339-346.

Berlin, A. *Zephaniah*. AB 24a. London: Doubleday, 1994.

Bernhardt, K.-H. *Das Problem der altorientalischen Königsideologie im Alten Testament: unter besonderer Berücksichtigung der Geschichte der Psalmenexegese dargestellt und kritisch gewürdigt*. VTSup 8. Leiden: Brill, 1961.

Bersani, L., and U. Dutoit. *The Forms of Violence: Narrative in Assyrian Art and Modern Culture*. New York, N.Y.: Schocken Books, 1985.

Birch, B.C. "Divine character and the formation of moral community in the book of Exodus". Pages 119-135 in *The Bible in Ethics: The Second Sheffield Colloquium*. Edited by M.D. Carroll R., M. Davies and J.W. Rogerson. JSOTSup 207. Sheffield: Sheffield Academic Press, 1995.

---. *Let Justice Roll Down: The Old Testament, Ethics, and Christian Life*. Louisville, Ky.: Westminster John Knox, 1988.

---. "Old Testament narrative and moral address". Pages 75-91 in *Canon, Theology and Old Testament Interpretation: Essays in Honor of Brevard S. Childs*. Edited by G.M. Tucker, D.L. Petersen and R.R. Wilson. Philadelphia, Pa.: Fortress, 1988.

Black, J., A.R. George, and J.N. Postgate, eds. *A Concise Dictionary of Akkadian*. 2d (corrected) ed. Wiesbaden: Harrassowitz, 2000.

Bloch-Smith, E. *Judahite Burial Practices and Beliefs about the Dead*. JSOTSup 123. Sheffield: JSOT, 1992.

Boadt, L. *Reading the Old Testament*. Mahwah, N.J.: Paulist Press, 1984.

Boling, R.G., and G.E. Wright. *Joshua: A New Translation*. AB 6. Garden City, N.Y.: Doubleday, 1982.

Borger, R. *Beiträge zum Inschriftenwerk Assurbanipals*. Wiesbaden: Harrassowitz, 1996.

---. *Die Inschriften Asarhaddons, Königs von Assyrien*. AfOB 9. Graz: Ernst Weidner, 1956.

Brett, M.G. "Literacy and domination: G.A. Herion's sociology of history writing". Pages 109-134 in *Social-Scientific Old Testament Criticism*. Edited by D.J. Chalcraft. BS 47. Sheffield: Sheffield Academic Press, 1997. Reprinted from *JSOT* 37 (1987): 15-40.

---. "Nationalism and the Hebrew Bible". Pages 136-163 in *The Bible in Ethics: The Second Sheffield Colloquium*. Edited by M.D. Carroll R., M. Davies and J.W. Rogerson. JSOTSup 207. Sheffield: Sheffield Academic Press, 1995.

Brettler, M.Z. *The Creation of History in Ancient Israel*. London: Routledge, 1995.

---. "Images of YHWH the warrior in Psalms". *Semeia* 61 (1993): 135-165.

---. "The new biblical historiography". Pages 43-50 in *Israel's Past in Present Research: Essays on Ancient Israelite Historiography*. Edited by V.P. Long. SBTS 7. Winona Lake, Ind.: Eisenbrauns, 1999.

Brichto, H.C. *Toward a Grammar of Biblical Poetics: Tales of the Prophets*. Oxford: Oxford University Press, 1992.

Brinkman, J.A. *Prelude to Empire: Babylonian Society and Politics, 747-626 B.C.* OPBF 7. Philadelphia, Pa.: The Babylonian Fund, 1984.

---. "Sennacherib's Babylonian problem: an interpretation". *JCS* 25 (1973): 89-95.

---. "Through a glass darkly: Esarhaddon's retrospects on the downfall of Babylon". *JAOS* 103 (1983): 35-42.

Brown, W.P. "The moral cosmologies of creation". Pages 11-26 in *Character Ethics and the Old Testament: Moral Dimensions of Scripture*. Edited by M.D. Carroll R. and J.E. Lapsley. London: Westminster John Knox, 2007.
Brueggemann, W. *Deuteronomy*. AOTC. Nashville, Tenn.: Abingdon, 2001.
---. *First and Second Samuel*. Interpretation. Louisville, Ky.: John Knox, 1990.
de Bruin, W.M. "Die Freistellung vom Militärdienst in Deut. xx 5-7: Die Gattung der Wirkungslosigkeitssprüche als Schlüssel zum Verstehen eines alten Brauches". *VT* 49 (1999): 21-33.
Buber, M. "Imitatio dei". Pages 32-43 in *Mamre: Essays in Religion*. Translated by G. Hort. London: Oxford University Press, 1946.
Burman, M.N. "Punishment and justification". *Ethics* 118 (2008): 258-290.
Butler, T.C. *Joshua*. WBC 7. Waco, Tex.: Word, 1983.

Carroll R., M.D. "'He has told you what is good': moral formation in Micah". Pages 103-118 in *Character Ethics and the Old Testament: Moral Dimensions of Scripture*. Edited by M.D. Carroll R. and J.E. Lapsley. London: Westminster John Knox, 2007.
Cathcart, K.J. *Nahum in the Light of Northwest Semitic*. BO 36. Rome: Pontificio Istituto Biblico, 1973.
---. "Treaty-curses and the book of Nahum". *CBQ* 34 (1973): 179-187.
Cazeaux, J. *Le refus de la guerre sainte: Josué, Juges et Ruth*. LD 174. Paris: Éditions du Cerf, 1998.
Chapman, C.R. *The Gendered Language of Warfare in the Israelite-Assyrian Encounter*. HSM 62. Winona Lake, Ind.: Eisenbrauns, 2004.
Chapman, M.D. "Ideology, theology and sociology: from Kantsky to Meeks". Pages 41-65 in *The Bible in Ethics: The Second Sheffield Colloquium*. Edited by M.D. Carroll R., M. Davies and J.W. Rogerson. JSOTSup 207. Sheffield: Sheffield Academic Press, 1995.
Childs, B.S. *Introduction to the Old Testament as Scripture*. London: SCM, 1979.
---. *Isaiah*. OTL. London: Westminster John Knox, 2001.
Christensen, D.L. "The acrostic of Nahum reconsidered". *ZAW* 87 (1975): 17-30.
---. *Deuteronomy 1-11*. WBC 6a. Dallas, Tex.: Word, 1991.
---. *Deuteronomy 21:10-34:12*. WBC 6b. Nashville, Tenn.: Thomas Nelson, 2002.
---. *Prophecy and War in Ancient Israel: Studies in the Oracles Against the Nations in Old Testament Prophecy*. Berkeley, Ca.: BIBAL, 1975.
Clements, R.E. *Jeremiah*. Interpretation. Atlanta, Ga.: John Knox, 1988.
Clifford, R.J. *Psalms 1-72*. AOTC. Nashville, Tenn.: Abingdon, 2002.
---. *Psalms 73-150*. AOTC. Nashville, Tenn.: Abingdon, 2003.
Clines, D.J.A. "Ethics and deconstruction, and, the ethics of deconstruction". Pages 77-106 in *The Bible in Ethics: The Second Sheffield Colloquium*. Edited by M.D. Carroll R., M. Davies and J.W. Rogerson. JSOTSup 207. Sheffield: Sheffield Academic Press, 1995.
Cogan, M. *Imperialism and Religion: Assyria, Judah and Israel in the Eighth and Seventh Centuries B.C.E.* SBLMS 19. Missoula, MT: Scholars Press, 1974.
Cogan, M., and H. Tadmor. *II Kings: A New Translation with Introduction and Commentary*. AB 11. Garden City, N.Y.: Doubleday, 1998.

Coggins, R.J. "Prophecy – true and false". Pages 80-94 in *Of Prophets' Visions and the Wisdom of Sages*. Edited by D.J.A. Clines and H.A. McKay. JSOTSup 162. Sheffield: JSOT, 1993.

Cole, S.W. "The destruction of orchards in Assyrian warfare". Pages 29-40 in *Assyria 1995: Proceedings of the 10th Anniversary Symposium of the Neo-Assyrian Text Corpus Project*. Edited by S. Parpola and R.M. Whiting. Helsinki: Helsinki University Press, 1997.

Cook, P. *The Redactional Development of Isaiah 18-20*. University of Oxford D.Phil. thesis, 2009.

Cooper, J. "Assyrian prophecies, the Assyrian tree, and the Mesopotamian origins of Jewish monotheism, Greek philosophy, Christian theology, Gnosticism, and much more". *JAOS* 120 (2000): 430-444.

Coote, R.B. *Amos Among the Prophets: Composition and Theology*. Philadelphia, Pa.: Fortress, 1981.

Cortese, E. "Theories concerning Dtr: a possible rapprochement". Pages 179-190 in *Pentateuchal and Deuteronomistic Studies: Papers Read at the XIIIth IOSOT Congress, Leuven 1989*. Edited by C. Brekelmans and J. Lust. BETL 94. Leuven: Leuven University Press, 1990.

Craigie, P.C. *The Book of Deuteronomy*. NICOT. Grand Rapids, Mich.: Eerdmans, 1981.

---. *The Problem of War in the Old Testament*. Grand Rapids, Mich.: Eerdmans, 1981.

---. *Psalms 1-50*. WBC 19. Waco, Tex.: Word, 1983.

---. "Recent evidence from Assyrian sources for Judean history from Uzziah to Manasseh". *JSOT* 28 (2004): 387-401.

Craigie, P.C., J.F. Drinkard and P.H. Kelley. *Jeremiah 1-25*. WBC 26. Waco, Tex.: Word, 1991.

Croft, S.J.L. *The Identity of the Individual in the Psalms*. JSOTSup 44. Sheffield: JSOT, 1987.

Cross, F.M. *Canaanite Myth and Hebrew Epic: Essays in the History of the Religion of Israel*. Cambridge, Mass.: Harvard University Press, 1973.

Crüsemann, F., W. Dietrich, and H.-C. Schmitt. "Gerechtigkeit-Gewalt-Leben: Was leistet eine Ethik des Alten Testaments?" Pages 145-169 in *Recht und Ethik im Alten Testament: Beiträge des Symposiums „Das Alte Testament und die Kultur der Moderne" anlässlich des 100. Geburtstags Gerhard von Rads (1901-1971), Heidelberg, 18.-21. Oktober 2001*. Edited by B.M. Levinson and E. Otto. ATM 13. Munich: Lit Verlag, 2004.

Curran, C.E. "Absolute norms in moral theology". Pages 139-174 in *Norm and Context in Christian Ethics*. Edited by G.H. Outka and P. Ramsey. London: SCM, 1969.

Curtis, J.E., and J.E. Reade, eds. *Art and Empire: Treasures from Assyria in the British Museum*. London: British Museum, 1995.

Dalley, S. *Esther's Revenge at Susa: From Sennacherib to Ahasuerus*. Oxford: Oxford University Press, 2007.

---. "Foreign chariotry and cavalry in the armies of Tiglath-Pileser III and Sargon II". *Iraq* 47 (1985): 31-48.

---. "The language of destruction and its interpretation". *BM* 36 (2005): 275-285.

---. *Myths from Mesopotamia: Creation, The Flood, Gilgamesh, and Others*. Oxford: Oxford University Press, 2000.

Davie, M.R. *The Evolution of War: A Study of its Rôle in Early Societies*. London: Oxford University Press, 1929.

Davies, A. *Double Standards in Isaiah: Re-evaluating Prophetic Ethics and Divine Justice*. BIS 46. Leiden: Brill, 2000.

Davies, E.W. "Ethics of the Hebrew Bible: the problem of methodology". *Semeia* 66 (1995): 43-53.

Davies, G.I. *Hosea*. NCB. Grand Rapids, Mich.: Eerdmans, 1992.

Davies, P.R. "'Ancient Israel' and history: a response to Norman Whybray". Pages 188-191 in *Israel's Past in Present Research: Essays on Ancient Israelite Historiography*. Edited by V.P. Long. SBTS 7. Winona Lake, Ind.: Eisenbrauns, 1999.

---. "Ethics and the Old Testament". Pages 164-173 in *The Bible in Ethics: The Second Sheffield Colloquium*. Edited by M.D. Carroll R., M. Davies and J.W. Rogerson. JSOTSup 207. Sheffield: Sheffield Academic Press, 1995.

---. *In Search of 'Ancient Israel'*. JSOTSup 148. Sheffield: JSOT, 1992.

---. "Method and madness: some remarks on doing history with the Bible". *JBL* 114 (1995): 699-705.

---. "This is what happens...". Pages 106-118 in *'Like a Bird in a Cage': The Invasion of Sennacherib in 701 BCE*. JSOTSup 363. Edited by L.L. Grabbe. Sheffield: Sheffield Academic Press, 2003.

Day, J. *God's Conflict with the Dragon and the Sea: Echoes of a Canaanite Myth in the Old Testament*. COP 35. Cambridge: Cambridge University Press, 1985.

---, ed. *In Search of Pre-Exilic Israel*. JSOTSup 406. London: T&T Clark, 2004.

De Odorico, M. *The Use of Numbers and Quantifications in the Assyrian Royal Inscriptions*. SAAS 3. Helsinki: Neo-Assyrian Text Corpus Project, 1995.

Del Monte, G.F. "The Hittite ḥerem". Pages 21-45 in *Memoriae Igor M. Diakonoff*. OC 8. Edited by L. Kogan, N. Koslova, S. Loesov and S. Tishchenko. Winona Lake, Ind.: Eisenbrauns, 2005.

Dever, W.G. "Histories and non-histories of ancient Israel: the question of the United Monarchy". Pages 65-94 in *In Search of Pre-Exilic Israel*. JSOTSup 406. Edited by J. Day. London: T&T Clark, 2004.

DeVries, S.J. *1 Kings*. WBC 12. Waco, Tex.: Word, 1985.

Dietrich, M. *The Babylonian Correspondence of Sargon and Sennacherib*. SAA 17. Helsinki: Helsinki University Press, 2003.

Dillard, R.B. *2 Chronicles*. WBC 15. Waco, Tex.: Word Books, 1987.

Dubovský, P. *Hezekiah and the Assyrian Spies: Reconstruction of the Neo-Assyrian Intelligence Services and its Significance for 2 Kings 18-19*. BO 49. Rome: Pontificio Istituto Biblico, 2006.

Dutcher-Walls, P. "The social location of the Deuteronomists: a sociological study of factional politics in late pre-exilic Judah". *JSOT* 52 (1991): 77-94.

Eaton, J.H. *Kingship and the Psalms*. SBT(SS) 32. London: SCM, 1976.

Eichrodt, W. *Theology of the Old Testament*. Translated by J.A. Baker. 2 vols. OTL. London: SCM, 1961-1967.

Elgavish, D. "The division of the spoils of war in the Bible and in the ancient Near East". *ZABR* 8 (2002): 242-273.

Engnell, I. *Studies in Divine Kingship in the Ancient Near East*. Uppsala: Almqvist & Wiksell, 1943.

Eph'al, I. "On warfare and military control in the ancient Near Eastern empires: a research outline". Pages 88-106 in *History, Historiography and Interpretation: Studies in Biblical and Cuneiform Literatures*. Edited by H. Tadmor and M. Weinfeld. Leiden: E.J. Brill, 1983.

Fales, F.M. "The enemy in Assyrian royal inscriptions: 'the moral judgement'". Pages 425-436 in vol. 2 of *Mesopotamien und seine Nachbarn: politische und kulturelle Wechselbeziehungen im Alten Vorderasien vom 4. bis 1. Jahrtausend v. Chr. XXV. Rencontre assyriologique internationale Berlin, 3. bis 7. Juli 1978*. Edited by H.-J. Nissen and J. Renger. BBVO 1. Berlin: Dietrich Reimer Verlag, 1982.

---. "A literary code in Assyrian royal inscriptions: the case of Ashurbanipal's Egyptian campaigns". Pages 169-202 in *Assyrian Royal Inscriptions: New Horizons in Literary, Ideological, and Historical Analysis: Papers of a Symposium held in Cetona (Siena), June 26-28, 1980*. Edited by F.M. Fales. OAC 17. Rome: Istituto per l'Oriente, 1981.

Fales, F.M., and J.N. Postgate. *Imperial Administrative Records, Part II: Provincial and Military Administration*. SAA 11. Helsinki: Helsinki University Press, 1995.

Faust, A., and E. Weiss. "Judah, Philistia, and the Mediterranean world: reconstructing the economic system of the seventh century B.C.E.". *BASOR* 338 (2005): 71-92.

Fensham, C.F. "Common trends in curses of near-eastern treaties and *kudurru*-inscriptions compared with the maledictions of Amos and Isaiah". *ZAW* 75 (1963): 155-175.

Flandin, E. *Monument de Ninive*. 5 vols. Paris: Imprimerie Nationale, 1849-1850.

Foster, B.R. *Before the Muses: An Anthology of Akkadian Literature*. 3d ed. Bethesda, Md.: CDL, 2005.

Frahm, E. *Einleitung in die Sanherib-Inschriften*. AfOB 26. Vienna: Institut für Orientalistik der Universität Wien, 1997.

---. "Images of Assyria in nineteenth- and twentieth-century Western scholarship". Pages 74-94 in *Orientalism, Assyriology and the Bible*. Edited by S.W. Holloway. HBM 10. Sheffield: Sheffield Phoenix, 2006.

Frame, G. *Babylonia 689-627 B.C.: A Political History*. Istanbul: Nederlands Historisch-Archaeologisch Instituut, 1992.

Frame, G., and A.R. George. "The royal libraries of Nineveh: new evidence for king Assurbanipal's tablet collecting". *Iraq* 67 (2005): 265-284. Vol. 2 of *Nineveh: Papers of the XLIXe Rencontre Assyriologique Internationale London 7-11 July 2003*.

Frankfort, H. *Kingship and the Gods: A Study of Ancient Near Eastern Religion as the Integration of Society and Nature*. Chicago, Ill.: University of Chicago Press, 1948.

Freedman, D.N. "Between God and Man: Prophets in Ancient Israel". Pages 57-88 in *Prophecy and Prophets: The Diversity of Contemporary Issues in Scholarship*. Edited by Y. Gitay. SS. Atlanta, Ga.: Scholars, 1997.

Freedman, D.N., and R. Frey. "False Prophecy is True". Pages 82-87 in *Inspired Speech: Prophecy in the Ancient Near East: Essays in Honor of Herbert B. Huffmon*. Edited by J. Kaltner and L. Stulman. JSOTSup 378. London: T&T Clark, 2004.

Frick, F.S. "*Cui bono?* – History in the service of political nationalism: the Deuteronomistic History as political propaganda". *Semeia* 66 (1995): 79-92.

Fuchs, A. *Die Inschriften Sargons II. aus Khorsabad*. Göttingen: Cuvillier, 1994.

Fuchs, A., and S. Parpola. *The Correspondence of Sargon II, Part III: Letters from Babylonia and the Eastern Provinces*. SAA 15. Helsinki: Helsinki University Press, 2001.

Garelli, P. "La conception de la royauté en Assyrie". Pages 1-11 in *Assyrian Royal Inscriptions: New Horizons in Literary, Ideological, and Historical Analysis: Papers of a Symposium held in Cetona (Siena), June 26-28, 1980*. Edited by F.M. Fales. OAC 17. Rome: Istituto per l'Oriente, 1981.

Geertz, C. *The Interpretation of Cultures: Selected Essays*. London: Fontana, 1973.

Gehman, H.S. "Natural law and the Old Testament". Pages 109-122 in *Biblical Studies in Memory of H.C. Alleman*. Edited by J.M. Myers, O. Reimherr and H.N. Bream. Locust Valley, N.Y.: J.J. Augustin, 1960.

Gelb, I.J., et al. *The Assyrian Dictionary*. Chicago, Ill.: University of Chicago, 1956-.

Gerstenberger, E.S. *Theologies in the Old Testament*. Translated by J. Bowden. London: T&T Clark, 2002.

Gillingham, S.E. *The Poems and Psalms of the Hebrew Bible*. OBS. Oxford: Oxford University Press, 1994.

Goetze, A. "Warfare in Asia Minor". *Iraq* 25 (1963): 124-130.

Goldingay, J. *Approaches to Old Testament Interpretation*. ICT. Leicester: Inter-Varsity, 1981.

Good, R.M. "The just war in ancient Israel". *JBL* 104 (1985): 385-400.

Gordon, R.P. "From Mari to Moses: prophecy at Mari and in ancient Israel". Pages 63-79 in *Of Prophets' Visions and the Wisdom of Sages*. Edited by D.J.A. Clines and H.A. McKay. JSOTSup 162. Sheffield: JSOT, 1993.

Gottwald, N.K. "'Holy war' in Deuteronomy: analysis and critique". *RE* 61 (1965): 296-310.

---. "Theological education as a theory-praxis loop: situating the book of Joshua in a cultural, social ethical, and theological matrix". Pages 107-118 in *The Bible in Ethics: The Second Sheffield Colloquium*. Edited by M.D. Carroll R., M. Davies and J.W. Rogerson. JSOTSup 207. Sheffield: Sheffield Academic Press, 1995.

---. *The Tribes of Yahweh: A Sociology of the Religion of Liberated Israel, 1250-1050 B.C.E.* London: SCM, 1980.

Grabbe, L.L. "Prophets, priests, diviners and sages in ancient Israel". Pages 43-62 in *Of Prophets' Visions and the Wisdom of Sages*. Edited by D.J.A. Clines and H.A. McKay. JSOTSup 162. Sheffield: JSOT, 1993.

---, ed. *'Like a Bird in a Cage': The Invasion of Sennacherib in 701 BCE*. JSOTSup 363. Sheffield: Sheffield Academic Press, 2003.

Gray, J. *I & II Kings*. OTL. 3d ed. London: SCM, 1977.

---. *Joshua, Judges and Ruth*. NCB. London: Thomas Nelson, 1967.

---. "The kingship of God in the prophets and psalms". *VT* 11 (1961): 1-29.
Grayson, A.K. "Assyrian royal inscriptions: literary characteristics". Pages 35-47 in *Assyrian Royal Inscriptions: New Horizons in Literary, Ideological, and Historical Analysis: Papers of a Symposium held in Cetona (Siena), June 26-28, 1980*. Edited by F.M. Fales. OAC 17. Rome: Istituto per l'Oriente, 1981.
---. *Assyrian Rulers of the Early First Millennium BC II (858-745 BC)*. Vol. 3 of *The Royal Inscriptions of Mesopotamia*. London: University of Toronto Press, 1996.
Green, A. "Ancient Mesopotamian religious iconography". Pages 1837-1856 in vol. 3 of *Civilizations of the Ancient Near East*. Edited by J.M. Sasson. 4 vols. Peabody, Mass.: Hendrickson, 2000.
Greengus, S. "Some issues relating to the comparability of laws and the coherence of the legal tradition". Pages 60-87 in *Theory and Method in Biblical and Cuneiform Law: Revision, Interpolation and Development*. Edited by B.M. Levinson. JSOTSup 181. Sheffield: Sheffield Academic Press, 1994.
Gunkel, H. *An Introduction to the Psalms: The Genres of the Religious Lyric of Israel*. Completed by J. Begrich. Translated by J.D. Nogalski. MLBS. Macon, Ga.: Mercer University Press, 1998.

Haas, V. "Die Dämonisierung des Fremden und des Feindes im Alten Orient". Pages 37-44 in *Anniversary Volume Dedicated to Rudolph Ranoszek on his Eighty-fifth Birthday*. Edited by E. Tryjarski. *RO* 41.2. Warsaw: Państwowe Wydawnictwo Naukowe, 1980.
Hackett, J.A. *The Balaam Text from Deir 'Allā*. HSM 31. Chico, Ca.: Scholars, 1984.
Haglund, E. *Historical Motifs in the Psalms*. CBOT 23. Stockholm: CWK Gleerup, 1984.
Haldar, A. *Studies in the Book of Nahum*. Leipzig: Otto Harrassowitz, 1947.
Hallo, W.W. "An Assurbanipal text recovered". *IMJ* 6 (1987): 33-37.
---. "Biblical history in its Near Eastern setting: the contextual approach". Pages 1-26 in *Essays on the Comparative Method*. Edited by C.D. Evans, W.W. Hallo and J.B. White. SC 1. Pittsburg, Pa.: Pickwick, 1980.
Hallo, W.W., and K.L. Younger Jr., eds. *Archival Documents from the Biblical World*. COS 3. Leiden: Brill, 2000.
---. *Monumental Inscriptions from the Biblical World*. COS 2. Leiden: Brill, 2000.
Hamilton, M. "Religion and meaning". Pages 177-184 in *The Sociology of Religion: Theoretical and Comparative Perspectives*. 2d ed. London: Routledge, 2001.
Hammershaimb, E. "On the ethics of the Old Testament prophets". Pages 75-101 in *Congress Volume: Oxford 1959*. VTSup 7. Leiden: Brill, 1960.
Harris, M.J. *Divine Command Ethics: Jewish and Christian Perspectives*. PID. London: RoutledgeCurzon, 2003.
Hasel, M.G. *Military Practice and Polemic: Israel's Laws of Warfare in Near Eastern Perspective*. Berrien Springs, Mich.: Andrews University Press, 2005.
Hausmann, J. "„Gott ist König über die Völker." Der Beitrag von Ps 47 zum Thema Israel und die Völker". Pages 91-102 in vol. 1 of *Vielseitigkeit des Alten Testaments: Festschrift für Georg Sauer zum 70. Geburtstag*. 2 vols. Edited by J.A. Loader and H.V. Kieweler. WAS 1. Frankfurt-am-Main: Peter Lang, 1999.
Hawk, L.D. *Joshua*. BerO. Collegeville, Minn.: Liturgical Press, 2000.

Hayes, J.H. *Amos the Eighth Century Prophet: His Times and his Preaching*. Nashville, Tenn.: Abingdon, 1988.

---. "The history of the study of Israelite and Judaean history: from the Renaissance to the present". Pages 7-42 in *Israel's Past in Present Research: Essays on Ancient Israelite Historiography*. Edited by V.P. Long. SBTS 7. Winona Lake, Ind.: Eisenbrauns, 1999.

---. "The usage of oracles against foreign nations in ancient Israel". *JBL* 87 (1968): 81-92.

Hempel, J. "Ethics in the OT". Pages 153-161 in vol. 2 of *Interpreter's Dictionary of the Bible*. Edited by G.A. Buttrick. 4 vols. New York, N.Y.: Abingdon, 1962.

---. *Das Ethos des Alten Testaments*. BZAW 68. Berlin: A. Töpelmann, 1938.

Herion, G.A. "The impact of modern and social science assumptions in the reconstruction of Israelite history". Pages 78-108 in *Social-Scientific Old Testament Criticism*. Edited by D.J. Chalcraft. BS 47. Sheffield: Sheffield Academic Press, 1997. Reprinted from *JSOT* 34 (1986): 3-33.

Herrmann, S. "The devaluation of the Old Testament as a historical source: notes on a problem in the history of ideas". Pages 346-355 in *Israel's Past in Present Research: Essays on Ancient Israelite Historiography*. Edited by V.P. Long. SBTS 7. Winona Lake, Ind.: Eisenbrauns, 1999.

Hertzberg, H.W. *I & II Samuel*. OTL. Translated by J. Bowden. London: SCM, 1964.

Hobbs, T.R. *2 Kings*. WBC 13. Waco, Tex.: Word Books, 1985.

---. *A Time for War: A Study of Warfare in the Old Testament*. OTS 3. Wilmington, Del.: Michael Glazier, 1989.

Holloway, S.W. *Aššur is King! Aššur is King! Religion in the Exercise of Power in the Neo-Assyrian Empire*. CHANE 10. Leiden: Brill, 2002.

Horst, F. "Naturrecht und Altes Testament". Pages 235-259 in *Gottes Recht: gesammelte Studien zum Recht im Alten Testament: aus Anlass der Vollendung seines 65. Lebensjahres*. TB 12. Edited by H.W. Wolff. Munich: Kaiser, 1961.

Houston, W. "The character of YHWH and the ethics of the Old Testament: is *imitatio dei* appropriate?" *JTS* 58 (2007): 1-25.

Hrouda, B. "Der assyrische Streitwagen". *Iraq* 25 (1963): 155-158.

Huffmon, H.B. "A company of prophets: Mari, Assyria, Israel". Pages 47-70 in *Prophecy in its Ancient Near Eastern Context: Mesopotamian, Biblical, and Arabian Perspectives*. Edited by M. Nissinen. SBLSS 13. Atlanta, Ga.: SBL, 2000.

---. "The one and the many: prophets and deities in the ancient Near East". Pages 116-131 in *Propheten in Mari, Assyrien und Israel*. Edited by M. Köckert and M. Nissinen. FRLANT 201. Göttingen: Vandenhoeck & Ruprect, 2003.

---. "The origins of prophecy". Pages 171-186 in *Magnalia Dei, The Mighty Acts of God: Essays on the Bible and Archaeology in Memory of G. Ernest Wright*. Edited by F.M. Cross, W.E. Lemke and P.D. Miller, Jr. Garden City, N.Y.: Doubleday, 1976.

Jacob, E. "Les bases théologiques de l'éthique de l'Ancien Testament". Pages 39-51 in *Congress Volume: Oxford 1959*. VTSup 7. Leiden: Brill, 1960.

Janzen, W. *Old Testament Ethics: A Paradigmatic Approach*. Louisville, Ky.: Westminster John Knox, 1994.
Japhet, S. *I & II Chronicles*. OTL. London: SCM, 1993.
Jaruzelska, I. "Amos et Osée face aux rois d'Israel". Pages 145-176 in *Prophètes et rois: Bible et Proche-Orient*. Edited by A. Lemaire. LDHS. Paris: Éditions du Cerf, 2001.
Jensen, J. *Isaiah 1-39*. OTM. Wilmington, Del.: Michael Glazier, 1984.
Jepsen, A. "צדק und צדקה im Alten Testament". Pages 78-89 in *Gottes Wort und Gottes Land: Hans-Wilhelm Hertzberg zum 70. Geburtstag am 16. Januar 1965 dargebracht von Kollegen, Freunden und Schülern*. Edited by H.G. Reventlow. Göttingen: Vandenhoeck & Ruprecht, 1965.
Jeremias, J. *Kultprophetie und Gerichtsverkündigung in der späten Königszeit Israels*. WMANT 35. Neukirchen-Vluyn: Neukirchener Verlag, 1970.
---. *Der Prophet Amos*. ATD 24.2. Göttingen: Vandenhoeck & Ruprecht, 1995.
---. *Der Prophet Hosea*. ATD 24.1. Göttingen: Vandenhoeck & Ruprecht, 1983.
Johnson, B. "ṣāḏaq". Columns 898-926 in vol. 6 of *Theologisches Wörterbuch zum Alten Testament*. Edited by H.-J. Fabry and H. Ringgren. 10 vols. Berlin: Kohlhammer, 1989.
Johnston, L. "Old Testament morality". *CBQ* 20 (1958): 19-25.
Jones, G.H. *1 and 2 Kings*. NCB. 2 vols. Basingstoke: Marshall, Morgan & Scott, 1984.
---. "'Holy war' or 'Yahweh war'?". *VT* 25 (1975): 642-658.
Jones, P. "Divine and non-divine kingship". Pages 330-342 in *A Companion to the Ancient Near East*. Edited by D.C. Snell. Oxford: Blackwell, 2005.
Jost, R. "God of love/God of vengeance, or Samson's 'Prayer for Vengeance'". Pages 117-125 in *Judges: A Feminist Companion to the Bible*. Edited by A. Brenner. FCB(SS). Sheffield: Sheffield Academic Press, 1999.

Kaiser, O. *Isaiah 1-12*. OTL. 2d edn., completely rewritten. Translated by J. Bowden. London: SCM, 1983.
---. *Isaiah 13-39*. OTL. Translated by R.A. Wilson. London: SCM, 1974.
Kaiser Jr., W.C. *Toward Old Testament Ethics*. Grand Rapids, Mich.: Zondervan, 1983.
Kang, S.-M. *Divine War in the Old Testament and in the Ancient Near East*. BZAW 177. Berlin: Walter de Gruyter, 1989.
Keel, O. "Powerful symbols of victory – the parts stay the same, the actors change". Translated by A. Rima. *JNSL* 25.2 (1999): 205-240.
Kelle, B.E. *Ancient Israel at War 853-586 BC*. EH 67. Oxford: Osprey, 2007.
Keller, C.A. "Die theologische Bewältigung der geschichtlichen Wirklichkeit in der Prophetie Nahums". *VT* 22 (1972): 399-419.
Keller, C.A., and R. Vuilleumier. *Michée, Nahoum, Habacuc, Sophonie*. CAT 116. Paris: Delachaux & Niestlé, 1971.
Keown, G.L., P.J. Scalise, and T.G. Smothers. *Jeremiah 26-52*. WBC 27. Waco, Tex.: Word, 1995.
Kim, E.K. "Holy war ideology and the rapid shift of mood in Psalm 3". Pages 77-93 in *On the Way to Nineveh: Studies in Honor of George M. Landes*. Edited by S.L. Cook and S.C. Winter. Atlanta, Ga.: Scholars, 1999.
Klein, R.W. *1 Samuel*. WBC 10. Waco, Tex.: Word, 1983.

Klengel, H. "Krieg, Kriegsgefangene". Pages 241-246 in vol. 6 of *Reallexikon der Assyriologie*. 11 vols. Berlin: Walter de Gruyter, 1980-1983.

Klingbeil, M. *Yahweh Fighting from Heaven: God as Warrior and as God of Heaven in the Hebrew Psalter and Ancient Near Eastern Iconography*. OBO 169. Göttingen: Vandenhoeck & Ruprecht, 1999.

Koch, K. "Gibt es ein Vergeltungsdogma im Alten Testament?" *ZTK* 52 (1955): 1-42.

---. "ṣdq gemeinschafttreu/heilvoll sein". Columns 507-530 in vol. 2 of *Theologisches Handwörterbuch zum Alten Testament*. 2 vols. Edited by E. Jenni and C. Westermann. Munich: Chr. Kaiser Verlag, 1976.

Korošec, V. "The warfare of the Hittites – from the legal point of view". *Iraq* 25 (1963): 159-166.

Knauf, E.A. "Does 'Deuteronomistic Historiography' (DtrH) exist?" Pages 388-398 in *Israel Constructs its History: Deuteronomistic Historiography in Recent Research*. Edited by A. de Pury, T. Römer and J.-D. Macchi. JSOTSup 306. Sheffield: Sheffield University Press, 2000.

Knight, D.A. "Cosmogony and order in the Hebrew tradition". Pages 133-157 in *Cosmogony and Ethical Order: New Studies in Comparative Ethics*. Edited by R.W. Levin and F.E. Reynolds. London: University of Chicago Press, 1985.

---. "The social basis of morality and religion in ancient Israel". Pages 151-169 in *Language, Theology and the Bible: Essays in Honour of James Barr*. Edited by S.E. Balentine and J. Barton. Oxford: Clarendon, 1994.

Knoppers, G.N. "Jerusalem at war in Chronicles". Pages 57-76 in *Zion, City of Our God*. Edited by R.S. Hess and G.J. Wenham. Cambridge: Eerdmans, 1999.

Kraus, H.-J. *Psalms 1-59: A Commentary*. Translated by H.C. Oswald. Minneapolis, Minn.: Augsburg, 1988.

---. *Theology of the Psalms*. Translated by K. Crim. Minneapolis, Minn.: Augsburg, 1986.

Kreuzer, S. "Zur Hermeneutik ethischer Aussagen des Alten Testaments". Pages 233-249 in *Recht und Ethos im Alten Testament: Gestalt und Wirkung: Festschrift für Horst Seebass zum 65. Geburtstag*. Edited by S. Beyerle, G. Mayer and H. Strauß. Neukirchen-Vluyn: Neukirchener Verlag, 1999.

Kristiansen, K. "Ideology and material culture: an archaeological perspective". Pages 72-100 in *Marxist Perspectives in Archaeology*. Edited by M. Spriggs. NDA. Cambridge: Cambridge University Press, 1984.

Kuhrt, A. "Israelite and Near Eastern historiography". Pages 257-279 in *Congress Volume: Oslo 1998*. Edited by A. Lemaire and M. Sæbø. VTSup 80. Leiden: Brill, 2000.

Labat, R. *Le poème babylonien de la creation*. Paris: Librairie d'Amérique et d'Orient, 1935.

LaFont, S. "Ancient Near Eastern laws: continuity and pluralism". Pages 91-118 in *Theory and Method in Biblical and Cuneiform Law: Revision, Interpolation and Development*. Edited by B.M. Levinson. JSOTSup 181. Sheffield: Sheffield Academic Press, 1994.

Lambert, W.G. "The Assyrian recension of Enūma Eliš". Pages 77-79 in *Assyrien im Wandel der Zeiten: XXXIXe Rencontre Assyriologique Internationale,*

Heidelberg 6.-10. Juli 1992. Edited by H. Waetzoldt and H. Hauptmann. HSAO 6. Heidelberg: Heidelberger Orientverlag, 1997.

---. "The great battle of the Mesopotamian religious year: the conflict in the Akītu house (a summary)". *Iraq* 25 (1963): 189-190.

---. "Mesopotamian sources and pre-exilic Israel". Pages 352-365 in *In Search of Pre-Exilic Israel: Proceedings of the Oxford Old Testament Seminar*. Edited by J. Day. JSOTSup 406. London: T&T Clark, 2004.

Lanfranchi, G.B., and S. Parpola. *The Correspondence of Sargon II, Part II: Letters from the Northern and Northeastern Provinces*. SAA 5. Helsinki: Helsinki University Press, 1990.

Launderville, P. "Anti-monarchical ideology in Israel in light of Mesopotamian parallels". Pages 119-128 in *Imagery and Imagination in Biblical Literature: Essays in Honor of Aloysius Fitzgerald, F.S.C.* CBQMS 32. Edited by L. Boadt and M.S. Smith. Washington, D.C.: Catholic Biblical Association of America, 2001.

Layard, A.H. *The Monuments of Nineveh*. London: John Murray, 1853.

---. *A Second Series of the Monuments of Nineveh*. London: John Murray, 1853.

Lemaire, A. "Toward a redactional history of the book of Kings". Translated by S.W. Heldenbrand. Pages 446-461 in *Reconsidering Israel and Judah: Recent Studies on the Deuteronomistic History*. Edited by G.N. Knoppers and J.G. McConville. SBTS 8. Winona Lake, Ind.: Eisenbrauns, 2000. Reprinted from "Vers l'histoire de la redaction des livres des Rois". *ZAW* 98 (1986): 221-236.

Lemche, N.P. *The Israelites in History and Tradition*. LAI. London: SPCK, 1998.

Levine, B.A. "Assyrian ideology and Israelite monotheism". *Iraq* 67 (2005): 411-427. Vol. 2 of *Nineveh: Papers of the XLIXe Rencontre Assyriologique Internationale London 7-11 July 2003*.

Levine, L.D. "Manuscripts, texts and the study of the Neo-Assyrian royal inscriptions". Pages 49-70 in *Assyrian Royal Inscriptions: New Horizons in Literary, Ideological, and Historical Analysis: Papers of a Symposium held in Cetona (Siena), June 26-28, 1980*. Edited by F.M. Fales. OAC 17. Rome: Istituto per l'Oriente, 1981.

---. "Preliminary remarks on the historical inscriptions of Sennacherib". Pages 58-75 in *History, Historiography and Interpretation: Studies in Biblical and Cuneiform Literatures*. Edited by H. Tadmor and M. Weinfeld. Leiden: Brill, 1984.

Licht, J. "Biblical historicism". Pages 107-120 in *History, Historiography and Interpretation: Studies in Biblical and Cuneiform Literatures*. Edited by H. Tadmor and M. Weinfeld. Leiden: Brill, 1984.

Lie, A.G. *The Inscriptions of Sargon II, King of Assyria*. Paris: Librairie Orientaliste Paul Geuthner, 1929.

Limburg, J. *Hosea-Micah*. Interpretation. Atlanta, Ga.: John Knox, 1988.

Lind, M.C. *Yahweh is a Warrior: The Theology of Warfare in Ancient Israel*. Scottdale, Penn.: Herald, 1980.

van der Lingen, A. *Les guerres de Yahvé: L'implication de YHWH dans les guerres d'Israël selon les livres historiques de l'Ancien Testament*. LD 139. Paris: Éditions du Cerf, 1990.

Linville, J.R. "What does 'it' mean? Interpretation at the point of no return in Amos 1-2". *BI* 8 (2000): 400-424.

Liverani, M. "Critique of variants and the titulary of Sennacherib". Pages 225-257 in *Assyrian Royal Inscriptions: New Horizons in Literary, Ideological, and Historical Analysis: Papers of a Symposium held in Cetona (Siena), June 26-28, 1980*. Edited by F.M. Fales. OAC 17. Rome: Istituto per l'Oriente, 1981.

---. "The ideology of the Assyrian empire". Pages 297-318 in *Power and Propaganda: A Symposium on Ancient Empires*. Edited by M.T. Larsen. Mesopotamia 7. Copenhagen: Akademisk Forlag, 1979.

---. *Israel's History and the History of Israel*. Translated by C. Peri and P.R. Davies. BW. London: Equinox, 2005.

---. "The Medes at Esarhaddon's court". *JCS* 47 (1995): 57-62.

---. "Memorandum on the approach to historiographic texts". *Or* 42 (1973): 178-194.

---. *Myth and Politics in Ancient Near Eastern Historiography*. Edited by Z. Bahrani and M. van de Mieroop. SEANE. Ithaca, NY: Cornell University Press, 2004.

---. "Propaganda". Pages 474-477 in vol. 5 of *Anchor Bible Dictionary*. 6 vols. Edited by D.N. Freedman. London: Doubleday, 1992.

Livingstone, A. *Court Poetry and Literary Miscellanea*. SAA 3. Helsinki: Helsinki University Press, 1989.

Lloyd, S. *The Art of the Ancient Near East*. WAL. Norwich: Thames & Hudson, 1961.

Lohfink, N. "ḥāram; ḥērem". Pages 180-199 in vol. 5 of *Theological Dictionary of the Old Testament*. Edited by G.J. Botterweck and H. Ringgren. 15 vols. Translated by D.E. Green. Grand Rapids, Mich.: Eerdmans, 1986.

---. "Der »heilige Krieg« und der »Bann« in der Bibel". *IKZ* 89 (1989): 104-112.

Long, V.P., ed. *Israel's Past in Present Research: Essays on Ancient Israelite Historiography*. SBTS 7. Winona Lake, Ind.: Eisenbrauns, 1999.

Luckenbill, D.D. *The Annals of Sennacherib*. OIP 2. Chicago, Ill.: University of Chicago Press, 1924.

---. *Historical Records of Assyria from the Earliest Times to Sargon*. Vol. 1 of *Ancient Records of Assyria and Babylonia*. Chicago, Ill.: University of Chicago Press, 1926-1927.

Luukko, M., and G. Van Buylaere. *The Political Correspondence of Esarhaddon*. SAA 16. Helsinki: Helsinki University Press, 2002.

Macintosh, A.A. "A consideration of Hebrew גער". *VT* 19 (1969): 471-479.

---. *A Critical and Exegetical commentary on Hosea*. ICC. Edinburgh: T&T Clark, 1997.

Malamat, A. "Conquest of Canaan: Israelite conduct of war according to biblical tradition". Pages 68-96 in *History of Biblical Israel: Major Problems and Minor Issues*. CHANE 7. Leiden: Brill, 2001.

Malcolm, L. "Divine commands". Pages 112-129 in *The Oxford Handbook of Theological Ethics*. Edited by G. Meilaender and W. Werpehowski. Oxford: Oxford University Press, 2005.

Malul, M. *The Comparative Method in Ancient Near Eastern and Biblical Legal Studies*. AOAT 227. Neukirchen-Vluyn: Neukirchener Verlag, 1990.

Mannheim, K. *Ideology and Utopia: An Introduction to the Sociology of Knowledge*. ILP. Translated by L. Wirth and E. Shils. New York, N.Y.: Harcourt, Brace & Co, 1936.

Marcus, M.I. "Art and ideology in ancient western Asia". Pages 2487-2506 in vol. 4 of *Civilizations of the Ancient Near East*. Edited by J.M. Sasson. 4 vols. Peabody, Mass.: Hendrickson, 2000.

---. "Geography as visual ideology: landscape, knowledge, and power in Neo-Assyrian art". Pages 193-202 in *Neo-Assyrian Geography*. QGS 5. Edited by M. Liverani. Rome: Università di Roma, 1995.

Mason, R. *Old Testament Pictures of God*. RSG 2. Macon, Ga.: Smyth & Helwys, 1993.

---. *Propaganda and Subversion in the Old Testament*. London: SPCK, 1997.

Maul, S.M. "Der assyrische König – Hüter der Weltordnung". Pages 65-77 in *Gerechtigkeit: Richten und Retten in der abendländischen Tradition und ihrer altorientalischen Ursprüngen*. Edited by J. Assmann, B. Janowski and M. Welker. Munich: Wilhelm Fink Verlag, 1998.

---. "'Wenn der Held (zum Kampfe) auszieht...' Ein Ninurta-Eršemma". *Or* 60 (1991): 312-334.

May, H.G. "Aspects of the imagery of world dominion and world state in the Old Testament". Pages 57-76 in *Essays in Old Testament Ethics (J. Philip Hyatt, In Memoriam)*. Edited by J.L. Crenshaw and J.T. Willis. New York, N.Y.: Ktav, 1974.

---. "Some cosmic connotations of mayim rabbîm, 'many waters'". *JBL* 74 (1955): 9-21.

Mayer, W.R. "Ein Mythos von der Erschaffung des Menschen und des Königs". *Or* 56 (1987): 55-68.

---. *Politik und Kriegskunst der Assyrer*. ALASP 9. Münster: Ugarit-Verlag, 1995.

---. "Sargons Feldzug gegen Urartu – 714 v. Chr.: Text und Übersetzung". *MDOG* 115 (1983): 65-132.

Mayes, A.D.H. "Deuteronomistic ideology and the theology of the Old Testament". Pages 456-480 in *Israel Constructs its History: Deuteronomistic Historiography in Recent Research*. Edited by A. de Pury, T. Römer and J.-D. Macchi. JSOTSup 306. Sheffield: Sheffield University Press, 2000.

---. "Deuteronomistic royal ideology in Judges 17-21". *BI* 9 (2001): 241-258.

---. *Deuteronomy*. NCB. London: Marshall, Morgan & Scott, 1981.

---. "Prophecy and society in Israel". Pages 25-42 in *Of Prophets' Visions and the Wisdom of Sages*. Edited by D.J.A. Clines and H.A. McKay. JSOTSup 162. Sheffield: JSOT, 1993.

---. *The Story of Israel between Settlement and Exile: A Redactional Study of the Deuteronomistic History*. London: SCM, 1983.

Mays, J.L. *Amos*. OTL. London: SCM, 1969.

---. *Hosea*. OTL. London: SCM, 1969.

---. *Micah*. OTL. London: SCM, 1976.

McCann, J.C. *Judges*. Interpretation. Louisville, Ky.: John Knox, 2002.

---. *The Shape and Shaping of the Psalter*. JSOTSup 159. Sheffield: JSOT, 1993.

McCarter Jr., K.P. *I Samuel*. AB 8. Garden City, N.Y.: Doubleday, 1980.

---. *II Samuel*. Anchor Bible 9. Garden City, NY: Doubleday, 1984.

McCarthy, D.J. "The wrath of Yahweh and the structural unity of the Deuteronomistic History". Pages 97-110 in *Essays in Old Testament Ethics (J. Philip Hyatt, In Memoriam)*. Edited by J.L. Crenshaw and J.T. Willis. New York, N.Y.: Ktav, 1974.

McConville, J.G. *Deuteronomy*. Apollos 5. Leicester: Inter-Varsity, 2002.

McKeating, H. *The Books of Amos, Hosea and Micah*. CBC. Cambridge: Cambridge University Press, 1971.

---. "Sanctions against adultery in ancient Israelite society, with some reflections on methodology in the study of Old Testament ethics". *JSOT* 11 (1979): 57-72.

McKenzie, S.L. *The Trouble with Kings: The Composition of the Book of Kings in the Deuteronomistic History*. Leiden: Brill, 1991.

Meilaender, G., and W. Werpehowski, eds. *The Oxford Handbook of Theological Ethics*. Oxford: Oxford University Press, 2005.

Mein, A. *Ezekiel and the Ethics of Exile*. OTM. Oxford: Oxford University Press, 2001.

Mendenhall, G.E. "The 'vengeance' of Yahweh". Pages 69-104 in *The Tenth Generation: The Origins of the Biblical Tradition*. London: Johns Hopkins University Press, 1973.

Mettinger, T.N.D. *King and Messiah: The Civil and Sacral Legitimation of Israel's Kings*. CBOT 8. Lund: CWK Gleerup, 1976.

Millar, J.G. *Now Choose Life: Theology and Ethics in Deuteronomy*. NSBT 6. Leicester: Apollos, 1998.

Miller, P.D. *Deuteronomy*. Interpretation. Louisville, Ky.: John Knox, 1990.

---. *The Divine Warrior in Early Israel*. HSM 5. Cambridge, Mass.: Harvard University Press, 1975.

---. "Faith and ideology in the Old Testament". Pages 464-479 in *Magnalia Dei, The Mighty Acts of God: Essays on the Bible and Archaeology in Memory of G. Ernest Wright*. Edited by F.M. Cross, W.E. Lemke and P.D. Miller. Garden City, N.Y.: Doubleday, 1976.

---. "God the warrior: a problem in biblical interpretation and apologetics". *Interpretation* 19 (1965): 39-46.

Mitchell, H.G. *The Ethics of the Old Testament*. UCPRE. HER. Cambridge: Cambridge University Press, 1912.

Mobley, G. *The Empty Men: The Heroic Tradition of Ancient Israel*. ABRL. London: Doubleday, 2005.

Moenikes, A. "Psalm 2,7b und die Göttlichkeit des israelitischen Königs". *ZAW* 111 (1999): 619-621.

Möller, K. *A Prophet in Debate: The Rhetoric of Persuasion in the Book of Amos*. JSOTSup 372. Sheffield: Sheffield Academic Press, 2003.

Morgan, R., with J. Barton. *Biblical Interpretation*. OBS. Oxford: Oxford University Press, 1988.

Mowinckel, S. "General oriental and specific Israelite elements in the Israelite conception of the sacral kingdom". Pages 283-293 in *The Sacral Kingship: Contributions to the Central Theme of the VIIIth International Congress for the History of Religions (Rome, April 1955)*. SHR 4. Leiden: Brill, 1959.

---. *The Psalms in Israel's Worship*. Translated by D.R. Ap-Thomas. 2 vols. Oxford: Basil Blackwell, 1962.

Myers, J.M. *II Chronicles*. AB 13. Garden City, N.Y.: Doubleday, 1965.

Na'aman, N. "Ekron under the Assyrian and Egyptian empires". *BASOR* 332 (2003): 81-91.
---. "Historical and Chronological Notes on the Kingdoms of Israel and Judah in the Eighth Century B.C.". *VT* 36 (1986): 71-92.
---. "Population changes in Palestine following Assyrian deportations". Pages 200-219 in *Ancient Israel and its Neighbors: Interaction and Counteraction*. Vol. 1 of *Collected Essays*. Winona Lake, Ind.: Eisenbrauns, 2005.
---. "The province system and settlement patterns in southern Syria and Palestine in the Neo-Assyrian period". Pages 220-237 in *Ancient Israel and its Neighbors: Interaction and Counteraction*. Vol. 1 of *Collected Essays*. Winona Lake, Ind.: Eisenbrauns, 2005.
Nadali, D. "The representation of foreign soldiers and their employment in the Assyrian army". Pages 222-244 in *Ethnicity in Ancient Mesopotamia: Papers Read at the 48th Rencontre Assyriologique Internationale*. Edited by W.H. van Soldt. UNHAIL 102. Leiden: Nederlands Instituut voor het Nabije Oosten, 2005.
Nelson, R.D. *The Double Redaction of the Deuteronomistic History*. JSOTSup 18. Sheffield: JSOT, 1981.
---. *First and Second Kings*. Interpretation. Louisville, Ky.: John Knox, 1987.
---. *The Historical Books*. IBT. Nashville, Tenn.: Abingdon, 1998.
---. *Joshua*. OTL. Louisville, Ky.: Westminster John Knox, 1997.
---. "Josiah in the book of Joshua". *JBL* 100 (1981): 531-540.
Nicholson, E.W. *Deuteronomy and Tradition*. Oxford: Basil Blackwell, 1967.
Niditch, S. *War in the Hebrew Bible: A Study in the Ethics of Violence*. Oxford: Oxford University Press, 1993.
Nineham, D. *The Use and Abuse of the Bible: A Study of the Bible in an Age of Rapid Cultural Change*. LPR. London: Macmillan, 1976.
Nissinen, M. "Comparing prophetic sources: methodological perspectives". Old Testament Seminar, Oxford. 15 May 2006.
---. "Falsche Prophetie in neuassyrischer und deuteronomistischer Darstellung". Pages 172-195 in *Das Deuteronomium und seine Querbeziehungen*. SFEG 62. Edited by T. Veijola. Göttingen: Vandenhoeck & Ruprecht, 1996.
---. "Das kritische Potential in der altorientalischen Prophetie". Pages 1-32 in *Propheten in Mari, Assyrien und Israel*. Edited by M. Köckert and M. Nissinen. FRLANT 201. Göttingen: Vandenhoeck & Ruprecht, 2003.
---. "Prophets and the divine council". Pages 4-19 in *Kein Land für sich allein: Studien zum Kulturkontakt in Kanaan, Israel/Palästina und Ebirnâri für Manfred Weippert zum 65. Geburtstag*. Edited by U. Hübner and E.A. Knauf. OBO 186. Göttingen: Vandenhoeck & Ruprecht, 2002.
---. *References to Prophecy in Neo-Assyrian Sources*. SAAS 7. Helsinki: Helsinki University Press, 1998.
---. "Die Relevanz der neuassyrischen Prophetie für die alttestamentliche Forschung". Pages 217-258 in *Mesopotamia – Ugaritica – Biblica: Festschrift für Kurt Bergerhof zur Vollendung seines 70. Lebenjahres am 7. Mai 1992*. AOAT

232. Edited by M. Dietrich and O. Loretz. Neukirchen-Vluyn: Neukirchener Verlag, 1993.
---. "The socioreligious role of the neo-Assyrian prophets". Pages 89-114 in *Prophecy in its Ancient Near Eastern Context: Mesopotamian, Biblical, and Arabian Perspectives*. Edited by M. Nissinen. SBLSS 13. Atlanta, Ga.: SBL, 2000.
---. "Spoken, written, quoted, and invented: orality and writtenness in ancient Near Eastern prophecy". Pages 235-272 in *Writings and Speech in Israel and Ancient Near Eastern Prophecy*. Edited by E. Ben Zvi and M.H. Floyd. SBLSS 10. Atlanta, Ga.: SBL, 2000.
---. "What is prophecy? An ancient Near Eastern perspective". Pages 17-37 in *Inspired Speech: Prophecy in the Ancient Near East: Essays in Honor of Herbert B. Huffmon*. Edited by J. Kaltner and L. Stulman. JSOTSup 378. London: T&T Clark, 2004.
Nissinen, M., C.L. Seow, and R.K. Ritner. *Prophets and Prophecy in the Ancient Near East*. WAW 12. Atlanta, Ga.: SBL, 2003.
Noble, P.R. "'I will not bring "it" back" (Amos 1:3): a deliberately ambiguous oracle?" *ET* 106 (1994-1995): 105-109.
Noort, E. "Das Kapitulationsangebot im Kriegsgesetz Dtn 20:10ff. und in den Kriegserzählungen". Pages 197-222 in *Studies in Deuteronomy: In Honour of C.J. Labuschagne on the Occasion of his 65th Birthday*. Edited by F. García Martínez, A. Hilhorts, J.T.A.G.M. van Ruiten and A.S. van der Woude. VTSup 53. Leiden: Brill, 1994.
Noth, M. *The Deuteronomistic History*. Translated by D.R. Ap-Thomas, J. Barton, J. Doull and M.D. Rutter. JSOTSup 15. Sheffield: JSOT, 1981.

O'Brien, M.A.. *The Deuteronomistic History Hypothesis: A Reassessment*. OBO 92. Göttingen: Vandenhoeck & Ruprecht, 1989.
O'Brien, J.M. *Nahum*. Readings. London: Sheffield Academic Press, 2002.
Oded, B. "'The command of the god' as a reason for going to war in the Assyrian royal inscriptions". Pages 223-230 in *Ah, Assyria...Studies in Assyrian History and Ancient Near Eastern Historiography Presented to Hayim Tadmor*. Edited by M. Cogan and I. Eph'al. SH 33. Jerusalem: Magnes, 1991.
---. *Mass Deportations and Deportees in the Neo-Assyrian Empire*. Wiesbaden: Dr. Ludvig Reichert Verlag, 1979.
---. *War, Peace and Empire: Justifications for War in Assyrian Royal Inscriptions*. Weisbaden: Dr Ludwig Reichert Verlag, 1992.
Olmstead, A. T. "The text of Sargon's annals". *AJSL* 47 (1931): 259-280.
Oppenheim, A.L. *Ancient Mesopotamia: Portrait of a Dead Civilization*. 2d ed. Completed by E. Reiner. London: University of Chicago Press, 1977.
---. "The city of Assur in 714 B.C.". *JNES* 19 (1960): 133-147.
---. "Neo-Assyrian and Neo-Babylonian empires". Pages 111-144 in *The Symbolic Instrument in Early Times*. Vol. 1 of *Propaganda and Communication in World History*. Edited by H.D. Lasswell, D. Lerner and H. Speier. Honolulu, Hawaii: University Press of Hawaii, 1979.
Ornan, T. "The godlike semblance of a king: the case of Sennacherib's rock reliefs". Pages 161-178 in *Ancient Near Eastern Art in Context: Studies in Honor of Irene J. Winter by Her Students*. Edited by J. Cheng and M.H. Feldman. CHANE 26. Leiden: Brill, 2007.

---. *The Triumph of the Symbol: Pictorial Representation of Deities in Mesopotamia and the Biblical Image Ban.* OBO 213. Göttingen: Vandenhoeck & Ruprect, 2005.

Oswalt, J.N. *The Book of Isaiah: Chapters 1-39.* NICOT. Grand Rapids, Mich.: Eerdmans, 1986.

Otto, E. "Aspects of legal reforms and reformulations in the cuneiform and Israelite law". Pages 160-196 in *Theory and Method in Biblical and Cuneiform Law: Revision, Interpolation and Development.* Edited by B.M. Levinson. JSOTSup 181. Sheffield: Sheffield Academic Press, 1994.

---. "Forschungsgeschichte der Entwürfe einer Ethik im Alten Testament". *VF* 36.1 (1991): 3-37.

---. *Krieg und Frieden in der Hebräischen Bibel und im Alten Orient: Aspekt für eine Friedensordnung in der Moderne.* TF 18. Berlin: Kohlhammer, 1999.

---. "Of aims and methods in Hebrew Bible ethics". *Semeia* 66 (1995): 161-172.

---. "Recht und Ethik im Alten Testament: Neue Studien zur Ethik des Alten Testaments". *ZABR* 9 (2003): 210-219.

---. *Theologische Ethik des Alten Testaments.* TW 3.2. Berlin: W. Kohlhammer, 1994.

---. "Town and rural countryside in ancient Israelite law: reception and redaction in cuneiform and Israelite law". *JSOT* 57 (1993): 3-22.

Overholt, T.W. "Cultural anthropology and the Old Testament". Pages 1-23 in *Cultural Anthropology of the Old Testament.* GBS. Minneapolis, Minn.: Fortress, 1996.

van Oyen, H. *Ethik des Alten Testaments.* GE 2. Gütersloh: Gütersloher Verlagshaus, 1967.

Parpola, S. *Assyrian Prophecies.* SAA 9. Helsinki: Helsinki University Press, 1997.

---. "Assyrian royal inscriptions and Neo-Assyrian letters". Pages 117-142 in *Assyrian Royal Inscriptions: New Horizons in Literary, Ideological, and Historical Analysis: Papers of a Symposium held in Cetona (Siena), June 26-28, 1980.* Edited by F.M. Fales. OAC 17. Rome: Isituto per l'Oriente, 1981.

---. *The Correspondence of Sargon II, Part I: Letters from Assyria and the West.* SAA 1. Helsinki: Helsinki University Press, 1987.

---. *Letters from Assyrian and Babylonian Scholars.* SAA 10. Helsinki: Helsinki University Press, 1993.

Paul, S.M. *Amos.* Hermeneia. Minneapolis, Minn.: Fortress, 1990.

---. "Amos 1:3-2:3: a concatenous literary pattern". *JBL* 90 (1971): 397-403.

Parrot, A. *Nineveh and Babylon.* Translated by E. Gilbert and J. Emmons. AM 2. Norwich: Thames & Hudson, 1961.

Perlitt, L. *Die Propheten Nahum, Habakuk, Zephanja.* ATD 25.1. Göttingen: Vandenhoeck & Ruprecht, 2004.

Petersen, D.L. "Defining prophecy and prophetic literature". Pages 33-44 in *Prophecy in its Ancient Near Eastern Context: Mesopotamian, Biblical, and Arabian Perspectives.* Edited by M. Nissinen. SBLSS 13. Atlanta, Ga.: SBL, 2000.

---. "Rethinking the nature of prophetic literature". Pages 23-40 in *Prophecy and Prophets: The Diversity of Contemporary Issues in Scholarship.* Edited by Y. Gitay. SS. Atlanta, Ga.: Scholars, 1997.

Pfeiffer, R.H. *State Letters of Assyria: A Transliteration and Translation of 355 Official Assyrian Letters dating from the Sargonid Period (722-625 B.C.).* AOS 6. New Haven, Conn.: American Oriental Society, 1935.

Polley, M.E. "Hebrew prophecy within the council of Yahweh, examined in its ancient Near Eastern setting". Pages 141-156 in *Essays on the Comparative Method.* Edited by C.D. Evans, W.W. Hallo and J.B. White. SC 1. Pittsburg, Pa.: Pickwick, 1980.

Pongratz-Leisten, B. *Herrschaftswissen im Mesopotamien: Formen der Kommunikation zwischen Gott und König in 2. und 1. Jahrtausend v.Chr.* SAAS 10. Helsinki: Neo-Assyrian Text Corpus Project, 1999.

---. *Ina Šulmi Īrub: die kulttopographische und ideologische Programmatik der akītu-Prozession in Babylonien und Assyrien im I. Jahrtausend v. Chr.* BF 16. Mainz: Zabern, 1994.

---. "The interplay of military strategy and cultic practice in Assyrian politics". Pages 245-252 in *Assyria 1995: Proceedings of the 10th Anniversary Symposium of the Neo-Assyrian Text Corpus Project.* Edited by S. Parpola and R.M. Whitings. Helsinki: Helsinki University Press, 1997.

Pope, S. "Reason and natural law". Pages 148-167 in *The Oxford Handbook of Theological Ethics.* Edited by G. Meilaender and W. Werpehowski. Oxford: Oxford University Press, 2005.

Porteous, N.W. "The basis of the ethical teaching of the prophets". Pages 143-156 in *Studies in Old Testament Prophecy, Presented to Professor Theodore H. Robinson by the Society for Old Testament Study on his Sixty-Fifth Birthday August 9th 1946.* Edited by H.H. Rowley. Edinburgh: T&T Clark, 1950.

Porter, J.R. "The legal aspects of the concept of 'corporate personality' in the Old Testament". *VT* 15 (1965): 361-380.

Postgate, J.N. "Assyria: the home provinces". Pages 1-17 in *Neo-Assyrian Geography.* Edited by M. Liverani. QGS 5. Rome: Università di Roma, 1995.

---. "The Assyrian army in Zamua". *Iraq* 62 (2000): 89-108.

---. "The land of Assur and the yoke of Aššur". Pages 199-215 in *The Land of Assur and the Yoke of Assur: Studies in Assyria 1971-2005.* Oxford: Oxbow, 2007. Reprinted from *WA* 23 (1992): 247-263.

Powell, M.A. "Merodach-baladan at Dur-Jakin: a note on the defense of Babylonian cities". *JCS* 34 (1982): 59-61.

Preuss, H.D. *Old Testament Theology.* Translated by L.G. Perdue. 2 vols. Edinburgh: T&T Clark, 1995-1996.

Pritchard, J.B. *The Ancient Near East in Pictures Relating to the Old Testament.* 2d ed. with suppl. Princeton, N.J.: Princeton University Press, 1969.

Provan, I.W. *Hezekiah and the Books of Kings: A Contribution to the Debate about the Composition of the Deuteronomistic History.* BZAW 172. Berlin: Walter de Gruyter, 1988.

---. "Ideologies, literary and critical: reflections on recent writing on the history of Israel". *JBL* 114 (1995): 585-606.

de Pury, A., and T. Römer. "Deuteronomistic Historiography (DH): history of research and debated issues". Pages 24-41 in *Israel Constructs its History: Deuteronomistic Historiography in Recent Research.* Edited by A. de Pury, T. Römer and J.-D. Macchi. JSOTSup 306. Sheffield: Sheffield University Press, 2000.

de Pury A., T. Römer and J.-D. Macchi, eds. *Israel Constructs its History: Deuteronomistic Historiography in Recent Research.* JSOTSup 306. Sheffield: Sheffield University Press, 2000.

von Rad, G. *Deuteronomy.* OTL. Translated by D. Barton. London: SCM, 1966.
---. "Deuteronomy and the holy war". Pages 45-59 in *Studies in Deuteronomy.* Translated by D. Stalker. SBT 9. London: SCM, 1953.
---. *Der Heilige Krieg im alten Israel.* ATANT 20. Zürich: Zwingli-Verlag, 1951. Reprinted as *Holy War in Ancient Israel.* Translated by M.J. Dawn. Grand Rapids, Mich.: Eerdmans, 1991.
Radner, K. *The Prosopography of the Neo-Assyrian Empire* (A). Vol. 1/1. Helsinki: Neo-Assyrian Text Corpus Project, 1998.
---. *The Prosopography of the Neo-Assyrian Empire* (B-G). Vol. 1/2. Helsinki: Neo-Assyrian Text Corpus Project, 1999.
Reade, J.E. "Ideology and propaganda in Assyrian art". Pages 319-328 in *Power and Propaganda: A Symposium on Ancient Empires.* Edited by M.T. Larsen. Mesopotamia 7. Copenhagen: Akademisk Forlag, 1979.
---. "Neo-Assyrian monuments in their historical context". Pages 143-167 in *Assyrian Royal Inscriptions: New Horizons in Literary, Ideological, and Historical Analysis: Papers of a Symposium held in Cetona (Siena), June 26-28, 1980.* Edited by F.M. Fales. OAC 17. Rome: Isituto per l'Oriente, 1981.
Reed, S. "Blurring the edges: a reconsideration of the treatment of enemies in Ashurbanipal's reliefs". Pages 101-130 in *Ancient Near Eastern Art in Context: Studies in Honor of Irene J. Winter by Her Students.* Edited by J. Cheng and M.H. Feldman. CHANE 26. Leiden: Brill, 2007.
Renger, J. "Neuassyrische Königsinschriften als Genre der Keilschriftliteratur – zum Stil und zur Kompositionstechnik der Inschriften Sargons II. von Assyrien". Pages 109-128 in *Keilschriftliche Literaturen: Assyriologique Internationale Münster, 8-12.7.1985.* Edited by K. Hecker and W. Sommerfield. Berlin: Dietrich Reimer, 1986.
Reynolds, F.E. *The Babylonian Correspondence of Esarhaddon.* SAA 18. Helsinki: Helsinki University Press, 2003.
Rivaroli, M. and L. Verderame. "To be a non-Assyrian". Pages 290-303 in *Ethnicity in Ancient Mesopotamia: Papers Read at the 48th Rencontre Assyriologique Internationale.* Edited by W.H. van Soldt. UNHAIL 102. Leiden: Nederlands Instituut voor het Nabije Oosten, 2005.
Roberts, J.J.M. "The end of war in the Zion tradition: the imperialistic background of an Old Testament vision of worldwide peace". Pages 119-128 in *Character Ethics and the Old Testament: Moral Dimensions of Scripture.* Edited by M.D. Carroll R. and J.E. Lapsley. London: Westminster John Knox, 2007.
---. "Myth *versus* history: relaying the comparative foundations". *CBQ* 38 (1976): 1-13.
---. *Nahum, Habakkuk, and Zephaniah.* OTL. Louisville, Ky.: Westminster John Knox, 1991.
Robinson, H.W. "The Hebrew conception of corporate personality". Pages 49-62 in *Werden und Wesen des Alten Testaments.* Edited by P. Volz, F. Stummer and J. Hempel. BZAW 66. Berlin: Alfred Töpelmann, 1936.

Robinson, O.P. *The Books of Nahum, Habakkuk and Zephaniah*. NICOT. Grand Rapids, Mich.: William B. Eerdmans, 1990.

Rodd, C.S. *Glimpses of a Strange Land: Studies in Old Testament Ethics*. OTS. London: T&T Clark, 2001.

---. "On applying a sociological theory to biblical studies". Pages 22-33 in *Social-Scientific Old Testament Criticism*. Edited by D.J. Chalcraft. BS 47. Sheffield: Sheffield Academic Press, 1997. Reprinted from *JSOT* 19 (1981): 95-106.

---. "Psalms". Pages 355-405 in *The Oxford Bible Commentary*. Edited by J. Barton and J. Muddiman. Oxford: Oxford University Press, 2001.

Rofé, A. "The laws of warfare in the book of Deuteronomy: their origins, intent and positivity". *JSOT* 32 (1985): 23-44.

Rogerson, J.W. *Anthropology and the Old Testament*. Oxford: Basil Blackwell, 1978.

---. "Discourse ethics and biblical ethics". Pages 17-26 in *The Bible in Ethics: The Second Sheffield Colloquium*. Edited by M.D. Carroll R., M. Davies and J.W. Rogerson. JSOTSup 207. Sheffield: Sheffield Academic Press, 1995.

---. "The Hebrew conception of corporate personality: a re-examination". *JTS* 21 (1970): 1-16.

---. "Old Testament ethics". Pages 116-131 in *Text in Context: Essays by Members of the Society for Old Testament Study*. Edited by A.D.H. Mayes. Oxford: Oxford University Press, 2000.

---. "The Old Testament view of nature: some preliminary questions". Pages 67-84 in *Instruction and Interpretation: Studies in Hebrew Language, Palestinian Archaeology and Biblical Exegesis*. OS 20. Leiden: Brill, 1977.

---. *Theory and Practice in Old Testament Ethics*. Edited by M.D. Carroll R. JSOTSup 405. London: T&T Clark, 2004.

Rose, M. "Deuteronomistic ideology and theology of the Old Testament". Pages 124-455 in *Israel Constructs its History: Deuteronomistic Historiography in Recent Research*. JSOTSup 306. Edited by A. de Pury, T. Römer and J.-D. Macchi. Sheffield: Sheffield University Press, 2000.

Rouillard-Bonraisin, H. "Ésaïe, Jérémie et la politique des rois de Juda". Pages 177-224 in *Prophètes et rois: Bible et Proche-Orient*. Edited by A. Lemaire. LDHS. Paris: Éditions du Cerf, 2001.

Rowlett, L.L. *Joshua and the Rhetoric of Violence: A New Historicist Approach*. JSOTSup 226. Sheffield: Sheffield Academic Press, 1996.

Rudolph, W. *Joel-Amos-Obadja-Jona*. KAT 13.2. Gütersloher: Verlagshaus Gerd Mohn, 1971.

Saggs, H.W.F. "Assyrian prisoners of war and the right to live". Pages 85-93 in *Vorträge gehalten auf der 28. Rencontre Assyriologique Internationale in Wien 6.-10. Juli 1981*. AfOB 19. Horn: Ferdinand Berger & Söhne, 1982.

---. "Assyrian warfare in the Sargonid period". *Iraq* 25 (1963): 145-154.

---. *The Nimrud Letters, 1952*. Vol. 5 of *Cuneiform Texts from Nimrud*. Trowbridge: British School of Archaeology in Iraq, 2001.

Schatz, W. *Genesis 14: Eine Untersuchung*. EHS 23.2 Frankfurt: Peter Lang, 1972.

Schmid, H.H. *Gerechtigkeit als Weltordnung: Hintergrund und Geschichte des alttestamentlichen Gerechtigkeitsbegriffes*. BHT 40. Tübingen: J.C.B. Mohr (Paul Siebeck), 1968.

---. "Rechtfertigung als Schöpfungsgeschehen: Notizen zur alttestamentlichen Vorgeschichte eines neutestamentlichen Themas". Pages 403-414 in *Rechtfertigung: Festschrift für Ernst Käsemann zum 70. Geburtstag*. Edited by J. Friedrich, W. Pöhlmann, and P. Stuhlmacher. Göttingen: Vandenhoeck & Ruprecht, 1976.

Schmidt, W.H. "Im Umfeld des Liebesgebots: Ethische Auswirkung der Unterscheidung: Tun Gottes und Tun des Menschen". Pages 145-154 in *Recht und Ethos im Alten Testament: Gestalt und Wirkung: Festschrift für Horst Seebass zum 65. Geburtstag*. Edited by S. Beyerle, G. Mayer and H. Strauß. Neukirchen-Vluyn: Neukirchener Verlag, 1999.

Schneider, T.J. *Judges*. BerO. Collegeville, Minn.: Liturgical, 2000.

Schökel, L.A. "Narrative art in Joshua-Judges-Samuel-Kings". Pages 255-278 in *Israel's Past in Present Research: Essays on Ancient Israelite Historiography*. Edited by V.P. Long. SBTS 7. Winona Lake, Ind.: Eisenbrauns, 1999.

Seitz, C.R. *Isaiah 1-39*. Interpretation. Louisville, Ky.: John Knox, 1993.

Seux, M.-J. *Hymnes et Prieres aux Dieux de Babylonie et d'Assyrie: Introduction, traduction et notes*. LAPO 8. Paris: Les Éditions du Cerf, 1976.

Seybold, K. *Nahum Habakuk Zephanja*. ZBK 24.2. Zürich: Theologischer Verlag, 1991.

---. *Profane Prophetie: Studien zum Buch Nahum*. SBS 135. Stuttgart: Verlag Katholisches Bibelwerk, 1989.

Shafer, A. "Assyrian royal monuments on the periphery: ritual and the making of imperial space". Pages 133-159 in *Ancient Near Eastern Art in Context: Studies in Honor of Irene J. Winter by Her Students*. Edited by J. Cheng and M.H. Feldman. CHANE 26. Leiden: Brill, 2007.

Sherriffs, D.C.T. "'A tale of two cities': Zion and Babylon". *TynB* 39 (1988): 19-57.

Shils, E. "Center and periphery". Pages 3-16 in *Center and Periphery: Essays in Macrosociology*. London: University of Chicago Press, 1975.

Smend, R. "Ethik III". Pages 423-435 in vol. 10 of *Theologische Realenzyklopädie*. 36 vols. Berlin: Walter de Gruyter, 1995.

---. *Jahwekrieg und Stämmebund: Erwägungen zur ältesten Geschichte Israels*. FRLANT 84. Göttingen: Vandenhoeck & Ruprecht, 1963.

---. "The law and the nations: a contribution to deuteronomistic tradition history". Translated by P.T. Daniels. Pages 95-110 in *Reconsidering Israel and Judah: Recent Studies on the Deuteronomistic History*. Edited by G.N. Knoppers and J.G. McConville. SBTS 8. Winona Lake, Ind.: Eisenbrauns, 2000. Reprinted from "Das Gesetz und die Völker: Ein Beitrag zur deuteronomistichen Redaktionsgeschichte". Pages 494-509 in *Probleme biblischer Theologie: Gerhard von Rad zum 70. Geburtstag*. Edited by H.W. Wolff. Munich: Chr. Kaiser, 1971.

Smith, J.M.P. *The Moral Life of the Hebrews*. London: Cambridge University Press, 1923.

Smith, J.M.P., W.H. Ward, and J.A. Bewer. *A Critical and Exegetical Commentary on Micah, Zephaniah, Nahum, Habakkuk, Obadiah and Joel*. ICC. Edinburgh: T&T Clark, 1948.

Smith, J.Z. *Imagining Religion: From Babylon to Jonestown*. CSHJ. London: University of Chicago Press, 1982.

Smith, M. "The present state of Old Testament studies". *JBL* 88 (1969): 19-35.
Smith, R.L. *Micah-Malachi*. WBC 32. Waco, Tex.: Word, 1984.
Smith, S., ed. *Assyrian Sculptures in the British Museum from Shalmaneser III to Sennacherib*. London: British Museum, 1938.
von Soden, W. *The Ancient Orient: An Introduction to the Study of the Ancient Near East*. Translated by D.G. Schley. Grand Rapids, Mich.: Eerdmans, 1994.
---. "Die Assyrer und der Krieg". *Iraq* 25 (1963): 131-144.
Soggin, J.A. *Introduction to the Old Testament: from its Origins to the Closing of the Alexandrian Canon*. Translated by J. Bowden. London: SCM, 1980.
---. *Joshua*. OTL. Translated by R.A. Wilson. London: SCM, 1972.
---. *Judges*. OTL. Translated by J. Bowden. London: SCM, 1981.
Spieckermann, H. *Juda unter Assur in der Sargonidenzeit*. FRLANT 129. Göttingen: Vandenhoeck & Ruprecht, 1982.
Spohn, W.C. "Scripture". Pages 93-111 in *The Oxford Handbook of Theological Ethics*. Edited by G. Meilaender and W. Werpehowski. Oxford: Oxford University Press, 2005.
Sprinkle, J.M. "Deuteronomic „just war" (Deut 20,10-20) and 2 Kings 3,27". *ZABR* 6 (2000): 285-301.
Starbuck, S.R.A. *Court Oracles in the Psalms: The So-Called Royal Psalms in their Ancient Near Eastern Context*. SBLDS 172. Atlanta, Ga.: SBL, 1999.
Starr, I. "Historical omens concerning Ashurbanipal's war against Elam". *AfO* 32 (1985): 60-67.
---. *Queries to the Sungod: Divination and Politics in Sargonid Assyria*. SAA 4. Helsinki: Helsinki University Press, 1990.
Stern, P.D. *The Biblical Ḫerem: A Window on Israel's Religious Experience*. BJS 211. Atlanta, Ga.: Scholars, 1991.
Stolz, F. *Jahwes und Israels Kriege: Kriegstheorien und Kriegserfahrungen im Glauben des alten Israel*. ATANT 60. Zürich: Theologischer Verlag, 1972.
Streck, M. *Assurbanipal und die letzten assyrischen Könige bis zum Untergange Nineveh's*. Vol. 2. Leipzig: J.C. Hinrichs, 1916.
Stuhlman, L. *Jeremiah*. AOTC. Nashville, Tenn.: Abingdon, 2005.
Sweeney, M.A. "The critique of Solomon in the Josianic edition of the Deuteronomistic History". *JBL* 114 (1995): 607-622.

Tadmor, H. "History and ideology in the Assyrian royal inscriptions". Pages 13-33 in *Assyrian Royal Inscriptions: New Horizons in Literary, Ideological, and Historical Analysis: Papers of a Symposium held in Cetona (Siena), June 26-28, 1980*. Edited by F.M. Fales. OAC 17. Rome: Isituto per l'Oriente, 1981.
---. *The Inscriptions of Tiglath-Pileser III King of Assyria: Critical Edition, with Introductions, Translations and Commentary*. Jerusalem: The Israel Academy of Sciences and Humanities, 1994.
---. "World dominion: the expanding horizon of the Assyrian empire". Pages 55-62 in vol. 1 of *Landscapes: Territories, Frontiers and Horizons in the Ancient Near East: Papers Presented to the XLIV Rencontre Assyriologique Internationale, Venezia, 7-11 July 1997*. Edited by L. Milano, S. de Martino, F.M. Fales and G.B. Lanfranchi. HANEM 3/1. Padoua: Sargon srl, 1999.
Tadmor, H. and M. Weinfeld, eds. *History, Historiography and Interpretation: Studies in Biblical and Cuneiform Literatures*. Leiden: Brill, 1983.

Talmon, S. "The comparative method in biblical interpretation: principles and problems". Pages 11-49 in *Literary Studies in the Hebrew Bible: Form and Content*. Leiden: Brill, 1993. Reprinted from pages 320-356 in *Congress Volume: Göttingen 1977*. VTSup 29. Leiden: Brill, 1978.

Talon, P. *Enūma Eliš: The Standard Babylonian Creation Myth*. SAACT 4. Helsinki: Neo-Assyrian Text Corpus Project, 2005.

Tate, M.E. *Psalms 51-100*. WBC 20. Dallas, Tex.: Word, 1990.

Thompson, T.L. *The Bible in History: How Writers Create a Past*. London: Jonathan Cape, 1999.

---. "A neo-Albrightean school in history and biblical scholarship?" *JBL* 114 (1995): 683-698.

Tigay, J.H. *Deuteronomy*. JPS. Philadelphia, Pa.: Jewish Publication Society, 1996.

van der Toorn, K. "From the mouth of the prophet: the literary fixation of Jeremiah's prophecies in the context of the ancient Near East". Pages 191-202 in *Inspired Speech: Prophecy in the Ancient Near East: Essays in Honor of Herbert B. Huffmon*. Edited by J. Kaltner and L. Stulman. JSOTSup 378. London: T&T Clark, 2004.

---. "Mesopotamian prophecy between immanence and transcendence: a comparison of Old Babylonian and Neo-Assyrian prophecy". Pages 71-88 in *Prophecy in its Ancient Near Eastern Context: Mesopotamian, Biblical, and Arabian Perspectives*. Edited by M. Nissinen. SBLSS 13. Atlanta, Ga.: SBL, 2000.

Tuell, S.S. *First and Second Chronicles*. Interpretation. Louisville, Ky.: John Knox, 2001.

Van Seters, J. *In Search of History: Historiography in the Ancient World and the Origins of Biblical History*. London: Yale University Press, 1983.

---. "Joshua's campaign of Canaan and Near Eastern historiography". Pages 170-180 in *Israel's Past in Present Research: Essays on Ancient Israelite Historiography*. Edited by V.P. Long. SBTS 7. Winona Lake, Ind.: Eisenbrauns, 1999.

Van Wyk, W.C. "Allusions to 'prehistory' and history in the book of Nahum". Pages 222-232 in *De Fructu Oris Sui: Essays in Honour of Adrianus van Selms*. Edited by I.H. Eybers, F.C. Fensham, D.J. Labuschagne, W.C. Van Wyk and A.H. Van Zyl. POS 9. Leiden: Brill, 1971.

de Vaux, R. *Ancient Israel: Its Life and Institutions*. Translated by J. McHugh. London: Darton, Longman and Todd, 1961.

Villard, P. "Les prophètes à l'époque néo-assyrienne". Pages 55-84 in *Prophètes et rois: Bible et Proche-Orient*. Edited by A. Lemaire. LDHS. Paris: Éditions du Cerf, 2001.

Vriezen, T.C. *An Outline of Old Testament Theology*. Translated by S. Neuijen. Oxford: Basil Blackwell, 1960.

Walton, J.H. *Ancient Near Eastern Thought and the Old Testament: Introducing the Conceptual World of the Hebrew Bible*. Nottingham: Apollos, 2007.

Walzer, M. *Just and Unjust Wars: A Moral Argument with Historical Illustrations*. New York, N.Y.: Penguin Books, 1977.

Waterman, L. *Royal Correspondence of the Assyrian Empire: Translated into English, with a Transliteration of the Text and a Commentary*. Vols. 1-2. UMSMS 17-20. Ann Arbor, Mich.: University of Michigan, 1930.

Waters, M.W. "A letter from Ashurbanipal to the elders of Elam (BM 132980)". *JCS* 54 (2002): 79-86.

Watts, J.D.W. *The Books of Joel, Obadiah, Jonah, Nahum, Habakkuk and Zephaniah*. CBC. Cambridge: Cambridge University Press, 1975.

---. *Isaiah 1-33*. WBC 24. Waco, Tex.: Word, 1985.

---. "Jerusalem: an example of war in a walled city (Isaiah 3-4)". Pages 210-215 in *'Every City shall be Forsaken': Urbanism and Prophecy in Ancient Israel and the Near East*. Edited by L.L. Grabbe and R.D. Haak. JSOTSup 330. Sheffield: Sheffield Academic Press, 2001.

Weber, M. *Ancient Judaism*. Translated by H.H. Gerth and D. Martindale. Glencoe, Ill.: Free Press, 1952.

Weidner, E.F. "Assyrische Beschreibungen der Kriegs-Reliefs Aššurbânipalis". *AfO* 8 (1932-1933): 175-208.

Weinfeld, M. "Divine intervention in war in ancient Israel and in the ancient Near East". Pages 121-147 in *History, Historiography and Interpretation: Studies in Biblical and Cuneiform Literatures*. Edited by H. Tadmor and M. Weinfeld. Leiden: Brill, 1983.

---. "'Justice and righteousness' in ancient Israel against the background of 'social reforms' in the ancient Near East". Pages 491-520 in vol. 2 of *Mesopotamien und seine Nachbarn: politische und kulturelle Wechselbeziehungen im Alten Vorderasien vom 4. bis 1. Jahrtausend v. Chr. XXV. Rencontre assyriologique internationale Berlin, 3. bis 7. Juli 1978*. Edited by H.-J. Nissen and J. Renger. BBVO 1. Berlin: Dietrich Reimer Verlag, 1978.

---. *Social Justice in Ancient Israel and in the Ancient Near East*. Jerusalem: Magnes, 1995.

Weippert, H. "'Histories' and 'history': promise and fulfillment in the deuteronomistic historical work". Translated by P.T. Daniels. Pages 47-61 in *Reconsidering Israel and Judah: Recent Studies on the Deuteronomistic History*. Edited by G.N. Knoppers and J.G. McConville. SBTS 8. Winona Lake, Ind.: Eisenbrauns, 2000.

Weippert, M. "Assyrische Prophetien der Zeit Asarhaddons und Assurbanipals". Pages 71-115 in *Assyrian Royal Inscriptions: New Horizons in Literary, Ideological, and Historical Analysis: Papers of a Symposium held in Cetona (Siena), June 26-28, 1980*. Edited by F.M. Fales. OAC 17. Rome: Isituto per l'Oriente, 1981.

---. "Die Bildsprache der neuassyrischen Prophetie". Pages 55-93 in *Beiträge zur prophetischen Bildsprache in Israel und Assyrien*. Edited by H. Weippert, K. Seybold and M. Weippert. OBO 64. Göttingen: Vandenhoeck & Ruprecht, 1985.

---. "'Heiliger Krieg' in Israel und Assyrien: Kritische Anmerkungen zu Gerhard von Rads Konzept des 'Heiligen Kriegs im alten Israel'". *ZAW* 84 (1982): 460-493.

---. "'König, fürchte dich nicht!': Assyrische Prophetie im 7. Jahrhundert v.Chr.". *Or* 71 (2007): 1-54.

Weissbach, F.H. "Zu den Inschriften der Säle im Palaste Sargon's II. von Assyrien". *ZDMG* 72 (1918): 161-185.

Weissert, E. "Creating a political climate: literary allusions to *Enūma Eliš* in Sennacherib's account of the battle of Halule". Pages 191-202 in *Assyrien im Wandel der Zeiten: XXXIXe Rencontre Assyriologique Internationale, Heidelberg 6.-10. Juli 1992*. Edited by H. Waetzoldt and H. Hauptmann. HSAO 6. Heidelberg: Heidelberger Orientverlag, 1997.

Wenham, G.J. "The ethics of the Psalms". Pages 175-194 in *Interpreting the Psalms: Issues and Approaches*. Edited by P.S. Johnston and D.G. Firth. Leicester: Apollos, 2005.

---. "The gap between law and ethics in the Bible". *JJS* 48 (1997): 17-29.

---. *Story as Torah: Reading the Old Testament Ethically*. OTS. Edinburgh: T&T Clark, 2000.

Westbrook, R. "What is the Covenant Code?" Pages 15-36 in *Theory and Method in Biblical and Cuneiform Law: Revision, Interpolation and Development*. Edited by B.M. Levinson. JSOTSup 181. Sheffield: Sheffield Academic Press, 1994.

Westermann, C. *Isaiah 40-66*. OTL. London: SCM, 1969.

Wevers, J.W. "War, Methods of". Pages 801-805 in vol. 4 of *Interpreter's Dictionary of the Bible*. Edited by G.A. Buttrick. 4 vols. New York, N.Y.: Abingdon, 1962.

---. "Weapons and implements of war". Pages 820-825 in vol. 4 of *Interpreter's Dictionary of the Bible*. Edited by G.A. Buttrick. 4 vols. New York, N.Y.: Abingdon, 1962.

Whybray, R.N. "What do we know about ancient Israel?" Pages 181-187 in *Israel's Past in Present Research: Essays on Ancient Israelite Historiography*. Edited by V.P. Long. SBTS 7. Winona Lake, Ind.: Eisenbrauns, 1999.

Wildberger, H. *Isaiah 1-12: A Continental Commentary*. Translated by T.H. Trapp. Minneapolis, Minn.: Fortress, 1991.

---. *Isaiah 13-27: A Continental Commentary*. Translated by T.H. Trapp. Minneapolis, Minn.: Fortress, 1997.

Williamson, H.G.M. *1 and 2 Chronicles*. NCB. London: Marshall, Morgan & Scott, 1982.

Wilson, G.H. *The Editing of the Hebrew Psalter*. SBLDS 76. Chico, Ca.: Scholars Press, 1985.

Wilson, R.R. "Approaches to Old Testament ethics". Pages 62-74 in *Canon, Theology, and Old Testament Interpretation: Essays in Honor of Brevard S. Childs*. Edited by G.M. Tucker, D.L. Petersen and R.R. Wilson. Philadelphia, Pa.: Fortress, 1988.

---. "Ethics in conflict: sociological aspects of ancient Israelite ethics". Pages 193-206 in *Text and Tradition: The Hebrew Bible and Folklore*. Edited by S. Niditch. SS. Atlanta, Ga.: Scholars, 1990.

---. "Sources and methods in the study of ancient Israelite ethics". *Semeia* 66 (1995): 55-63.

Winckler, H. *Die Keilschrifttexte Sargons*. Leipzig: Eduard Pfeiffer, 1888.

Winter, I.J. "Aesthetics in ancient Mesopotamian art". Pages 2569-2582 in vol. 4 of *Civilizations of the Ancient Near East*. Edited by J.M. Sasson. 4 vols. Peabody, Mass.: Hendrickson, 2000.

---. "Art *in* empire: the royal image and the visual dimensions of Assyrian ideology". Pages 359-382 in *Assyria 1995: Proceedings of the 10th Anniversary Symposium of the Neo-Assyrian Text Corpus Project*. Edited by S. Parpola and R.M. Whitings. Helsinki: Helsinki University Press, 1997.

---. "*Le palais imaginaire*: scale and meaning in the iconography of Neo-Assyrian cylinder seals". Pages 51-88 in *Images as Media: Sources for the Cultural History of the Near East and the Eastern Mediterranean (Ist millennium BCE)*. Edited by C. Uehlinger. OBO 175. Göttingen: Vandenhoeck & Ruprecht, 2000.

---. "The program of the throneroom of Assurnasirpal II at Nimrud". Pages 15-32 in *Essays on Near Eastern Art and Archaeology in Honor of Charles Kyrle Wilkinson*. Edited by P.O. Harper and H. Pittman. New York, N.Y.: Metropolitan Museum of Art, 1983.

Wolff, H.W. *Dodekapropheton I: Hosea*. BKAT 14.1. Neukirchen-Vluyn: Neukirchener Verlag, 1976.

---. *Hosea*. Hermeneia. Edited by P.D. Hanson. Translated by G. Stansell. Philadelphia, Pa.: Fortress, 1974.

---. *Joel and Amos*. Hermeneia. Edited by S.D. McBride Jr. Translated by W. Janzen, S.D. McBride Jr., and C.A. Muenchow. Philadelphia, Pa.: Fortress, 1977.

---. *Micah the Prophet*. Translated by R.D. Gehrke. Philadelphia, Pa.: Fortress, 1981.

Wright, C.J.H. *Old Testament Ethics for the People of God*. Leicester: Inter-Varsity, 2004.

Wright, G.E. *The Old Testament Against its Environment*. London: SCM Press, 1950.

Wyatt, N. "Arms and the king: the earliest allusions to the *Chaoskampf* motif and their implications for the interpretation of the Ugaritic and biblical traditions". Pages 151-189 in *'There's Such Divinity Doth Hedge a King': Selected Essays of Nicholas Wyatt on Royal Ideology in Ugaritic and Old Testament Literature*. SOTSMS. Aldershot: Ashgate, 2005.

---. "Degrees of divinity: some mythical and ritual aspects of West Semitic kingship". Pages 191-220 in *'There's Such Divinity Doth Hedge a King': Selected Essays of Nicholas Wyatt on Royal Ideology in Ugaritic and Old Testament Literature*. SOTSMS. Aldershot: Ashgate, 2005.

Yadin, Y. *The Art of Warfare in Biblical Lands in the Light of Archaeological Discovery*. London: Weidenfeld and Nicolson, 1963.

Younger Jr., K.L. *Ancient Conquest Accounts: A Study in Ancient Near Eastern and Biblical History Writing*. JSOTSup 98. Sheffield: JSOT, 1990.

Zaccagnini, C. "The enemy in the Neo-Assyrian royal inscriptions: the 'ethnographic' description". Pages 409-424 in vol. 2 of *Mesopotamien und seine Nachbarn: politische und kulturelle Wechselbeziehungen im Alten Vorderasien vom 4. bis 1. Jahrtausend v. Chr. XXV. Rencontre assyriologique internationale Berlin, 3. bis 7. Juli 1978*. Edited by H.-J. Nissen and J. Renger. BBVO 1. Berlin: Dietrich Reimer Verlag, 1978.

Zawadski, S. "Hostages in Assyrian royal inscriptions". Pages 449-458 in *Immigration and Emigration within the Ancient Near East: Festschrift E. Lipiński*. Edited by K. van Lerherghe and A. Schoors. OLA 65. Leuven: Peeters Publishers and Department of Oriental Studies, 1995.

Zehnder, M. *Umgang mit Fremden in Israel und Assyrien: Ein Beitrag zur Anthropologie des »Fremden« im Licht antiker Quellen*. BWANT 168. Stuttgart: Kohlhammer, 2005.

Zenger, E. *A God of Vengeance? Understanding the Psalms of Divine Wrath*. Translated by L.M. Maloney. Louisville, Ky.: Westminster John Knox, 1996.

Zenger, J. "Neuassyrische Königsinschriften als Genre der Keilschriftliteratur – Zum Stil und zur Kompositionstechnik der Inschriften Sargons II. von Assyrien". Pages 109-128 in *Keilschriftliche Literaturen: Ausgewählte Vorträge der XXII. Rencontre Assyriologique Internationale Münster, 8-12.7.1985*. Edited by K. Hecker and W. Sommerfield. BBVO 6. Berlin: Dietrich Reimer, 1986.

Zimmern, H. "Marduks (Ellis, Aššurs) Geburt im babylonischen Weltschöpfungsepos". *MVAG* 21 (1916): 213-225.

ben Zvi, E. "Malleability and its limits: Sennacherib's campaign against Judah as a case-study". Pages 73-105 in *'Like a Bird in a Cage': The Invasion of Sennacherib in 701 BCE*. Edited by L.L. Grabbe. JSOTSup 363. Sheffield: Sheffield Academic Press, 2003.

Index of ancient sources

Biblical texts

Akkadian texts

Palace reliefs

Index of modern authors

www.ingramcontent.com/pod-product-compliance
Lightning Source LLC
Chambersburg PA
CBHW070027100426
42740CB00013B/2621
* 9 7 8 3 1 1 0 4 8 5 9 6 7 *